An Historical Bibliography of Egyptian Prehistory

compiled by

Kent R. Weeks

with the editorial assistance of

Catharine Roehrig
Joel Paulson
Frank T.F. Ho

Published for
The American Research Center in Egypt
by
Eisenbrauns
Winona Lake, Indiana

American Research Center in Egypt / Catalogs, No. 6

Library of Congress Cataloging-in-Publication Data

Weeks, Kent R.
An historical bibliography of Egyptian prehistory.

1. Man, Prehistoric—Egypt—Bibliography.
2. Egypt—Antiquities—Bibliography. I. Title.
Z5113.W43 1985 [GN865.E3] 016.932 85-9075
ISBN 0-936770-11-2

1117 SIA Building, Columbia University, New York, NY 10027

Printed in the United States of America

Contents

Introduction . . . . *v*

Abbreviations . . . . *xix*

A – Z *1*

Supplement *137*

Introduction

This bibliography was begun over ten years ago as a personal effort to organize material that will someday, it is hoped, result in a book surveying the archaeology of Egypt through the end of the Old Kingdom. The number of references that have come to be entered, however, preclude any thought of including the bibliography as an appendix to such a book. That, and this compiler's belief that many of the obscure publications that it includes are worth recalling to historians of Egyptology, have combined to give the bibliography a life of its own.

Having logged 2,515 entries, it would be nice to argue that the bibliography is a complete one. Unfortunately, that certainly is not the case. Obscure references still lie hidden on library shelves; well-known references may be excluded because, being so familiar, they stand before us unseen. But it seems fair to state that *almost* everything appears in this collection.

And an eclectic collection it is. Questions about Egypt's prehistory, its Early Dynastic Period, and the process by which it grew from the one to the other, have brought out both the best and the worst in a tradition of scholarship that has covered the whole gamut of disciplines, a tradition that has been extant for over two centuries. Nevertheless, even the obscure and vague items among these references have historical interest, and not a few of them contain information or interpretations that scholars may profitably study even today.

Although nearly all of the references included here have been seen by us, read and, in about 60% of the cases, summarized for our own use, the preparation of abstracts for inclusion here was a desirable goal that of necessity was abandoned. Instead, a highly selective guide to some of the more important subjects discussed has been added to this introduction. While by no means complete, it should assist those interested in specific subjects to locate the less obvious, less well-known, discussions of various topics.

It is with great pleasure that I express my thanks to four students at the University of California, Berkeley, who helped in the later stages of this project. Ms. Catharine Roehrig checked many of the bibliographic entries for accuracy, Mr. Joel Paulson, (assisted for a time by Mr. James Petersen), was responsible for the arduous task of typesetting the manuscript. Mr. Frank T. F. Ho undertook the computer typesetting needed for this work, and also was responsible for the typographical layout of the book. Funding for the computer typsetting needed for this project was made possible through grants from the University of California, Berkeley.

By good fortune it was possible, during the course of this work, to make use of a number of libraries, in Luxor, Cairo, London, New York, and Berkeley. To the staffs of those libraries I extend my thanks for their aid.

BIBLIOGRAPHY Standard Egyptological bibliographies, such as those of Pratt, Federn or Janssen (but with the notable exception of Kemp's now-defunct *Egyptology Titles*), have covered prehistoric Egypt only cursorily, usually noting only articles that appeared in Egyptological journals. A 19th century attempt to deal with sources for the study of Egyptian races [2227] is of some historical interest. More useful, although incomplete and with numerous errors, is the bibliography of Bachatly [125] and the more recent North African compilation by Mauny and Balout [1403]. Hayes's excellent bibliographic commentaries [1010], though now dated and limited to pre-Neolithic material, remain of great value. *Index Libycus* [2042] deals only peripherally with Egypt, but contains many useful sources, especially on the subject of petroglyphs. (Egyptian petroglyphs are treated more fully, however, in [616]).

Bibliographies of various individual scholars may sometimes be found in *Who Was Who in Egyptology* [626]. Authors listed in our bibliography who are to be found in that work will have arrow brackets < > following their names. These enclose the *WWWE* page reference. A bibliography of Elise Baumgartel appears in [674].

HISTORY OF EGYPTIAN PREHISTORICAL RESEARCH The first discovery of the Stone Age in Egypt was made just over eleven decades ago, perhaps by Arcelin [74-81], perhaps by Hamy [970-71] and Lenormant [976-78, 1307-9]. (The question of priority is dealt with in occasional scattered references, e.g., [834-36, 1584]). Some further details of the work of these scholars have been published by Naville [1574] and in bibliographies of Hamy [530] and Lenormant [171]. At the time of their discoveries, not all scholars agreed that the tools found actually were prehistoric. Indeed, Chabas [519], (cf. [79, 1376]) and, especially, Lepsius [1311], strongly argued that they were not. Mariette was one of the first to accept the prehistoric date of these finds [1379, 1574].

Other principal 19th-century works on Egyptian prehistory include [972, 1013, 1335-37, 1380-81, 1816, 1843, 1931-33]. Broad surveys of this early work may be found in [309, 510, 600-2, 876, 2455, 2465] and, more recently, in [1058].

Prehistoric surveys with an emphasis on the question of Egyptian origins and race (q.v.) include [895, 934, 973-75]. A strong emphasis on Biblical explanation may be seen in [1399, 1645, 1647-48]. The role of the theories of G. E. Smith is outlined in [704-5, 875].

General surveys of the Palaeolithic (q.v.) also contain much historical information.

GEOLOGICAL STUDIES Although much of their work is now dated, the studies of Sanford and Arkell [1993-96, 1998-99, 2001, 2004-5], with commentaries in [9, 323], still are a major part of the foundation of Egyptian geological research. Their data have been significantly revised by Passarge [1666] and Butzer [381-420 passim].

Surveys of Egyptian Pleistocene geology include [103, 936, 981, 1012, 1117, 1989, 2291]. Dated, but still of interest, is [1010].

The relationship between geological studies and Egyptology is dealt with in [486, 1788, 1882, 1972]. The geology of the oases is discussed in [390, 1985]; of the Fayum in [849-50 852, 855, 858, 1318, 1405]; of Nubia in [393, 413, 878, 1020-22]. Dating of pluvial periods is discussed in [1011, 1988].

We list in this bibliography only those works dealing with Egyptian geology as it relates to human occupation, and to a few works of general interest. Of the latter, a basic reference is [1984].

CLIMATOLOGICAL STUDIES The role of climate in the development of Egyptian culture has been remarked upon even by early Graeco-Roman travellers, but its formal study, especially for predynastic times, dates only from the last eighty years. Among the earliest works are an overview of the problem [909]; a survey of Huntington's theories of climate's influence on the development of civilization [1103-4]; and studies by Petrie [1748-49]. More recently, several studies of general climatic patterns in North Africa and the Near East have appeared: [377-80, 392, 403, 410, 415, 419, 672, 1854, 1948, 2134] and others. Kees's study [1193], of course, is a classic discussion of climate's role in Egypt, and [909, 1108, 1536] also contain data of value. B. Bell's paper [2488], the first of several that she has written on Egyptian climate, together with Butzer's recent *LdÄ* articles [e.g., 403] bring this aspect of climatological work up to date.

Several studies of Western Desert and Libyan climatic history have been published. In addition to site-specific studies on Cyrenaica [1357], Kurkur Oasis [2269], and Nubia [1649], there are a number of more general reports: [1049, 1087, 1090, 1536, 1545, 1677, 1949, 1997, 2268, 2385-86, 2448-49, 2480, 2482-83]. Rain charms are discussed in [1583].

THE RIVER NILE Probably no river in the world has been more discussed more frequently than the Nile. Works dealing especially with its geological and hydrological history, however, are less common. On these subjects, general works include the classic studies by Passarge [1666], Sanford and Arkell [1998, 2003-5], and Butzer [406-8 (articles in *LdÄ*), 417-19], the early work of Blanckenhorn [267], and more recent studies such as [991, 1986, 1990, 2001]. Fascinating new data from satellite photography may be found in [1363].

The relation of Nile development to human cultural history is discussed in [1193, 1237, 2001, 2449, 2488].

GENERAL WORKS ON THE PREHISTORIC PERIOD Surveys of Egyptian culture before Dynasty I are numerous. A few have become minor classics: [193, 460, 536-42, 1010, 1058, 1108, 1147-48, 1401, 1474, 2254, 2273, 2378]. Others include: [72, 87, 103, 106, 114, 230, 265, 291, 319, 337, 364, 375-76, 421, 461, 508-9, 522, 528, 642-43, 646, 659, 678, 746-47, 794, 848, 861, 984, 995, 997, 999, 1008, 1013, 1038, 1045, 1050, 1081, 1106-11, 1115, 1133, 1164, 1177, 1216, 1251, 1276, 1278-82, 1309, 1338, 1356, 1378, 1397, 1412, 1433, 1455, 1457, 1471-88 passim, 1516, 1533, 1561, 1629, 1651, 1657, 1682-83, 1686, 1714, 1750-53, 1883, 1888, 1903, 1940, 1958, 1965-69, 2046-48, 2079-82, 2254, 2369, 2376, 2407, 2415, 2425, 2445-46].

Surveys of the problems of prehistoric chronology include [426, 1108, 1416]. See also [1109].

Collections of Egyptian stone tools are described in [330, 1811, 2027].

Relations between Egypt and Africa during this time are discussed in [13, 155, 158, 425, 427, 431, 552-53, 557, 574-76, 579, 587-89, 598, 744, 786-87, 1227, 1285, 1358, 1669, 2222, 2449]. Relations with Western Asia and the northeast Mediterranean are treated in [368, 462, 558, 767, 837-38, 1098, 1515].

Discussions of physical anthropology and the origins of Palaeolithic populations include [348, 526, 611, 621-25, 657, 989-90].

CHRONOLOGY OF THE PREDYNASTIC AND EARLY DYNASTIC This complex subject, whose data seem to change regularly, is treated generally for the palaeolithic in works cited above and with greater emphasis on the Neolithic and Early Dynastic in [229, 531, 693, 699, 782-83, 1009-10, 1023, 1114, 1149, 1163, 1255-56, 1314, 1416, 1437, 1563, 1718-19, 1779, 1821, 1845, 1918, 2132, 2270, 2396, 2499].

Chronology which has been established through the study of ancient annals and texts is treated in [169, 595, 606, 699, 847, 871-72, 900, 1031, 1375, 1615, 1622, 1663-65, 1752, 2226, 2462].

The use of C-14 dating, long unpopular with Egyptologists, has now come to be an important archaeological tool. Its value and its problems are discussed in [166, 426, 429-30, 650, 652, 1000, 1435, 1840, 2167]. Thermoluminescence dating is the subject of [507, 2515]. Seriation is treated in [596], the dating of petroglyphs through seriation techniques in [613-15, 1498].

Chronological problems in Nubia and the Sudan are discussed in [104, 1010,

2418]; of Libya and North Africa generally in [422-23, 426, 429-30, 649, 652, 739, 783, 903, 1088, 1090, 1114, 2338].

THE PALAEOLITHIC A number of descriptive works deal with Palaeolithic implements generally. Several describe museum collections made before data was systematically taken on such implements [210, 597, 966, 1716, 1884, 1970, 2019]. Several articles attempt to arrange this material sequentially [596, 2006, 2203, 2222, 2261, 2273, 2320]; others deal with wide-ranging field surveys [373, 466, 490, 800]. Schweinfurth's collecting activities are noted in [2064-68]. Surveys of the Theban hills are described in [636, 641, 963, 1835, 2073, 2075-76, 2079]. Collections from Helwan are discussed in [593]; from Nubia in [1225, 1388]; from the Libyan Desert in [1357, 1362, 1445, 2267]. The quarries exploited during the Palaeolithic are noted in [191, 1243, 2121].

General descriptions of tools and of the techniques of their manufacture may be found in several studies: [190, 192, 603, 648, 659, 940, 964-65, 1010, 1014, 1081, 1127, 1242-43, 1351, 1443, 1485, 1530-31, 1562, 1633, 1745, 1761, 1832-33, 1914, 2001, 2056, 2100, 2119-20, 2128-29, 2208, 2217, 2220, 2273, 2279, 2290-91, 2313, 2321].

The Lower Palaeolithic The discoveries of Arcelin are surveyed in [74-81] and historically relevant discussions may be found in [309, 1012-14]. Museum collections are described in [209, 296, 597, 784]. Relations between Egypt and Africa and the Near East during this period are discussed in [268-69, 295, 785, 798-99, 882, 1361, 2100]. General articles on the period include [190-92, 294, 310-12, 343, 373, 458, 525, 587-88, 596, 1971, 2099] and, most recently, [2496]. Hominid remains are noted in [578, 640]. Site surveys include those in the Fayum [270]; around Cairo [305-8, 314]; in Upper Egypt and Nubia [315, 546, 954-55, 1012-14, 1328, 1816, 2291-92]. See also [313, 1367-68] on the Chalossian. Of considerable historical interest, of course, are the studies of Hamy [970-78] and Lenormant [1307-9].

The Middle Palaeolithic The most recent survey of this period is [2490]. Earlier works include [210, 268-69, 294-96, 309-13, 372, 497, 596-97, 1361, 2256-57, 2279, 2294-95, 2315, 2379, 2400, 2403, 2412]. Mousterian industries are discussed in [156, 796, 933, 1040, 1384]. On chronology see also [2379]. Site surveys include, for the Fayum [270]; Helwan [306]; Maadi and the environs of Cairo [307-8, 314, 1451]; Aswan [315]; Sudan [546, 933, 954-55, 1384]; el-Kab [2283-93].

The Upper Palaeolithic The historical background of work on this period may be found in [309, 519]. Museum collections are described in [210, 597]. General articles on the period include [309, 312, 373, 462, 596, 1106, 1109, 1111, 1139, 1380, 1791, 1954, 2041, 2174, 2180, 2182, 2309-11, 2406, 2512]. The tools themselves are described in [336, 370, 2040]; skeletal materials in [374]. Chronology is discussed in [2173, 2396, 2421, 1106]; relations beyond Egypt in [1894, 2193]; climatic conditions in [2385, 2387].

Sites in the Sinai are described in [177-78]; in Lower Egypt in [314, 630]; in Upper Egypt in [305-8, 315, 383, 1799, 2395]. Nubia and the Western Desert are discussed in [310-11, 457, 566-70, 580, 870, 1092, 1113, 1340-41, 1366, 1383, 1386, 2373-74]. The site of Kom Ombo is the subject of [2172, 2175-77, 2316]; Nag Hammadi of [2299-2301, 2303, 2305, 2307-8]. The Aterian industry is described in [766, 1377, 2276, 2413]; the Halfan in [1382], and in articles noted above. On cattle pastoralism see [1368]; on the possible use of grain [2380-81, 2397, 2414, 2419].

The Sebilian The discovery of this industry is treated in [2302, 2306]. Microburins are discussed in [2312, 2314]; associated faunal remains in [549]. Site surveys include [998] on the Nile Valley; [985] on Dishna; [1001] on el-Kilh; [2317] on Kom Ombo; [316] on the Delta; and [1385] on Second Cataract material. See also references in earlier paragraphs.

THE EPI-PALAEOLITHIC Articles on this period are included in the preceding section.

FLORAL AND FAUNAL REMAINS Material, mostly of the Neolithic and Early Dynastic, but occasionally of earlier periods as well, has been infrequently the subject of specialized and detailed study. General works in the field include [854, 870, 1332, 1519, 1609, 1874, 2181, 2383, 2428]. Studies of the vegetation of Egypt and North Africa (not including the brief references in site reports), include [300, 939, 958-59, 1024-25, 1614, 2133, 2181, 2380-81, 2383, 2428, 2489].

Faunal remains have been discussed in [549-51, 833, 869, 1105, 1197, 1199, 1332, 1520, 1693]. Articles on specific animals include those on camels [495]; dogs [1080]; cats [1501, 1521]; pigs [1198, 1611]; snails [1340-41]; fish [937, 1649, 1960]; and birds [154]. Articles on the appearance of domesticated animals in Egypt include [301, 697, 1237, 1650, 1840, 1875, 2168, 2181, 2383, 2428]. The archaeological occurrence of animal fats is noted in [817].

PETROGLYPHS The work of Egypt's inhabitants from Palaeolithic times to the modern day, these fascinating traces of human occupation are widely distributed geographically. They most recently have been studied by Davis in a series of articles [613-16] that attempt to order their study chronologically and bibliographically.

General discussions of petroglyphs in northeast Africa (including the Nile Valley) may be found in [108, 134-40, 304, 325, 327, 380, 513, 515-16, 616, 673, 1221, 1250, 1712, 2179]. Their dating has been discussed in [513, 517, 613-15, 1489, 1492, 1498]. Their usefulness in reconstructing climatic conditions is examined in [380].

The petroglyphs of Egypt (or, rather, a portion of them), have been published in [228, 514, 533, 585, 614-16, 1943-44, 2088, 2459-61].

Nubian petroglyphs, because of the several salvage programs conducted there, are among the most extensively recorded: [16, 19, 244, 514, 517, 544, 614, 681-83, 1035-36, 1119, 1240, 1332, 1556-57, 1590, 1662, 1945, 2296].

The Western Desert and Libya also have been surprisingly well published: [68, 326, 453-55, 583, 662, 820-24, 841, 910-24, 1086, 1089, 1091, 1094, 1207, 1438,

1489-98, 1500, 1526, 1539, 1618, 1676, 1697, 1699, 1897, 1920-26, 1929-30, 2028, 2136-38, 2140, 2356].

THE NEOLITHIC Surveys of this crucial period include [114, 193, 206, 262, 312, 431, 587-88, 698, 780, 999, 1110, 1308, 1548, 2435]. Its stone tools are described in [596-97, 938, 2201, 2350]. The Neolithic population of Egypt is treated in [986-87]; foreign relations are outlined in [1596, 2181]; chronology in [650, 1840]. Descriptions of Neolithic sites (see also the separate entries below) include [1047, 1245] for Lower Egypt; [1151] for Upper Egypt; [1015] for the Sudan; and [318, 1096, 1246-47, 2135] for Egypt and/or Africa generally.

Theories of agricultural origins in the Nile Valley include those by Braidwood [317], Butzer [409-10], Clarke [554, 556], Cohen [572], and others [17, 968, 984, 993, 1110, 1248, 1673, 1826, 1872, 1879, 1981-84, 2133, 2263a, 2383] and the brief discussion in *LdÄ* [347]. The domestication of wheat and barley is discussed in [669, 2205, 2380-81, 2397, 2409, 2411, 2414, 2416-17, 2419, 2428]; of animals in [577, 685, 737, 744, 787, 877, 983, 1367, 1402, 1875].

THE FAYUM The geology and geography of the Fayum and of Lake Moeris have been frequently discussed from the 19th century [335] onward. Articles on general geology include [849-50, 1318, 2000, 2003, 2402]; on the Lake and Depression [502, 506, 852, 858, 2002]; on the Neolithic period [500, 855, 1405, 1775, 1987]. Surveys of the geography of the Fayum may be found in [151, 1193, 2426]. Palaeolithic remains in the Fayum are discussed in [123, 126, 184, 597]. The Fayum Neolithic is the subject of early works by Seton-Karr [2124] and Petrie [1773, 1775, 1790]. Caton-Thompson's is a standard work [505]. Other discussions include [212, 270, 472-73, 480-85, 501, 597, 851, 1420, 1594, 1803]. Neolithic pottery is described in [450, 801]; faunal remains in [154].

MERIMDE BENI-SALAME The early work of Hermann Junker is to be found reported in [1132, 1134, 1136-41] and summarized in [200]. General comments on the site may be found in [188, 203, 1286, 1413-14] and in *LdÄ* [703]. The skeletal remains from the site are discussed in [655, 658, 1210]; the architecture in [148]; the bone tools in [1266]; stone tools in [2021]; pottery in [1264-65, 1267]; faunal remains in [1198]. Fortunately, the unsatisfactory excavation of this site, its incomplete publication, and the loss of much of the data and many of the artifacts during World War II, are now being compensated for by recent re-excavation of this important home of early agriculturalists [127, 702]. A four-volume report on this work by J. Eiwanger, et al., is in preparation: *AV* 47, 51, 59, 60.

EL-OMARI Palaeolithic materials have been surveyed by Bovier-Lapierre in [305-7]. The work of Debono is discussed in [627, 629, 634]. General remarks may be found in [2273].

HELWAN Schweinfurth's early reports are still of much interest [2059, 2061]. Of historical interest also is Reil's 1876 commentary on stone tools [1881]. Debono's work here was published in [627, 629-30]. Human remains from the site are described in [656]. General remarks may be found in [2273].

DEIR TASA No longer considered a valid culture, but rather a part of the Badarian, materials from the 'type site' are treated in [358, 830] and, generally, in [2273].

BADARIAN Early surveys of the site of el-Badari were undertaken by Reinach [1895] and by Petrie [1766, 1771]. The standard work is that of Brunton [349-51, 353, 355, 363, 535] which catalogues many of the objects found here [352, 354]; see also [874, 892, 967]. Skeletal remains are discussed in [1459-60]; tatooing of female figurines in [1200]; dating in [507]. General discussions include [193, 2273], and articles in *LdÄ* [217, 1155].

THE NAQADA CULTURE This most-discussed period of Upper Egyptian prehistory has been the subject of several early studies [2431, 2433, 2435]; of works by Petrie and Quibell [1795], by Baumgartel [193, 205-6], by Vandier [2273], by Kantor [1160], by Kees [1193], and by Kaiser [1147, 1158]. Its chronology is the subject of [204-5, 474, 476, 1149, 1721, 1754, 2020-21]. Its role in the development of urbanism is treated in [2093]; its African relations in [1122]. Tomb distribution is the subject of [478]. A general survey of this important material may be found in *LdÄ* [1033].

Naqada Cemeteries General works on the cemeteries of this period include [121, 131, 199, 204, 361, 735, 764 (which also covers craniometry), 950, 1592, 1893], and *LdÄ* article [1216]. Among the necropoleis that have been published are: Abusir [277, 1441-42]; Abydos [25-31, 1685, 1861]; el-Amrah [1861]; Armant [1447]; Badari [349-50, 355, 363]; Diospolis Parva [1715, 1721]; Gerzeh [1797]; Harageh [735]; Khozam [1196]; el-Mahasna [121]; Matmar [361]; Naqada [199, 204-5, 788, 865, 1033, 1592, 1795, 2018].

Naqada Villages Two recent general works by Kemp [1210, 1214] are of importance. Descriptive summaries of most sites may be found in [2273]. Abydos [475, 479, 806, 817, 1193]; el-Amrah [941]; Helwan [306, 479, 593]; el-Hamamiyeh [217 (an *LdÄ* article), 2515]; Hierakonpolis [3-4, 5 (an *LdÄ* article), 15, 201, 202 and 207 (on ivories), 228 (on petroglyphs), 356 (on the town site), 383, 753-54, 791, 868, 958 (on the flora), 979-80, 1053-62 (recent works by Hoffman, et al.), 1150 (by Kaiser), 1193 (by Kees), 1259, 1272, 1398, 1540, 1711, 1846, 2048, 2071, 2492]; Maadi [34-47, 1156 (an *LdÄ* article), 1347, 1406-13, 1417, 1419]; el-Mahasna [863-64]; Wadi Digla [49-50].

Naqada Pottery There are many articles on the ceramics of the Naqada culture, and no general book on Egyptian prehistory, archaeology or art fails to comment on at least the black-topped red ware and the decorated vessels. Techniques of manufacture and studies of the clays used in the various classes include [15, 396, 956, 1342]. Collections of vessels are described in [195, 209, 251, 303, 469, 874, 2353,

2430]; and general studies include [113 (an article in *LdÄ*), 303, 805, 1121, 1316, 1576, 1736, 2273]. The decoration of vessels is discussed in [92, 118, 209, 438, 792, 829, 1866 (which offers a Jungian view), 1938]; their typology, on which subject much work is currently being done: [441, 1593, 1684, 1727, 1757, 1793].

'B' Black-topped red ware: [92, 193, 437, 768-69, 1129, 1342, 1344, 1593, 1721, 1793, 1817, 1912, 2273].

'C' White cross-line: [121, 193, 205, 251, 349, 359, 438, 694, 1196, 1679, 1721, 1727, 1754, 1757, 1793, 1849, 1861, 1866, 2021, 2025, 2027, 2259, 2273, 2349, 2469]. On forged examples: [357].

'D' Decorated ware: This well-known predynastic pottery, among the most attractive ever produced in Egypt, has been discussed frequently. Among the general articles are: [193, 251, 283, 694, 804, 1196, 1447, 1579, 1604, 1754, 1757, 1793, 1795, 2026-27, 2030, 2065, 2258, 2273]. Forgeries are discussed in [357, 1671]. The representations of boats on these vessels is the subject of [283-84, 444, 692, 694, 1255, 1480, 1579, 1754, 1793, 2028, 2273]; arguments that they are not boats at all may be found in [534, 1573, 1870, 2243, 2492]. The ensigns these boats display and the palm branches on their prows are described and interpreted in [1078, 1125, 1322, 1604, 1741, 1809, 2230, 2273, 2510]. The so-called 'plant of Naqada,' is treated in [1263, 2223, 2273], and also in [1070, 1073, 1322, 1579, 1604, 1606-7, 1609, 1614, 1671] and, most recently, in [2492]. Examples of its occurrence are fairly common: [251, 284, 438, 756, 1196, 1754, 1793, 2065, 2273].

'F' Fancy ware and theriomorphic vessels: Discredited by Federn [1593], this class is discussed in [193, 349, 438, 864, 891, 1160, 1593, 1721, 1757, 1793, 2020, 2027, 2273].

'N' Nubian ware: [193, 1593, 1721, 1757, 1793, 2021, 2273].

'P' Polished red ware: [1593, 1757, 2273].

'R' Rough ware: [1196, 1593, 1757, 2027, 2273].

'W' Wavy-handled ware: This important class of pottery has been widely discussed: [53, 193, 804, 1016, 1043, 1133, 1159, 1414, 1593, 1721, 1743, 1757, 1793, 1795-96, 2021, 2273].

Naqada Stone Vessels The most recent survey of these famous vessels is [1217]. Their dating is discussed in [209]; their techniques of manufacture in [450, 1342]; and general articles include [105, 182-83, 193, 349, 1172, 1343, 1754, 1797, 2025, 2444].

Hierakonpolis Painted Tomb This perplexing structure, of which still only little is known in spite of Kemp's important article [1212], has been discussed frequently: [69, 284, 302, 829, 1160, 1670, 1851, 2513].

Palettes Although many palettes are to be dated to the Early Dynastic Period, it is appropriate to note them here since so many seem to relate (at least in the subject-matter of their reliefs) to the transition between the Predynastic and Dynasty I.

Undecorated palettes, moreover, are often of Predynastic date. Articles dealing with undecorated examples include: [349, 359, 437-38, 468, 1754, 1757, 1795, 1861, 2444, 2473]. Articles dealing with decorated palettes are common: [96, 221, 259, 290, 438-39, 594, 812, 879, 982, 1006, 1195, 1293, 1296, 1298, 1300, 1517, 1524, 1602, 1680, 1757, 1786, 1862, 1936, 2113, 2234, 2427, 2513]. The Libyan Palette also is discussed in [1195, 2113, 2206]. The palettes from Hierakonpolis are also treated in [221, 897, 1195, 1294, 1846, 1851, 1863, 2049, 2096, 2102, 2104, 2200, 2252, 2513].

Carved Ivories The subject is discussed generally or with reference to specific pieces in [193, 207, 225, 438, 771, 868, 1007, 1069, 1160, 1754, 1768, 1936, 1947, 2149, 2273, 2326, 2328, 2331, 2333]. The Gebel el-Arak knife handle is discussed in [225-26, 284, 644, 812, 1160, 1431, 2027], and in an unlisted paper delivered by Hans Goedicke at the Annual Meeting of ARCE in 1968.

Sculpture General discussions include [438, 2273, 2513]. Models of boats are treated in [284, 1255, 1754, 1785, 1861, 2027]. Zoomorphic pieces are treated in [438, 470, 1068, 1198, 1726]; anthropomorphic figures in [121, 349, 359, 1200, 1564, 2263-64].

Maceheads Among the numerous references to these objects, most of them parts of general works on Egyptian history and art, are: [201, 437-38, 1123, 1540, 1851, 2049].

THEORIES OF THE ORIGIN OF EGYPTIAN CIVILIZATION This has been a constantly recurring subject in Egyptological research. Until recently, it was assumed that Egypt's dynastic culture was an import into the Nile Valley, perhaps coming from Asia [1869], perhaps from Libya [2050], perhaps from Atlantis [2370], or even from outer space. Many have remarked on the Semitic affinities of Egyptian culture [174-5, 1064], many on the Biblical stories that purportedly explained its source [839, 1868]. A number of scholars have seen close ties to Mesopotamia or Asia generally [176, 459, 780, 1065-67, 1566, 1928, 2342-43]. That there was an African tie also has been remarked upon, nearly seventy years ago by Naville [1575], and more recently by Sheikh Anta Diop and his followers [176, 664-68, 1827]. In a reversal of this often-described cultural flow, G. Elliott Smith and his occasional later supporters saw ancient Egypt as the source for all other developments of 'higher cultures' [1694-96, 2165].

Broad theories of civilization's origins have dealt at some length with the Egyptian example [317, 573, 999, 1095, 1103-4, 1234-35, 1239, 1338, 1672, 1690, 1828, 2108, 2209, 2251, 2425, 2453]. One recurring theme has been the role of irrigation in this development [411, 414, 442, 2038, 2463]. More general discussions that deal with the Egyptian data include [197, 249-50 271, 320, 322, 433-34, 443, 999, 1058, 1062, 1567, 1731-32, 1763, 1789, 1865, 2014, 2052, 2241, 2254, 2363, 2365, 2369, 2436, 2445, 2453, 2511].

PHYSICAL ANTHROPOLOGY AND THE SO-CALLED DYNASTIC RACE No subject has generated more theories or been discussed over a longer period of time than the question of who the people were who founded Egyptian civilization. Ancient Egypt has always been looked upon as something very special, and it has seemed to many writers that its creators, too, must have been a special breed. A widespread reluctance, especially in the 19th century, to admit any African influence in Egypt led to theories that seem today to be far-fetched. During the 19th century, several anthropological studies were conducted in hopes of obtaining 'scientific' data to resolve these divergent views. They are numerous: [62, 72, 232, 249-50, 271, 297, 331, 334, 338, 344, 590, 740, 873, 895-96, 975, 1118, 1260, 1288, 1312, 1320, 1350, 1370, 1376, 1505, 1508-09, 1574, 1627, 1656, 1659, 1674, 1700, 1704, 1713, 1755, 1804, 1815, 1822-23, 1841, 1844, 1867, 1896, 2044, 2106, 2225, 2227, 2236, 2238, 2298, 2464, 2475-78]. More recent general surveys on the subject include: [57, 233-34, 328, 332, 663, 670, 700, 716, 759, 889-90, 1100, 1102, 1131, 1144, 1146, 1853, 2280].

Anthropometry, especially craniometric studies, has long been a favorite technique to determine the racial affinities of the Egyptians, although there are few today who would not seriously doubt the validity of these early approaches. (On this subject, and with some valuable comments on the Egyptian material, see [2493]. The material confronted there is dealt with in [1510-14]). Studies include: [82, 110, 185-87, 527, 599, 758, 760, 795, 1082, 1457, 1507, 1549-53, 1638, 1660, 1856-58, 2043, 2141, 2151, 2204, 2213, 2218-19, 2235, 2237, 2359, 2439, 2440-42]. Skeletal material from the Palaeolithic in Egypt and Nubia is treated in [374, 933, 1876, 2374]. Among numerous studies of Neolithic skeletons, many of them listed above, see [1037, 1088]. Early Dynastic material is treated in [1461, 1538], and in many of the articles listed above. Skeletons from Merimde Beni-Salame are discussed in [653, 656]; from Helwan in [654]; from Naqada in [746, 2018, 2359]; from Gebelen in [825-28, 1390-92]; from Abydos in [1660, 1856-58]; from el-Badari in [1459-60, 2204]; from Thebes in [1674, 2213]. See also [651, 1855, 2043, 2151, 2389].

Anthropometric or anthroposcopic similarities between Egypt and Nubia are discussed in general works and in [185-86, 246, 266, 1623, 2166, 2274]. Supposed connections with Libya are dealt with in [247, 342, 1859]. The question of skin color is singled out for treatment in [219]; of blood groups [880]; of dentition [949, 2150]; of hair [2337]. A possible Black African origin is discussed in [664-68, 1632, 2219]. Palaeopathology of early skeletal remains is treated in [2374, 2439]; supposed syphilitic lesions in [840, 1330-31, 2153]. Supposed ties with African pygmies are discussed in [2215-16].

Many discussions of the so-called 'Dynastic Race,' rather than relying upon anthropometric data, have chosen instead to treat representational art, Biblical interpretations, linguistic data, or other material as primary. Among the more general of such studies are: [655, 716, 733, 1066, 1202, 1222, 1365, 1598, 1691, 1713, 1722, 1729, 1787, 1841-42, 1845, 1956, 2018, 2068-70, 2095-96, 2117, 2225, 2280, 2359-60, 2440-42]. Those making extensive use of ancient Egyptian art or textual references include [339, 341, 563-64, 818, 974, 1131, 1252, 1755, 1774, 1782, 1824, 2007, 2242].

Numerous homelands for the 'Dynastic Race' have been proposed. Some have argued that it was in Asia [170, 952], some the Caucasus [117, 342, 1462], some the Near East [57, 149, 586, 1566-73]. Others have preferred Europe [2, 1500], or Africa [149, 242-43, 272, 591, 684, 701, 886-87, 1052, 1289, 1313, 1317, 1373, 1504, 1528, 1575, 1624, 1631, 1859, 1950, 2091, 2095, 2101, 2298, 2475-78]. Studies of Biblical references to man's origins include [61, 64-5, 953, 1289, 2013, 2239, 2456, 2467]. The possible transmission of Egyptian culture to other areas of the world, suggested by G.E. Smith, is treated in [180, 2151-66 passim].

THE FOLLOWERS OF HORUS Questions concerning a possible predynastic union of Egypt, and the nature of Egypt's earliest rulers still are unresolved. The former have been discussed in [321, 337, 2048] and in most general studies of early Egypt. The nature of the *Šmsw Ḥr* is the subject of [214, 1026, 1077, 1179, 1181, 1183, 1323, 1429, 1597, 2111] and, most recently in [1152] and two *LdÄ* articles [2037, 2228].

CANNIBALISM Discussions of whether this custom, or that of decapitation, were practiced in Egypt include [22, 67, 168, 365, 434, 761, 1952, 2431]. One also should see J. Spiegel, in *AÄA* 23 (1971): 438-39, and L. Zabkar, *SAOC* 34 (1968): 70-71.

The practice of tatooing is discussed in [645, 1200, 1720]. Deformation generally is the subject of *LdÄ* article [1051]. Tracheotomies are dealt with in [2329].

EARLY RELIGIOUS BELIEFS AND MORTUARY PRACTICES General discussions of predynastic and Early Dynastic religious practices are common: [32, 278, 365, 635, 832, 947, 1076, 1123, 1142, 1145, 1168-69, 1177, 1185-87, 1189-90, 1238, 1321, 1325, 1394, 1422-26, 1465, 1467, 1640, 1776, 1917, 1937].

Among discussions of the Memphite Theology, we note [738, 744, 810, 1143]. Egyptian deities in the earliest periods are discussed generally in [2188, 2352]. Among discussions of specific gods, Seth is dealt with in [1178, 1611, 2479]; Horus in [751, 845, 1178, 1181-84]; Min in [194, 196]; Osiris in [1028, 1613, 1778]; Bes in [1120]; Amon in [1124]; Anubis in [1187]; Mafdet in [231].

General surveys of mortuary customs include: [21, 112 (an *LdÄ* article), 433, 477-78, 695-96, 844, 1546, 1820, 1909, 2034, 2148]. 'Dolmens' are the subject of [189, 2155, 2157].

Early Dynastic tombs are treated in [131, 148, 707-27 passim, 808, 1268- 73 passim, 1909, 2361].

Tombs at Abydos are discussed in [23-32, 449, 957, 1157, 1193, 1577, 1583, 1660, 1679, 1717, 1723-24, 1730, 1737, 1829-30, 1836, 1858, 1899]; Naqada in [280, 865, 1476]; Abusir in [277, 1441-42, 1522]; Saqqara in [707-31, 1173, 1191-92, 1268-73]; Helwan in [1105, 1175, 1974-80].

SCULPTURE AND PAINTING General works on the art of the predynastic and Early Dynastic periods include: [11-12, 258, 437-38, 442, 448, 612, 660, 770, 775, 829, 879, 1258, 1680, 1946, 2033, 2187, 2206, 2355, 2450, 2457, 2513]. Collections and exhibitions of the art of this period are catalogued in [436, 765, 838, 1008, 1333, 1589, 1811, 2186, 2197, 2210]. More specific works on sculpture are: [252, 286, 289, 298, 677, 894, 948, 1079, 1306, 1864, 2076, 2078]. Painting is covered in [612, 770, 931-32, 1544, 1564, 2088].

METALLURGY General works include [1578, 1746, 1942, 2281]. Studies of the earliest appearance of copper and bronze include [235-40, 571, 1393, 1448-50, 1463, 1582, 1644, 1697, 1798, 1805, 1807, 1814, 1887, 1953, 2092, 2114-15]. The use of iron is discussed in [960-61, 1275, 1502, 1641, 1893, 2190, 2346-47, 2351].

THE EARLY DYNASTIC PERIOD All general works on Egypt deal in one degree or another with this material. In addition, studies of Menes may be found in [102, 280, 345-46, 741, 926, 1029, 1034, 1612, 2112, 2271, 2471-72]. Essays on other individuals of the First Dynasty incude [209, 216, 222-23, 263, 279, 281, 511, 709, 721, 846, 860, 897-98, 927, 1588]. General works on this period, or studies of specific elements of its culture are: [72, 114, 321, 714, 727, 731, 777, 899, 901-02, 925, 1042, 1044, 1153-54, 1167, 1174, 1209, 1214, 1224, 1270, 1426-27, 1590, 1610, 1615, 1717, 1813, 1829, 1936, 1981, 2113, 2282, 2363-69, 2486].

Aspects of the Second Dynasty are discussed in: [337, 727, 732, 776, 859, 904-5, 928-30, 1165, 1262, 1608, 1979-80, 2147, 2171, 2364-68].

TRADE AND FOREIGN CONTACTS General surveys: [119, 424, 1044, 1585, 1734, 2189, 2212]. Contacts with Nubia and the Sudan are discussed in [95, 811, 813, 1122, 1279, 1482]; with Libya [467]; with other parts of Africa [610, 647, 1122, 1279, 1334, 1482, 1547, 1575, 1624].

Trade with the ancient Near East in predynastic and Early Dynastic times is the subject of [255, 257, 273, 617, 675, 797, 804-7, 812, 1032, 1043, 1048, 1064-67, 1159, 1162, 1166, 1206, 1257, 1371, 1485, 1487, 1566, 1753, 1781, 1953, 2009, 2017, 2030, 2033, 2036, 2357-58, 2468, 2470-71, 2473-74].

Trade with European and Asiatic cultures: [124, 288, 452, 464-65, 468, 499, 532, 788-89, 816, 1439, 1500, 1586-87, 1767, 1772, 1869, 1953, 2450]. Contact with Crete, the Aegean and the Greek Mainland is discussed in [299, 745, 1639, 1688-89, 1892].

THE OASES AND THE WESTERN DESERT General discussions of the archaeology and history of these most interesting areas include: [134-40, 155-65, 172, 318, 326, 328, 409, 762-63, 804, 1003-5, 1017, 1045, 1049, 1074, 1083-86, 1097, 1106, 1201, 1206-7, 1219, 1253, 1283, 1310, 1314, 1348, 1356, 1361-63, 1440, 1489-99, 1616-21, 1628, 1819, 1922-27, 2058-61].

Kharga Oasis is treated in [150, 152, 213, 488-504 passim, 853-57, 1319, 1418, 2057, 2277]; Bahariya in [996]; Dakhla in [550, 2141, 2405, 2410]; Dongola in [401]; Kurkur in [390]; Siwa in [992, 994].

For the North Coast of Egypt, see [182-83]; for the Gilf Kebir [140, 211, 460-62, 1687]; for Gebel Uweinat [211, 453-55, 1369]; for Libya [163-64, 181, 247-48, 422-31,

581-84, 749-50, 814, 820-23, 831, 894, 903, 910-24, 1063, 1357-59, 1366-69, 1445, 1839, 1859, 1871, 1962, 2025, 2050].

NUBIA General studies and archaeological surveys include [6, 456-57, 729, 772-74, 868, 944, 1353, 1411, 1558-59, 1581, 1625-26, 1877-78, 1880, 1904, 1913, 2008, 2011-12, 2041, 2142-43, 2146, 2371-2423 passim].

Its flora and fauna are discussed in [154, 300, 870, 959, 1693]; its people in [7, 55, 185-86, 933, 1623, 1625]; its stone industries in [51, 55, 518, 520, 878, 954-55, 981, 1050, 1654-55, 1658, 2041, 2146, 2371-2413 passim]. The archaeology of Wadi Kubbaniya is treated in [160-62, 569, 870, 959, 1129, 1228-29, 2371-2423 passim].

KHARTOUM AND THE SUDAN The archaeology of this vast area is still largely unstudied. But several surveys have been conducted [83-104, 1011, 1906-7, 1911, 2094], and some syntheses of the Palaeolithic and Mesolithic [93, 1113, 1545-46] and of the Neolithic [92, 543] have appeared. One of the most important sites, of course, is that at Khartoum. It, and the site of Esh-Shaheinab, have been described and studied in [83-6, 88, 90-1, 99, 104, 543]. Artifacts from the Sudan are described in [8, 92, 94-6, 101, 1019].

Abbreviations

AÄA	*Archiv für ägyptische Archäologie,* Vienna.
AAI	*Annali dell'Africa Italiana,* Rome.
AAWLM	*Abhandlungen der Akadamie der Wissenschaften und der Literatur in Mainz,* Wiesbaden.
ADAW	*Abhandlungen der Deutschen Akadamie der Wissenschaft zu Berlin, Phil.-hist. Klasse,* Berlin. (Before 1945, *APAW.*)
ÄF	*Ägyptologische Forschungen,* Glückstadt, Hamburg and New York.
AfA	*Archiv für Anthropologie. Organ der deutschen Gesellschaft für Anthropologie, Ethnologie und Urgeschichte,* Braunschweig.
AfO	*Archiv für Orientforschung,* Berlin. (After vol. 15, Graz.)
AION	*Annali del Instituto Orientale di Napoli,* Naples.
AJA	*American Journal of Archaeology.*
AJSL	*American Journal of Semitic Languages and Literatures,* Chicago.
AKM	*Abhandlungen für die Kunde des Morgenlandes,* Leipzig. (After 1951, Wiesbaden.)
AnOr	*Analecta Orientalia,* Rome.
AnzAWW	*Anzeiger der Akademie der Wissenschaften in Wien,* Vienna. (After 1947, *AnzÖAW.*)
AnzÖAW	*Anzeiger der Österreichischen Akademie der Wissenschaften,* Vienna. (Before 1947, *AnzAWW.*)
AO	*Der alte Orient,* Leipzig.
APAW	*Abhandlungen der Preussischen Akademie der Wissenschaften,* Berlin. (After 1945, *ADAW.*)
ArOr	*Archiv Orientální,* Prague and Paris. (Vols. 14 and 15, Stuttgart and Paris.)
ASAE	*Annales du Service des Antiquités de l'Egypte,* Cairo.
ASN	Archaeological Survey of Nubia, Cairo.
AV	*Archäologische Veroffentlichungen,* Deutsches Archäologischen Instituts, Mainz. (Vols. 1-3, Cairo.)
BAAS	British Association for the Advancement of Science, London.

BASOR *Bulletin of the American Schools of Oriental Research,* New Haven.

BdE *Bibliothèque d'Etude,* Institut Français d'Archéologie Orientale, Cairo.

BE *Bibliothèque Egyptologique,* Cairo.

BIE *Bulletin de l'Institut d'Egypte.* (Before 1920, *Bulletin de l'Institut Egyptien.*)

BIFAO *Bulletin de l'Institut Français d'Archéologie Orientale,* Cairo.

BiOr *Bibliotheca Orientalis,* Leiden.

BMFA *Bulletin of the Museum of Fine Arts,* Boston.

BMMA *Bulletin of the Metropolitan Museum of Art,* New York.

BMRAH *Bulletin des Musées Royaux d'Art et d'Histoire (Bulletin van de Koninklijke Musea voor Kunst en Geschiedenis),* Brussels.

Bonner Geogr. Abh. *Bonner geographische Abhandlung,* Bonn.

BSAB *Bulletin de la Société Royale Belge d'Anthropolgogie,* Bruxelles.

BSAE *British School of Archaeology in Egypt,* London.

BSAL *Bulletin de la Société Linnéenne d'Anthropologie,* Lyon.

BSAP *Bulletin de la Société d'Anthropologie,* Paris.

BSFE *Bulletin de la Société Française d'Egyptologie,* Paris.

BSGE/BSRGE *Bulletin de la Société [Royale] Géographique d'Egypte,* Cairo.

BSGI *Bollettino Società Geografica Italiano,* Rome.

BSPF *Bulletin de la Société Préhistorique Française,* Paris.

BVMG *Bibliothèque du Vulgarisation du Musée Guimet,* Paris.

CAH *Cambridge Ancient History.* (Followed by edition: CAH^2 or CAH^3.)

CdE *Chronique d'Egypte,* Bruxelles.

CHE *Cahiers d'Histoire Egyptienne,* Cairo.

CRAIBL *Comptes Rendus à l'Académie des Inscriptions et Belles-Lettres,* Paris.

CrASP *Comptes-rendus à l'Académie des Sciences,* Paris.

DAWB *Denkschriften der Kaiserlichen Akadamie der Wissenschaften in Berlin, Phil.-hist. Klasse,* Berlin.

DAWW *Denkschriften der Kaiserlichen Akadamie der Wissenschaften in Wien, Phil.-hist. Klasse,* Vienna. (After 1950, *DÖAW.*)

DLZ *Deutsche Literaturzeitung,* Berlin, Leipzig.

DÖAW *Denkschrift der Österreichischen Akademie der Wissenschaften in Wien, Phil.-hist. Klasse,* Vienna. (Before 1950, *DAWW.*)

EEF Egypt Exploration Fund, London.

EES Egypt Exploration Society, London.

ERA Egyptian Research Account, London.

Expedition *Expedition: The Bulletin of the University Museum of the University of Pennsylvania,* Philadelphia.

FuF *Forschungen und Fortschritte,* Berlin.

GM *Göttinger Miszellen,* Göttingen.

IEJ — *Israel Exploration Journal,* Jerusalem.

ILN — *The Illustrated London News,* London.

IPEK — *Ipek: Jahrbuch für Prähistorische und Ethnographische Kunst,* Berlin and New York.

JA — *Journal Asiatique,* Paris.

JAOS — *Journal of the American Oriental Society,* New Haven.

JARCE — *Journal of the American Research Center in Egypt, Inc.,* Boston and Locust Valley.

JASOR — *Journal of the American Society of Oriental Research,* Toronto.

JEA — *Journal of Egyptian Archaeology,* London.

JEOL — *Jaarbericht van het Vooraziatisch-Egyptisch Genootschap (Gezelschap) 'Ex Oriente Lux',* Leiden.

JESHO — *Journal of the Economic and Social History of the Orient,* Leiden.

JMEOS — *Journal of the Manchester Egyptian and Oriental Society,* Manchester.

JNES — *Journal of Near Eastern Studies,* Chicago.

JRAI — *Journal of the Royal Anthropological Institute of Great Britain,* London.

JSSEA — *Journal of the Society for the Study of Egypian Antiquities,* Toronto.

Kush — *Kush: The Journal of the Sudan Antiquities Service,* Khartoum.

LAAA — *Liverpool Annals of Archaeology and Anthropology,* Liverpool.

LdÄ — *Lexikon der Ägyptologie,* Wiesbaden. (Ed. by Wolfgang Helck and Eberhard Otto.)

MAIBL — *Mémoires de l'Academie des Inscriptions et Belles-Lettres,* Paris.

MDAIK — *Mitteilungen des Deutschen Archäologischen Instituts, Abteilung Kairo,* Berlin and Wiesbaden; since 1970, Mainz. (Before 1944, *Mitteilungen des Deutschen Instituts für Ägyptische Altertumskunde in Kairo.*)

MDOG — *Mitteilungen der Deutschen Orientgesellschaft,* Berlin and Leipzig.

MIE — *Mémoires de l'Institut d'Egypte,* Cairo. (Before 1919, *Institut Egyptien.*)

MIFAO — *Mémoires publiés par les Membres de l'Institut Français d'Archéologie Orientale du Caire,* Cairo.

MIO — *Mitteilungen des Instituts für Orientforschung,* Berlin.

MonAeg — *Monumenta Aegyptiaca,* Brussels.

MonPiot — *Fondation Eugène Piot, Monuments et Mémoires publiés par l'Academie des Inscriptions et Belles-Lettres,* Paris.

MSAP — *Mémoires de la Société d'Anthropologie,* Paris.

MVAG — *Mitteilungen der Vorderasiatisch (-Ägyptisch)en Gesellschaft,* Leipzig and Berlin.

NARCE — *Newsletter: American Research Center in Egypt, Inc.*.

NAWG — *Nachrichten von der Akademie der Wissenschaften zu Göttingen, Phil.-hist. Klasse,* Göttingen. (After 1941, *NGWG.*)

NGWG — *Nachrichten von der Gesellschaft der Wissenschaften zu Göttingen, Phil.-hist. Klasse, Fachgruppe 1: Altertumswissenschaften,* Göttingen. (Before 1941, *NAWG.*)

Nyame Akuma — *Nyame Akuma: Newsletter of African Archaeology,* Department of Archaeology, University of Calgary, Alberta, Canada.

OIC — *Oriental Institute Communications,* University of Chicago, Chicago.

OIP — *Oriental Institute Publications,* University of Chicago, Chicago.

OLZ	*Orientalistische Literaturzeitung,* Berlin and Leipzig.
OMRO	*Oudeidkundige Mededeelingen uit het Rijksmuseum van Oudheden te Leiden,* Leiden.
OrSu	*Orientalia Suecana,* Uppsala.
PEQ	*Palestine Exploration Quarterly,* London. (Before 1937, *Palestine Exploration Fund's Quarterly Statement.*)
PPS	*Proceeding of the Prehistoric Society,* London.
PSBA	*Proceedings of the Society of Biblical Archaeology,* London.
PSEL	*Publications de la Société Egyptologique à l'Université d'Etat de Léningrad,* Leningrad.
RAr	*Revue Archéologique,* Paris.
Rev. Eg.	*Revue égyptologique,* Paris.
RC	*La Revue du Caire,* Cairo.
RdE	*Revue d'Egyptologie,* Cairo. (Before vol. 7, Paris.)
RecTrav	*Recueil de Travaux Rélatifs à la Philologie et à l'Archéologie Egyptiennes et Assyriennes,* Paris.
RSO	*Rivista degli Studi Orientali,* Rome.
SAS	*Sudan Antiquities Service, Occasional Papers,* Khartoum.
SAWW	*Sitzungsberichte der Akademie der Wissenschaften in Wien, Phil.-hist. Klasse,* Wien. (Before 1947, *Sitzungsberichte der Kaiserlichen Akademie der Wissenschaften.* After 1950, *SÖAW.*)
SBAW	*Sitzungsberichte der Bayerischen Akademie der Wissenschaften, Phil.-hist. Abteilung,* Munich.
SHAW	*Sitzungsberichte der Heidelberger Akademie der Wissenschaften, Phil.-hist. Klasse,* Heidelberg.
SNR	*Sudan Notes and Records,* Khartoum.
SÖAW	*Sitzungsberichte der Österreichischen Akademie der Wissenschaften in Wien, Phil.-hist. Klasse,* Vienna. (Before 1950, *SAWW.*)
TSBA	*Transactions of the Society of Biblical Archaeology,* London.
UCPAE	*University of California Publications in Archaeology and Ethnology,* Berkeley.
UCPEA	*University of California Publications in Egyptian Archaeology,* Berkeley.
UGAÄ	*Untersuchungen zur Geschichte und Altertumskunde Ägyptens,* Leipzig and Berlin. (After 1964, Hildesheim.)
WVDOG	*Wissenschaftliche Veröffentlichungen der Deutschen Orientgesellschaft,* Berlin and Leipzig.
WZKM	*Wiener Zeitschrift für die Kunde des Morgenlandes,* Vienna.
ZÄS	*Zeitschrift für Ägyptische Sprache und Altertumskunde,* Leipzig and Berlin.
ZDMG	*Zeitschrift der Deutschen Morgenländischen Gesellschaft,* Leipzig and Wiesbaden.

A

1 **D'Aconit, Georges.** Notes de préhistoire égyptienne. *Koninklijke Geschied- en Oudheidkundige Kring van Kortrijk., Handelingen,* n.s., 12 (1933): 126-31.

2 **Adamidi, Georges.** Les invasions de races européenes en Egypte dans les temps préhistoriques. *BIE,* 4th ser., 6 (1905): 77-89.

3 **Adams, Barbara.** *Ancient Hierakonpolis.* Warminster, 1974. [See also entry 4.]

4 ———. *Ancient Hierakonpolis Supplement.* Warminster, 1974.

Reviewed: [together with entry 3] *JEA* 61 (1975): 259-60 by Joan Crowfoot Payne.

5 ———. Hierakonpolis. *LdÄ* 2 (1975-): 1182-86.

———. See entry 1062.

Adams, Robert McC. See entry 1235.

6 **Adams, William Y.** *Nubia: Corridor to Africa.* Princeton, 1977.

7 ———. Geography and population of the Nile Valley. In: The Brooklyn Museum, *Africa in Antiquity,* 1: *The Essays.* (Brooklyn, 1978): 16-25.

Adamson, D.A. See entry 2448.

8 **Adamson, D.A., J.D. Clark** and **M.A.J. Williams.** Barbed bone points from central Sudan and the age of the 'Early Khartoum' Tradition. *Nature* 249 (1974): 120-23.

Addison. See entry 2429.

9 **Ahlmann, Hans W. von.** K.S. Sandfords undersökningar om utvecklingen av nidalen och den paleolitiska kulturen i denna. *Ymer* 56 (Stockholm, 1956): 176-83.

10 **Albîrunî.** *The Chronology of Ancient Nations. An English Version of the Arabic Text of the Athâr-ul-Bâkiya of Albîrunî, or 'Vestiges of the Past' Collected and Reduced to Writing by the Author in A.H. 390-1, A.D. 1000.* [Transl. and ed. with notes and index by Dr C. Edward Sachau.] London, 1879.

Albritton, Claude. See entries 1987, 2391 and 2392.

11 **Aldred, Cyril.** *Egypt to the End of the Old Kingdom.* London, 1965.

12 ———. *Egyptian Art.* Oxford, 1980.

13 **Alimen, H.** *Préhistoire de l'Afrique.* Paris, 1955. Transl. as *The Prehistory of Africa* by A.H. Broderick. London, 1957.

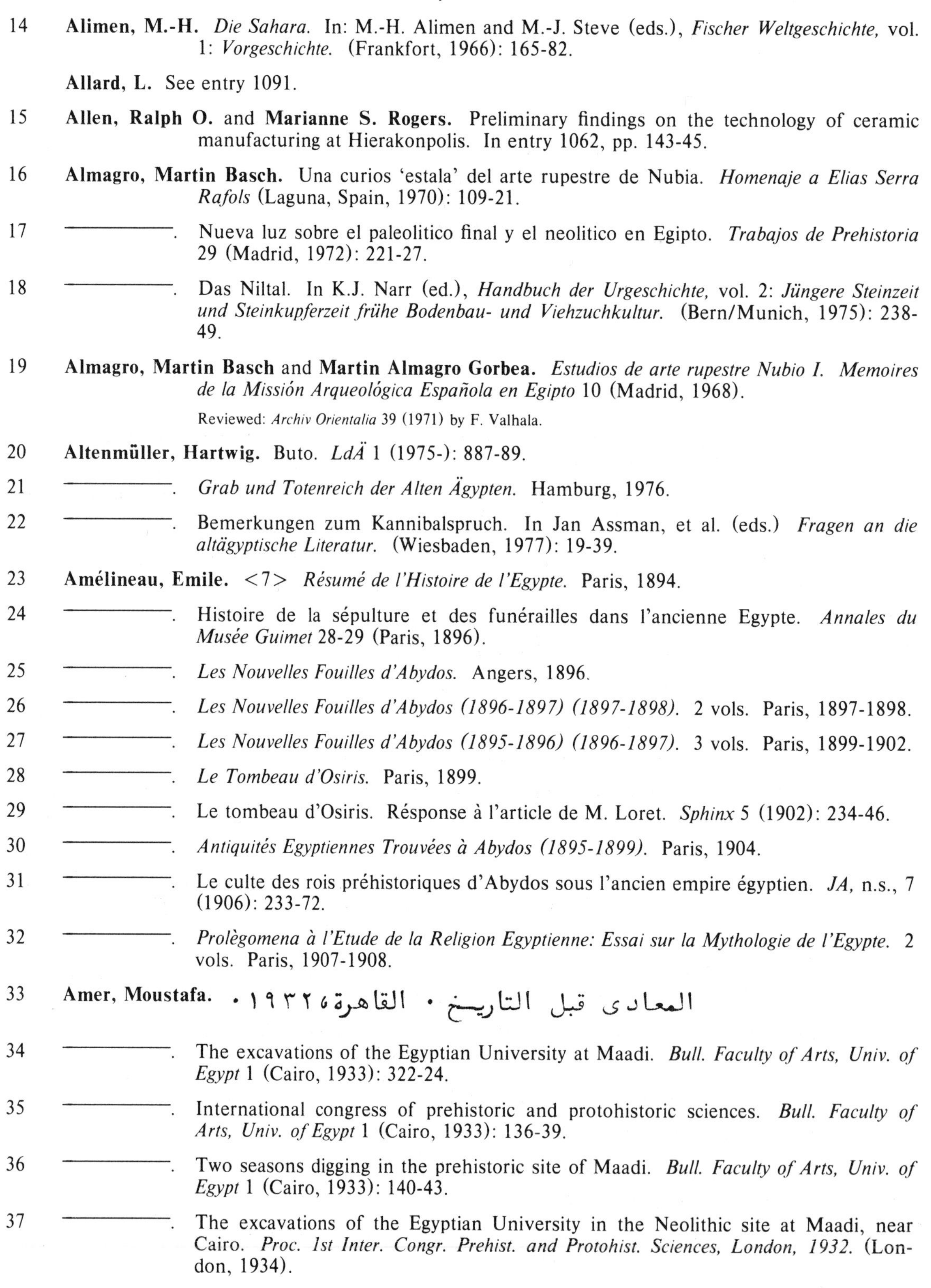

Reviewed: *Antiquity* 31 (1957): 49-51 by Sonia Cole.
Man 56 (1956): 142-43 by J.D. Clark.

14 **Alimen, M.-H.** *Die Sahara.* In: M.-H. Alimen and M.-J. Steve (eds.), *Fischer Weltgeschichte,* vol. 1: *Vorgeschichte.* (Frankfort, 1966): 165-82.

Allard, L. See entry 1091.

15 **Allen, Ralph O.** and **Marianne S. Rogers.** Preliminary findings on the technology of ceramic manufacturing at Hierakonpolis. In entry 1062, pp. 143-45.

16 **Almagro, Martin Basch.** Una curios 'estala' del arte rupestre de Nubia. *Homenaje a Elias Serra Rafols* (Laguna, Spain, 1970): 109-21.

17 ————. Nueva luz sobre el paleolitico final y el neolitico en Egipto. *Trabajos de Prehistoria* 29 (Madrid, 1972): 221-27.

18 ————. Das Niltal. In K.J. Narr (ed.), *Handbuch der Urgeschichte,* vol. 2: *Jüngere Steinzeit und Steinkupferzeit frühe Bodenbau- und Viehzuchkultur.* (Bern/Munich, 1975): 238-49.

19 **Almagro, Martin Basch** and **Martin Almagro Gorbea.** *Estudios de arte rupestre Nubio I. Memoires de la Missión Arqueológica Española en Egipto* 10 (Madrid, 1968).

Reviewed: *Archiv Orientalia* 39 (1971) by F. Valhala.

20 **Altenmüller, Hartwig.** Buto. *LdÄ* 1 (1975-): 887-89.

21 ————. *Grab und Totenreich der Alten Ägypten.* Hamburg, 1976.

22 ————. Bemerkungen zum Kannibalspruch. In Jan Assman, et al. (eds.) *Fragen an die altägyptische Literatur.* (Wiesbaden, 1977): 19-39.

23 **Amélineau, Emile.** <7> *Résumé de l'Histoire de l'Egypte.* Paris, 1894.

24 ————. Histoire de la sépulture et des funérailles dans l'ancienne Egypte. *Annales du Musée Guimet* 28-29 (Paris, 1896).

25 ————. *Les Nouvelles Fouilles d'Abydos.* Angers, 1896.

26 ————. *Les Nouvelles Fouilles d'Abydos (1896-1897) (1897-1898).* 2 vols. Paris, 1897-1898.

27 ————. *Les Nouvelles Fouilles d'Abydos (1895-1896) (1896-1897).* 3 vols. Paris, 1899-1902.

28 ————. *Le Tombeau d'Osiris.* Paris, 1899.

29 ————. Le tombeau d'Osiris. Résponse à l'article de M. Loret. *Sphinx* 5 (1902): 234-46.

30 ————. *Antiquités Egyptiennes Trouvées à Abydos (1895-1899).* Paris, 1904.

31 ————. Le culte des rois préhistoriques d'Abydos sous l'ancien empire égyptien. *JA,* n.s., 7 (1906): 233-72.

32 ————. *Prolègomena à l'Etude de la Religion Egyptienne: Essai sur la Mythologie de l'Egypte.* 2 vols. Paris, 1907-1908.

33 **Amer, Moustafa.** المعادى قبل التاريخ • القاهرة، ١٩٣٢ •

34 ————. The excavations of the Egyptian University at Maadi. *Bull. Faculty of Arts, Univ. of Egypt* 1 (Cairo, 1933): 322-24.

35 ————. International congress of prehistoric and protohistoric sciences. *Bull. Faculty of Arts, Univ. of Egypt* 1 (Cairo, 1933): 136-39.

36 ————. Two seasons digging in the prehistoric site of Maadi. *Bull. Faculty of Arts, Univ. of Egypt* 1 (Cairo, 1933): 140-43.

37 ————. The excavations of the Egyptian University in the Neolithic site at Maadi, near Cairo. *Proc. 1st Inter. Congr. Prehist. and Protohist. Sciences, London, 1932.* (London, 1934).

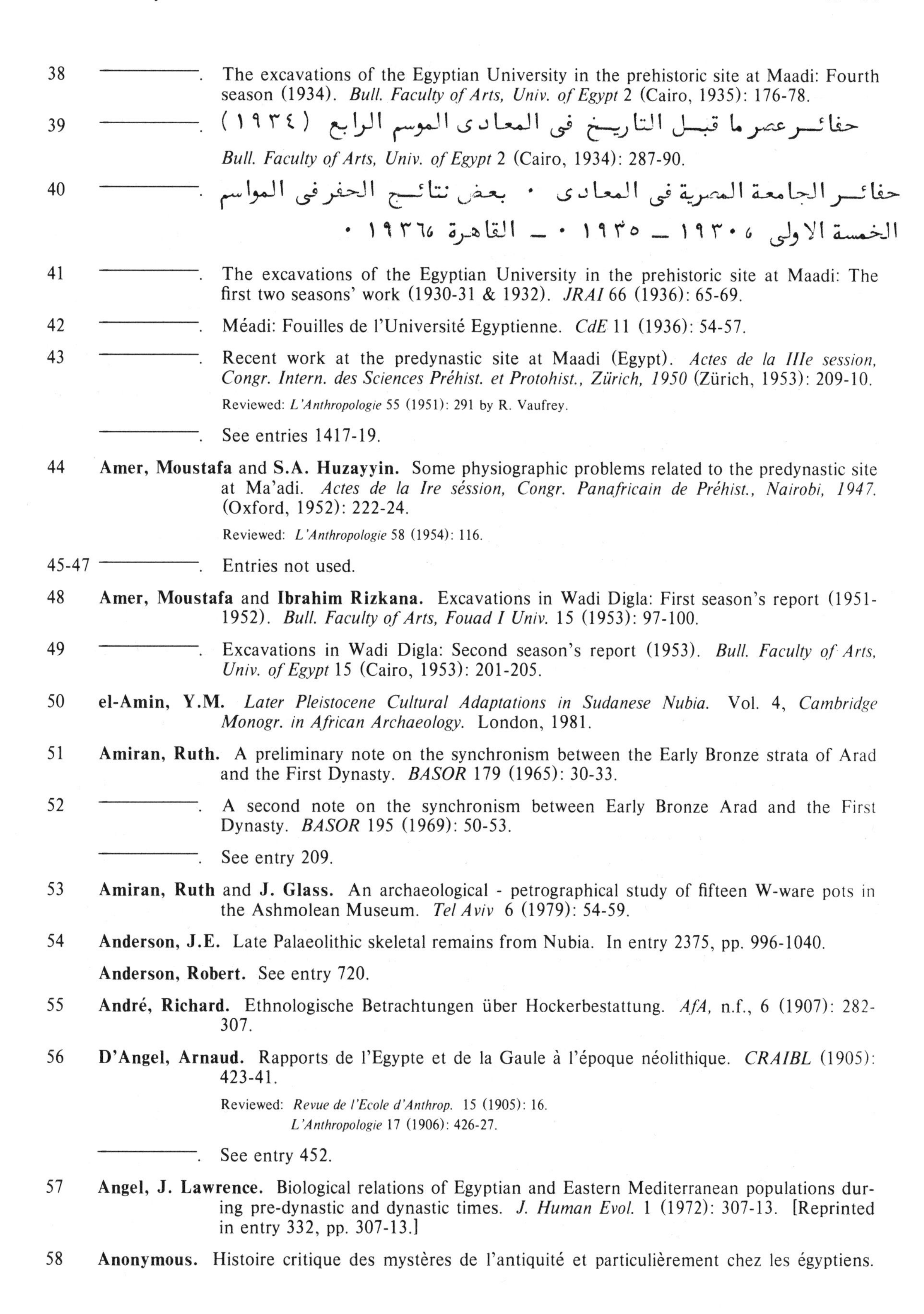

38 ————. The excavations of the Egyptian University in the prehistoric site at Maadi: Fourth season (1934). *Bull. Faculty of Arts, Univ. of Egypt* 2 (Cairo, 1935): 176-78.

39 ————. حفائر عصر ما قبل التاريخ فى المعادى الموسم الرابع (١٩٣٤)
Bull. Faculty of Arts, Univ. of Egypt 2 (Cairo, 1934): 287-90.

40 ————. حفائر الجامعة المصرية فى المعادى • بعض نتائج الحفر فى المواسم الخمسة الاولى ١٩٣٠، — ١٩٣٥ • — القاهرة ١٩٣٦ •

41 ————. The excavations of the Egyptian University in the prehistoric site at Maadi: The first two seasons' work (1930-31 & 1932). *JRAI* 66 (1936): 65-69.

42 ————. Méadi: Fouilles de l'Université Egyptienne. *CdE* 11 (1936): 54-57.

43 ————. Recent work at the predynastic site at Maadi (Egypt). *Actes de la IIIe session, Congr. Intern. des Sciences Préhist. et Protohist., Zürich, 1950* (Zürich, 1953): 209-10.
Reviewed: *L'Anthropologie* 55 (1951): 291 by R. Vaufrey.

————. See entries 1417-19.

44 **Amer, Moustafa** and **S.A. Huzayyin.** Some physiographic problems related to the predynastic site at Ma'adi. *Actes de la Ire séssion, Congr. Panafricain de Préhist., Nairobi, 1947.* (Oxford, 1952): 222-24.
Reviewed: *L'Anthropologie* 58 (1954): 116.

45-47 ————. Entries not used.

48 **Amer, Moustafa** and **Ibrahim Rizkana.** Excavations in Wadi Digla: First season's report (1951-1952). *Bull. Faculty of Arts, Fouad I Univ.* 15 (1953): 97-100.

49 ————. Excavations in Wadi Digla: Second season's report (1953). *Bull. Faculty of Arts, Univ. of Egypt* 15 (Cairo, 1953): 201-205.

50 **el-Amin, Y.M.** *Later Pleistocene Cultural Adaptations in Sudanese Nubia.* Vol. 4, *Cambridge Monogr. in African Archaeology.* London, 1981.

51 **Amiran, Ruth.** A preliminary note on the synchronism between the Early Bronze strata of Arad and the First Dynasty. *BASOR* 179 (1965): 30-33.

52 ————. A second note on the synchronism between Early Bronze Arad and the First Dynasty. *BASOR* 195 (1969): 50-53.

————. See entry 209.

53 **Amiran, Ruth** and **J. Glass.** An archaeological - petrographical study of fifteen W-ware pots in the Ashmolean Museum. *Tel Aviv* 6 (1979): 54-59.

54 **Anderson, J.E.** Late Palaeolithic skeletal remains from Nubia. In entry 2375, pp. 996-1040.

Anderson, Robert. See entry 720.

55 **André, Richard.** Ethnologische Betrachtungen über Hockerbestattung. *AfA,* n.f., 6 (1907): 282-307.

56 **D'Angel, Arnaud.** Rapports de l'Egypte et de la Gaule à l'époque néolithique. *CRAIBL* (1905): 423-41.
Reviewed: *Revue de l'Ecole d'Anthrop.* 15 (1905): 16.
L'Anthropologie 17 (1906): 426-27.

————. See entry 452.

57 **Angel, J. Lawrence.** Biological relations of Egyptian and Eastern Mediterranean populations during pre-dynastic and dynastic times. *J. Human Evol.* 1 (1972): 307-13. [Reprinted in entry 332, pp. 307-13.]

58 **Anonymous.** Histoire critique des mystères de l'antiquité et particulièrement chez les égyptiens.

(Paris, *An* 7 [Sept. 1798-Aug. 1799].)

59 ————. *Suggestions for the Application of the Egyptological Method to Modern History.* London, 1862.

60 ————. *To the Pyramids! A Series of Comic Sketches.* Bristol, 1863.

61 ————. *M.S.'s The Adamic Race. A Reply to 'Ariel', Drs. Young and Blackie.* New York, 1868.

62 ————. *S.H.M.'s The People of Africa. The Negro in Ancient History. The Koran. —African Mohammedanism. —Condition and Character of Negroes in Africa. —The Syrian (Arabic) College.* New York, 1871.

63 ————. Harmony of Egyptian and Mosaic Records. *London Quarterly and Holborn Review* 53 (1877): 265. [Reprinted in *Methodist Quarterly* 40 (1878): 709.]

64 ————. Races of North Africa and their religions. *Christian Remembrancer* 74 (1879): 261.

65 ————. Races of North Africa. *Eclectic Review* 58 (1881): 480. [Reprinted in *Irish Monthly* 47 (1879): 299.]

66 ————. Prehistoric man in Egypt and Syria. *The Builder* 46 (1884): 716.

67 ————. Prehistoric cannibalism in Egypt. *Biblia* 10 (1897): 290-93.

68 ————. Prehistoric art in the Libyan Desert. *Nature* 133 (1934): 20.

69 ————. *Prehistoric Wall-Painting in Egypt.* London, 1950. [A folio reproduction, with explanatory text, of the scenes in the Painted Tomb at Hierakonpolis.]

Reviewed: *BiOr* 8 (1951): 77-78.

70 ————. Une civilization pré-dynastique évoluée. *CHE,* 4th ser., fasc. 5-6 (1952): 238.

71 ————. Une découverte archéologique remontant à la première dynastie. *CHE,* 5th ser., fasc. 1 (1953): 93-94.

72 **Anoutchine, D.N.** *[The Stone Age in Egypt and its Prehistoric Population in the Light of Recent Research.] Bull. et Notices Archéol.* 3-4 (Moscow, 1898). [In Russian]

73 **Anthes, Rudolf.** König 'Schlange', <u>d</u>t-Schlange und Schlangengöttin Uto. *ZÄS* 83 (1958): 79-82.

74 **Arcelin, Adrian.** Letter à M. de Mortillet: L'Age de la pierre en Egypte. *RAr,* n.s., 20 (1869): 441.

75 ————. Réclamation relative à note récente de MM. Hamy et Lenormant sur la découverte des restes de l'âge de la pierre en Egypte. *CrASP* 69 (1869): 1312-13. [See also entry 976.]

76 ————. L'Industrie primitive en Egypte. *Rec. de Matériaux pour l'Hist. Primitive et Naturelle de l'Homme,* 2nd ser., 6 (1870): 27-29, 50, 102-8, 241, 238-40, 348-50.

77 ————. L'Industrie primitive en Egypte et en Syrie. Mission scientifique du Ministère de l'Instruction Publique. Rapports au Ministre. *Ann. de l'Acad. de Mâcon,* 1st ser., 9 (1870): 155.

78 ————. Lettre sur la question des silex taillés. *BIE* 13 (1872): 68-70.

79 ————. *L'Age de Pierre et la Classification Préhistorique d'après les Sources Egyptiennes: Résponse à MM. Chabas et Lepsius.* Paris, 1873.

80 ————. Les premiers habitants de l'Egypte. *C.r. du 4e Congr. Soc. Intern. des Catholiques* (1898): 23-51.

————. See Supplement entry 2487.

81 **Arcelin, Adrian, E.T. Hamy,** and **François Lenormant.** L'Age de pierre en Egypte. *Rec. de Matériaux pour l'Hist. Primitive et Naturelle de l'Homme,* 2nd ser., 5 (1869-1870): 27-43.

82 **Ardouin-Dumazat, V.E.** L'Anthropologie de l'Egypte, d'après M. Chantre. *La Geographie* 12 (1905): 102-8.

83 **Arkell, Anthony John.** Early Khartoum. *Antiquity* 21 (1947): 172-81.

84 ————. *Early Khartoum: An Account of the Excavations of an Early Occupation Site Carried Out by the Sudan Government Antiquities Service in 1944-45.* Oxford, 1949.
Reviewed: *Man* 50 (1950): 10.
Archaeology 3 (1950): 125-26.

85 ————. Excavations at Esh Shaheinab, Sudan, 1949. *PPS* 15 (1949): 42-49.

86 ————. The excavations of a Neolithic site at Esh Shaheinab. *SNR* 30 (1949): 212-21.

87 ————. The Old Stone Age in the Anglo-Egyptian Sudan. *SAS* 1 (Khartoum, 1949).

88 ————. The results of the excavation of an early site at Khartoum in 1944-45. *SNR*, suppl. to 30 (1949): 19-20.

89 ————. Varia Sudanica. *JEA* 36 (1950): 24-40.

90 ————. The late Acheulean of Esh Shaheinab. *Kush* 1 (1953): 30-34.

91 ————. *Shaheinab: An Account of the Excavation of a Neolithic Occupation Site.* Oxford, 1953.

92 ————. The Sudanese origin of the predynastic 'Black Incised' pottery. *JEA* 39 (1953): 76-79.

93 ————. A Khartoum Mesolithic site at Ed Damer. *Kush* 2 (1954): 91-92.

94 ————. An archaic representation of Hathor. *JEA* 41 (1955): 125-126.

95 ————. An early predynastic Sudanese bowl from Upper Egypt. *Kush* 3 (1955): 95-96.

96 ————. Modern designs on predynastic slate palettes. *JEA* 41 (1955): 126.

97 ————. The relations of the Nile Valley with the southern Sahara in Neolithic times. *IIe Session, Congr. Panafricain de Préhist., Alger* (Paris, 1955): 345-46.

98 ————. Some notes on the Sudanese Neolithic. *Kush* 4 (1956): 84-85.

99 ————. Khartoum's part in the development of the Neolithic. *Kush* 5 (1957): 8-12.

100 ————. Preliminary results of the British Ennedi Expedition, 1957. *Kush* 7 (1959): 15-26.

101 ————. The distribution in Central Africa of early Neolithic ware (Dotted Wavy Line Pottery) and its possible connections with the beginnings of pottery. *Actes de la Ire Session, Congr. Panafricain de Préhist., Leopoldville, Congo, 1959* (Tervareu, Belgium, 1962): 283-87.

102 ————. Was King Scorpion Menes? *Antiquity* 37 (1963): 31-35.

103 ————. The prehistory of the Nile Valley. In *Handbuch der Orientalistik,* 7 Abt., 1 Bd., 2 Abschnitt A, Lieferung 17 (Leiden/Köln, 1975).

104 ————. Dating Early Khartoum. In *Ägypten und Kusch.* (1977): 53-55.

105 **Arkell, Anthony John** and **E. Martin Burgess.** The reconstruction of a fluted porphyry bowl. *The Museum Journal* 54 (London, 1955): 287-90.

106 **Arkell, Anthony John** and **Peter J. Ucko.** Review of predynastic development in the Nile Valley. *Current Anthropology* 6 (1965): 145-66. [With comments by Elise Baumgartel, pp. 156-57.]

107 **Arkell, William J.** Prehistoric flints from Egypt. *Man* 31 (1931): 56.

108 ————. Rock paintings and drawings in northern Africa, 1933-1934. *Geogr. Rev.* 26 (New York, 1936): 153-55.

————. See entries 1999-2005.

109 ————. Entry not used.

Armelagos, George. See entries 110, 2274.

110 **Armelagos, George, G.H. Ewing, D.L. Greene** and **M.L. Papworth.** The physical anthropology of the Nile Valley. *Symposium on Nile Valley Prehistory, Intern. Assoc. for Quaternary Res.* (Boulder, Colorado, 1965). Unpublished.

111 **Arnold, Dieter.** Fajjum. *LdÄ* 2 (1975-): 87-93.

112 ————. Grab. *LdÄ* 2 (1975-): 826-37.

113 **Arnold, Dorothea.** Keramik. *LdÄ* 3 (1975-): 392-409.

114 **Asselbergh, Henri.** *Chaos en Beheerung: Documenten uit Aneolitisch Egypte.* Leiden, 1961.

115 **Atzler, M.** Randglossen zur ägyptischen Vorgeschichte. *JEOL* 22 (1971-72): 228-46.

116 **Aufrère, L.** *L'Aurore de l'Histoire sur les Déserts du Nord de l'Ancien Monde. La Vie dans la Région Désertique Nord-tropicale de l'Ancien Monde.* Paris, 1938.

Aumassip, G. See entry 1340.

Aurenche, O. See entry 1081.

117 **Avdiev, V.I.** Egypt and the Caucasus. *Ancient Egypt* (1933): 29-36.

118 ————. Geometrical ornament on archaic Egyptian pottery. *Ancient Egypt* (1935): 37-48.

119 ————. The origin and development of trade and cultural relations of ancient Egypt with neighboring countries. In *Papers Presented by the Soviet Delegation at the 23rd Intern. Congr. of Orientalists* (Moscow, 1954): 23-36.

Aymé, A. See entry 1377.

120 **Ayrton, Edward Russell** <13>. **C.T. Currelly,** and **A.E.P. Weigall.** *Abydos.* Part 3. *EES* 25. London, 1904.

121 **Ayrton, Edward Russell** and **W.L.S. Loat.** *Pre-dynastic Cemetery of El-Mahasna. EEF* 31. London, 1911.

B

122 **Bachatly, Charles Alexandre.** Two hitherto unknown prehistoric sites in Upper Egypt. *Man* 36 (1936): 15-16.

123 ———. Gisements capsiens au nord du Fayoum. *BIE* 19 (1937): 117-22.

124 ———. Relations between a prehistoric Transcaucasian and a modern Egyptian amulet. *Man* 38 (1938): 48.

125 ———. *Bibliographie de la Préhistoire Egyptienne (1869-1938).* Cairo, 1942.

Reviewed: *Man* 45 (1945): 114 by Elise J. Baumgartel.
Anthropos 37-40 (1942-1945): 958 by J. Maringer.

126 ———. Note complémentaire à propos des gisements capsiens au nord du Fayoum. *BIE* 32 (1951): 287-90.

127 **Badawi, Fathi Afifi.** Die Grabung der ägyptischen Altertümerverwaltung in Merimde-Benisalâme im Oktober-November 1976. *MDAIK* 34 (1978): 43-51.

128 **Badawy, Alexander.** *La Dessin Architectural chez les Anciens Egyptiens.* Cairo, 1948.

129 ———. La première architecture en Egypte. *ASAE* 51 (1951): 1-28.

130 ———. A propos du signe [hieroglyph]. *ASAE* 52 (1952): 137-44.

131 ———. *A History of Egyptian Architecture,* 1: *From the Earliest Times to the End of the Old Kingdom.* Giza, 1954.

Reviewed: *CdE* 61 (1956): 59-60 by A. Mekhitarian.

132 ———. Architekturdarstellung. *LdÄ* 1 (1975-): 399-420.

133 ———. Festungsanlage. *LdÄ* 2 (1975-): 194-203.

134 **Bagnold, R.A.** Journeys in the Libyan Desert, 1929 and 1930. *Geogr. J.* 78 (1931): 13-39.

135 ———. A further journey through the Libyan Desert. *Geogr. J.* 82 (1933): 211-35.

136 ———. *Libyan Sands: Travel in a Dead World.* London, 1935.

137 ———. An expedition to the Gilf Kebir and Uweinat, 1939. 1: Narrative of the journey. *Geogr. J.* 93 (1939): 281-87.

138 ———. *The Physics of Blown Sand and Desert Dunes.* London, 1941.

———. See entry 1678.

139 **Bagnold, R.A., J. Harding-King, D. Newbold** and **W.B.K. Shaw.** Journeys in the Libyan

Desert, 1929 and 1930. *Geogr. J.* 78 (1931): 524-35.

140 **Bagnold, R.A., R.F. Peel, O.H. Myers,** and **H.A. Winkler.** An expedition to the Gilf Kebir and Uweinat, 1938. *Geogr. J.* 93 (1939): 281-313.

141 **Baillet, Jules.** <15> L'Anthropophagie dans l'Egypte primitive. *BIFAO* 30 (1930): 65-72.
Reviewed: *Ancient Egypt* (1932): 61.

142 **Baillet, Jules** and **G.L. Chauvet.** *Silex Taillés du Nil et de la Charente.* Angoulême, 1899.

143 ————. *Sépultures Préhistoriques du Nil et de la Charente.* Angoulême, 1900.

144 **Bailloud, G.** Les peintres rupestres archaiques de l'Ennedi. *L'Anthropologie* 64 (1960): 3-4 and 211-34.

145 **Baines, John** and **Jaromir Málek.** *Atlas of Ancient Egypt.* Oxford, 1980.

146 **Baker, John R.** *Race.* Oxford, 1974.

Baker, M.J. See entry 422.

147 **Baker, Samuel White.** The races of the Nile Basin. *Trans. Ethnol. Soc.*, n.s., 5 (1867): 228-38.

148 **Balcz, H.** Die altägyptische Wandliederung. *MDAIK* 1 (1930): 38-92.

149 **Baldwin, John D.** *Prehistoric Nations; Or, Inquiries Concerning Some of the Great People and Civilizations of Antiquity, and Their Probable Relations to a Still Older Civilization of the Ethiopians or Cushites or Arabians.* London, 1869.

150 **Ball, John.** <16> *Kharga Oasis: Its Topography and Geology.* Cairo, 1900.

151 ————. The Fayum Depression. *Antiquity* 4 (1930): 467-71.
Reviewed: *Ancient Egypt* (1932): 30.

152 ————. Further remarks on Kharga Oasis. *Geogr. J.* 81 (1933): 532.

153 ————. *Contributions to the Geography of Egypt.* Cairo, 1939.

————. See entry 1319.

Ballais, Jean-Louis. See entries 1340 and 1341.

154 **Ballman, Peter.** Report on the avian remains from sites in Egyptian Nubia, Upper Egypt and the Fayum. In entry 2388, pp. 307-310.

————. See entry 870.

155 **Balout, L.** *Préhistoire de l'Afrique du Nord: Essai de Chronologie.* Paris, 1955.

156 ————. Données nouvelles sur le probléme du Moustèrien en Afrique du Nord. *Actes del V Congresso Panafricano de Prehistoria y de Estudio del Cuaternario, 1, Santa Cruz de Tenerife.* (1965): 137-46.

157 ————. Der Maghreb. In entry 14, pp. 148-65.

158 ————. The prehistory of North Africa. In J. Ki-Zerbo (ed.), *General History of Africa,* 1: *Methodology and African Prehistory.* (London and Berkeley, 1981): 568-84.

————. See entry 578.

159 **Banks, K. Morgan.** Ceramics of the Western Desert. In entry 2407, pp. 300-316.

160 ————. The grinding implements of Wadi Kubbaniya. In entry 2416, pp. 239-44.

161 ————. Report on site E-78-8. *Ibid.*, pp. 179-80.

162 ————. Report on site E-78-10. *Ibid.*, pp. 217-28.

————. See entries 1228 and 2438.

163 **Baramki, D.C.** Libya: Pre-historic archaeology (13 Sept. 1964 to 12 Sept. 1965). *UNESCO:*

Funds-in-Trust, LIBYAC 1 (Paris, 1965).

164 **Barich, B.E.** and **F. Mori.** Missione paletnologica italiana nel Sahara libico: Risultati della campagna 1969. *Origini* 4 (1970): 79-142.

165 **Barker, H., R. Burleigh** and **N. Meeks.** British Museum radiocarbon measurements, VII. *Radiocarbon* 13 (1971): 157-88.

166 **Barkley, Marylynn S.** Vertebral arch defects in ancient Egytian populations. *J. Human Evolution* (1978): 553-57.

Barrau, J. See entry 1826.

167 **Barsanti, E.** Ouverture de la pyramide de Zaouiét el-Aryân. *ASAE* 2 (1901): 92-94.

168 **Barta, Winfried.** Bemerkungen zur Bedeutung der in Pyramidenspruch 273/274 geschilderten Anthropophagie. *ZÄS* 106 (1979): 89-94.

169 ————. Die Chronologie der 1. bis 5. Dynastie nach den Angeben des Rekonstruieren Annalensteins. *ZÄS* 108 (1981): 11-23.

170 **Barthélemy, Jean Jacques.** *Mémoire dans Lequel on Prouve que les Chinois sont une Colonie Egyptienne.* Paris, 1758.

171 **Barthélemy, L.N.A.** François Lenormant. *Literatur-blatt für Orientalische Philologie* (1884): 440-47.

172 **Barthoux, J.** Paléogéographie de l'Egypte. *C.r. Congr. Intern. de Geogr.* 3 (1925): 68-100.

173 **Bartolomei, G.** Alcuni risultati delle ricerche sul quaternario del massiccio dell'Acacus-Tadrart (Fezzan meridionale). *Atti della . . . Riunione Scientifica dell'Instituto Italiano di Preistoria e Protostoria in Memoria de Francesco Zorzi 10.1965* (Verona, 1966): 15-22.

174 **Barton, George Aaron.** *Sketch of Semitic Origins.* New York, 1902.

175 ————. *Semitic and Hamitic Origins: Social and Religious.* Philadelphia, 1934.

176 ————. The origins of civilization in Africa and Mesopotamia: Their relative antiquity and interplay. *Proc. Amer. Phil. Soc.* 68 (1929): 303-12.

177 **Bar-Yosef, O.** The Epipalaeolithic in Palestine and Sinai. In entry 2388, pp. 363-78.

————. See entries 1800 and 1801.

178 **Bar-Yosef, O.** and **J.L. Phillips** (eds.). *Prehistoric Investigations in Gebel Maghara, Northern Sinai. Monographs of the Institute of Archaeology* 7 (Jerusalem, 1977).

179 **Bataillard, P.** Discussion sur le fer en Egypte. *BSAP*, 3rd ser., 4 (1883): 616-17.

180 **Bates, Oric.** <21> Dr. G. Elliot Smith and the Egyptian Race. *Cairo Science J.* 6 (1912): 108-11. [See also entry 2165.]

181 ————. *The Eastern Libyans.* Oxford, 1914.

182 ————. Archaic burials at Marsa Matrûh. *Ancient Egypt* (1915): 158-65.

183 ————. Excavations at Marsa Matrûh. *Harvard African Studies* 8 (1927): 123-97.

184 **Bates, Oric,** and **John E. Wolf.** A nephrite celt from the Fayûm. *Man* 15 (1915): 132-34.

185 **el Batrawi, Ahmed.** The racial history of Egypt and Nubia, I: The craniology of Lower Nubia from predynastic times to the sixth century B.C. *JRAI* 75 (1945): 81-101.

186 ————. The racial history of Egypt and Nubia, II: The racial relationships of the ancient and modern populations of Egypt and Nubia. *JRAI* 76 (1946): 131-56.

187 **el Batrawi, Ahmed** and **G.M. Morant.** A study of a First Dynasty series of skulls from Sakkara and of an Eleventh Dynasty series from Thebes. *Biometrika* 34 (1947): 18-27.

188 **Baudouin, Marcel.** La station du néolithique terminal de Merimde, près le Caire. *BSPF* 29 (1932): 352.

189 **Baumgartel, Elise J.** Dolmen und Mastaba. *Alten Orient,* Beiheft 6. (Leipzig, 1926).

190 ———. Neolitische Steingeräte in Form von Typen des älteren Paläolithikums. *Prähist. Zeits* 19 (Berlin, 1928): 101-9.

191 ———. Feuersteingeräte. *MDAIK* 2 (1932): 107-8.

192 ———. The flint quarries of Wady Sheykh (Campignien). *Ancient Egypt* (1939): 103-8.

193 ———. *The Cultures of Prehistoric Egypt.* 2 vols. Oxford, 1947-1960. With a 2nd ed. of vol. 1 publ. in 1955.

Reviewed: (vol. 1, 1st ed.): *AJA* 53 (1949): 76-79 by H.J. Kantor.
L'Anthropologie 54 (1950): 477-78 by E. Massoulard.
Antiquity 21 (1947): 166-68 by A.J. Arkell.
BECTHNK 3, 33 (1950): 160-65 by N.M. Postovskaya.
(vol. 1, 2nd ed.): *CdE* 61 (1956): 57-59 by Pierre Gilbert.
BiOr 8 (1951): 26-28 by Hans Stock.
CdE 24 (1949): 270-72 by E. Saccasyn della Santa.
CHE, 1st ser., 2 (1948): 209-10 by J. Leibovitch.
JEA 36 (1950): 115-16 by K.R. Maxwell-Hyslop.
J. des Savants (1948):92-93 by Jacques Vandier.
Man 48 (1948):45-46 by G. Caton-Thompson and J. Waechter.
RdE 7 (1950): 127-29 by R. Weill.
(vol. 2): *BiOr* 18 (1961): 189.
CdE 36 (1961): 151-53 by C. Vandersleyen.
Man 61 (1961): 166 by M.A. Murray.
OLZ 57 (1962): 129-33 by E. Otto.
Times Literary Supplement 60 (1961): 403.

194 ———. Herodotus on Min (A reinterpretation of Book II, 4: 99, and 145/6). *Antiquity* 21 (1947): 145-50.

195 ———. Fragments of prehistoric Egyptian pottery. *Man* 48 (1948): 59-60.

196 ———. The three colossi from Koptos and their Mesopotamian counterparts. *ASAE* 48 (1948): 533-53.

197 ———. Some notes on the origins of Egypt. *Archiv Orientálni* 20 (1952): 278-87.

198 ———. Predynastic architecture in Egypt. *Proc. 23rd Intern. Congr. Orient., London* 59 (1956).

Reviewed: *Bull. Fac. Arts, Egyptian Univ., Cairo* 16 (1955):103 by Alexander Badawy.
Wiener Völkerkundliche Mitt. 2 (1954): 219 by E. Winter.

199 ———. The predynastic cemetery at Nagada. *Antiquity* 39 (1965): 299.

200 ———. What do we know about the excavations at Merimde? *JAOS* 85 (1965): 502-11.

201 ———. Scorpion and rosette and the fragments of the large Hierakonpolis mace head. *ZÄS* 93 (1966): 9-13.

202 ———. About some ivory statuettes from the 'Main Deposit' at Hierakonpolis. *JARCE* 7 (1968): 7-14. [Abstr. in *Proc. 27th Intern. Congr. Orient., Wiesbaden* (1971): 117.]

203 ———. Merimda. *Proc. 26th Intern. Congr. Orient., New Delhi* 2 (1968): 3-5.

204 ———. The predynastic cemetery at Nagada. *ZÄS* 95 (1968):72.

205 ———. *Petrie's Naqada Excavations: A Supplement.* London, 1970.

Reviewed: *Antiquity* 46 (1972): 63 by H. Case.
BiOr 24 (1972): 176-78 by G. Godron.
JEA 58 (1972): 311-12 by B.J. Kemp.

206 ———. Predynastic Egypt. *CAH*^{3}, vol. 1, pt. 1, 9 (Cambridge, 1970, also in fasc. 1965): 463-97.

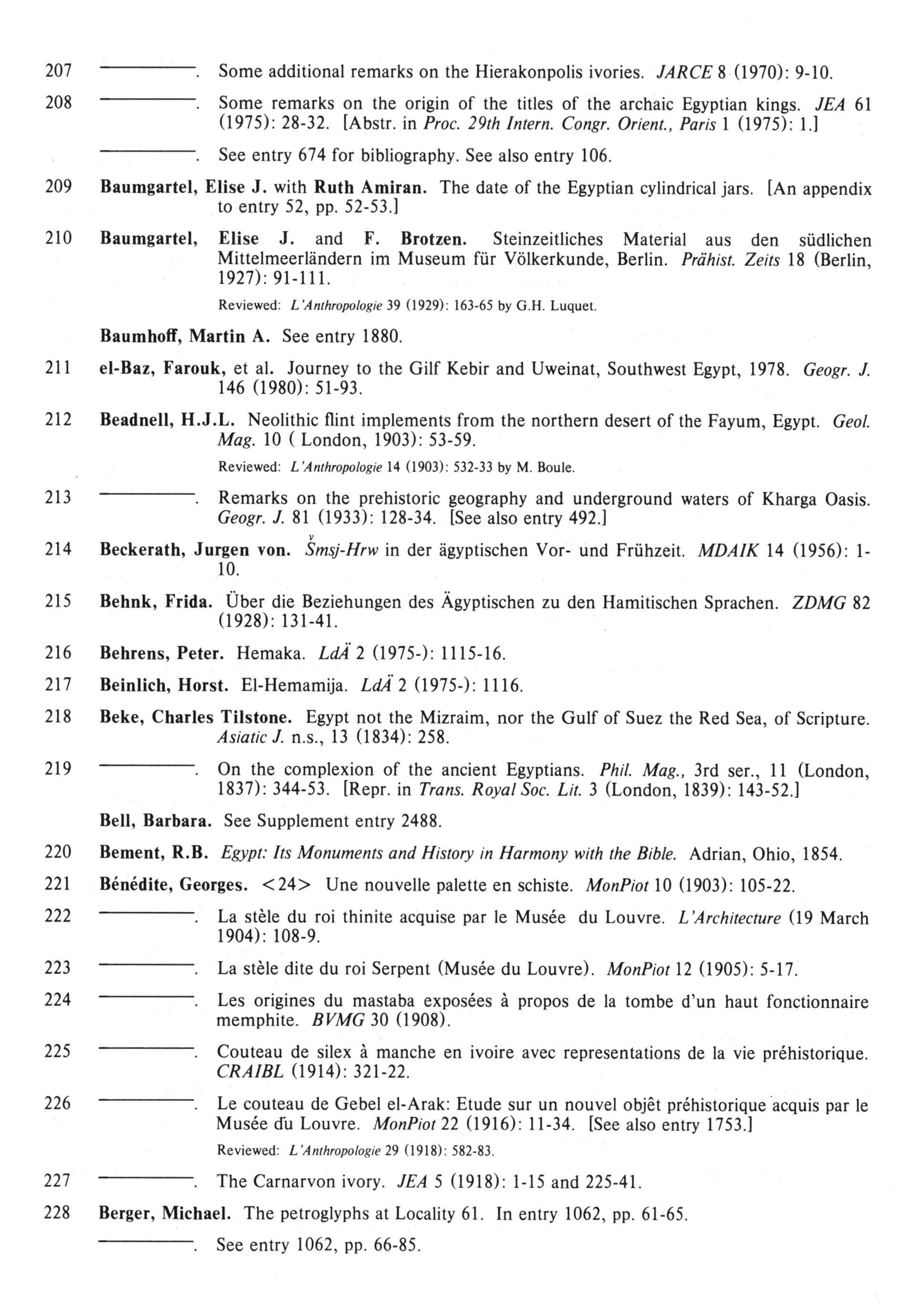

207 ————. Some additional remarks on the Hierakonpolis ivories. *JARCE* 8 (1970): 9-10.

208 ————. Some remarks on the origin of the titles of the archaic Egyptian kings. *JEA* 61 (1975): 28-32. [Abstr. in *Proc. 29th Intern. Congr. Orient., Paris* 1 (1975): 1.]

————. See entry 674 for bibliography. See also entry 106.

209 **Baumgartel, Elise J.** with **Ruth Amiran.** The date of the Egyptian cylindrical jars. [An appendix to entry 52, pp. 52-53.]

210 **Baumgartel, Elise J.** and **F. Brotzen.** Steinzeitliches Material aus den südlichen Mittelmeerländern im Museum für Völkerkunde, Berlin. *Prähist. Zeits* 18 (Berlin, 1927): 91-111.

Reviewed: *L'Anthropologie* 39 (1929): 163-65 by G.H. Luquet.

Baumhoff, Martin A. See entry 1880.

211 **el-Baz, Farouk,** et al. Journey to the Gilf Kebir and Uweinat, Southwest Egypt, 1978. *Geogr. J.* 146 (1980): 51-93.

212 **Beadnell, H.J.L.** Neolithic flint implements from the northern desert of the Fayum, Egypt. *Geol. Mag.* 10 (London, 1903): 53-59.

Reviewed: *L'Anthropologie* 14 (1903): 532-33 by M. Boule.

213 ————. Remarks on the prehistoric geography and underground waters of Kharga Oasis. *Geogr. J.* 81 (1933): 128-34. [See also entry 492.]

214 **Beckerath, Jurgen von.** *Šmsj-Hrw* in der ägyptischen Vor- und Frühzeit. *MDAIK* 14 (1956): 1-10.

215 **Behnk, Frida.** Über die Beziehungen des Ägyptischen zu den Hamitischen Sprachen. *ZDMG* 82 (1928): 131-41.

216 **Behrens, Peter.** Hemaka. *LdÄ* 2 (1975-): 1115-16.

217 **Beinlich, Horst.** El-Hemamija. *LdÄ* 2 (1975-): 1116.

218 **Beke, Charles Tilstone.** Egypt not the Mizraim, nor the Gulf of Suez the Red Sea, of Scripture. *Asiatic J.* n.s., 13 (1834): 258.

219 ————. On the complexion of the ancient Egyptians. *Phil. Mag.*, 3rd ser., 11 (London, 1837): 344-53. [Repr. in *Trans. Royal Soc. Lit.* 3 (London, 1839): 143-52.]

Bell, Barbara. See Supplement entry 2488.

220 **Bement, R.B.** *Egypt: Its Monuments and History in Harmony with the Bible.* Adrian, Ohio, 1854.

221 **Bénédite, Georges.** <24> Une nouvelle palette en schiste. *MonPiot* 10 (1903): 105-22.

222 ————. La stèle du roi thinite acquise par le Musée du Louvre. *L'Architecture* (19 March 1904): 108-9.

223 ————. La stèle dite du roi Serpent (Musée du Louvre). *MonPiot* 12 (1905): 5-17.

224 ————. Les origines du mastaba exposées à propos de la tombe d'un haut fonctionnaire memphite. *BVMG* 30 (1908).

225 ————. Couteau de silex à manche en ivoire avec representations de la vie préhistorique. *CRAIBL* (1914): 321-22.

226 ————. Le couteau de Gebel el-Arak: Etude sur un nouvel objêt préhistorique acquis par le Musée du Louvre. *MonPiot* 22 (1916): 11-34. [See also entry 1753.]

Reviewed: *L'Anthropologie* 29 (1918): 582-83.

227 ————. The Carnarvon ivory. *JEA* 5 (1918): 1-15 and 225-41.

228 **Berger, Michael.** The petroglyphs at Locality 61. In entry 1062, pp. 61-65.

————. See entry 1062, pp. 66-85.

229 **Berger, R.** Ancient Egyptian chronology. *Phil. Trans. Royal Soc.* 269 (London, 1970): 23-36.

————. See entry 1840.

230 **[Berlin Museum.]** *Vorgeschichtliche Altertümer Ägyptens.* Berlin, 1908.

231 **Bernard-Delapierre, Guy.** Une nouvelle mention de la déesse Mafdet sous la 1re dynastie. *RdE* 4 (1940): 220-21.

232 **Bernier, François.** Nouvelle division de la terre, par les differentes espèces ou races d'hommes qui l'habitant. *J. des Savants* 12 (1684): 148-55.

233 **Berry, A.C.** and **R.J. Berry.** Origins and relationships of the ancient Egyptians; Based on a study of non-metrical variations in the skull. *J. Human Evol.* 1 (1972): 199-208. [Repr. in entry 330, pp. 199-208.]

234 **Berry, A.C., R.J. Berry** and **P.J. Ucko.** Genetical changes in ancient Egypt. *Man* 2 (1967): 551-68.

Berry, R.J. See entries 233 and 234.

235 **Berthelot, M.** Sur les âges de cuivre et de bronze et sur le sceptre de Pépi Ier, roi d'Egypte. *J. des Savants* (1889): 567-73.

236 ————. Sur l'origine du bronze et sur le sceptre de Pépi Ier, roi d'Egypte. *Ann. de Chimie et de Physique,* 6th ser., 17 (1889).

237 ————. Sur quelques nouveaux objets de cuivre provenant de l'ancienne Egypte. *CrASP* 118 (1894): 464-66.

238 ————. Etude sur les métaux qui composent les objets de cuivre, de bronze, d'étain et d'argent découvertes par M. de Morgan dans les fouilles de Dahchour, ou provenant du Musée de Gizeh. *Ann. de Chimie et de Physique,* 7th ser., 4 (1895): 546-74.

239 ————. Sur les mines de cuivre de Sinai exploitées par les anciens Egyptiens. *CrASP* 123 (1896): 365-74.

240 ————. Outils et armes de l'âge de cuivre en Egypte: Procédés de fabrication: Nouvelles recherches. *CrASP* 124 (1897): 1119-25.

241 **Besançon, J.** *L'Homme et le Nil.* Paris, 1957.

242 **Bet-Arie, Y.** [A chalcolithic work station near Serabit el-Khadem.] *Qadmoniot* 8, 2-3 (30-31) (1975): 62-64. [In Hebrew]

243 **Biasutti, Renato.** Egiziani ed Etiopici. *Aegyptus* 6 (1925): 27-35.

244 ————. I contributi alla etnologia. *Comitato Geografico Nazionale Italiano: L'Opera degli Italiani per la Conoscenza dell'Egitto e per il suo Risorgimento Economico* (1926): 93-98.

245 **Bietak, Manfred** and **R. Engelmeyer.** Eine frühdynastische Abrisiedlung mit Felsbilden aus Sayala-Nubien. *DÖAW* 82 (1963).

246 **Billy, G.** Population changes in Egypt and Nubia. *J. Human Evol.* 6 (1977): 697-704.

247 **Bilsborough, A.** Late Pleistocene human remains from Cyrenaican Libya. *Man,* n.s., 6 (1971): 694-96.

248 **Birman, R. A.** Historic problem of the Libyan Desert. *Geogr. J.* 83 (1934): 456-63.

249 **Birch, Samuel.** <27> Sur l'origine des Egyptiens. *C.r. 1er Congr., des Orient Session I, II.* (Paris, 1876): 61-66.

250 **Bissing,** Freiherr von **Friedrich.** <28> Les origines de l'Egypte. *L'Anthropologie* 9 (1898): 241-58 and 408-17.

251 ————. *Catalogue Générale des Antiquities Egyptienne du Musée du Caire. Nos. 18065-18793.*

Tongefässe. Vienna, 1904.

252 ———. Les débuts de la statuaire en Egypte. *RAr,* 4th ser., 15 (1910): 244-62.

253 ———. Prähistorische Töpfe aus Indien und aus Äegypten. *SBAW* 22 (1911): 3-22.
Reviewed: *OLZ* 15 (1912): 317 by Max Müller.

254 ———. Vom Wasi es Saaba' Rigale bei Gebel Silsile. *SBAW* 24 (1913): 3-20.

255 ———. Probleme der Ägyptischen Vorgeschichte, 1: Ägypten und Mesopotamien. *AfO* 5 (1929): 49-81.

256 ———. Probleme der Ägyptischen Vorgeschichte, 2: Seltsame archaische Denkmaler. *AfO* 6 (1930): 1-11.

257 ———. Probleme der Ägyptischen Vorgeschichte, 3: Noch einmal Ägypten und Mesopotamien. *AfO* 7 (1931): 23-30.

258 ———. *Aegyptische Kunstgeschichte,* 1. Berlin and Charlottenburg, 1934.

259 ———. Seltene Formen frühzeitlichen Schminkpaletten. *ZÄS* 73 (1937): 56-60.

Bittel, Kurt. See entries 1420 and 2053.

260 **Blackman, Aylward Manley.** <29> Sacramental ideas and usages in ancient Egypt. *PSBA* 40 (1918): 57-66 and 86-91.

261 ———. Sacramental ideas and usages in ancient Egypt. *RecTrav* 39 (1920): 44-78.

262 ———. The predynastic and early dynastic period. In D. Ross (ed.), *The Art of Egypt through the Ages.* London, 1931.
Reviewed: *Ancient Egypt* 4 (1922): 121.

263 ———. Some remarks on a clay sealing found in the tomb of Hemaka. *AnOr* 7 (1938): 4-9.

264 **Blackman, Aylward M.** and **H.W. Fairman.** The myth of Horus at Edfou, 2. *JEA* 30 (1944): 5-32.

265 **Blanc, Nicole.** The peopling of the Nile Valley south of the 23rd parallel. In UNESCO, *The Peopling of Ancient Egypt and the Deciphering of Meroitic Script.* [Proc. of the symposium held in Cairo from 28 January to 3 February 1974] (Paris, 1978): 37-64. [Also published in French].

266 **Blanchard, Ralph Harrup.** <31> Prehistoric civilizations in Egypt. *Views and Reviews* 1 (1927): 49-51.

267 **Blanckenhorn, M.** Die Geschichte des Nilstroms in der Tertiär- und Quatärperiode, Sowie des paläolithischen Menschen in Ägypten. *Zeits. der Gesell. für Erdkunde.* 37 (1902): 694-722 and 753-762.

268 ———. Über die Steinzeit und die Feuersteinartefakte in Syrien-Palästina. *Zeits. für Ethnol.* 37 (1905): 447-72.

269 ———. Die steinzeit Palästina-Syriens und Nordafrikas. *Land der Bibel* 3 (Leipzig, 1921): 1-48 and 4 (1922): 1-45.
Reviewed: *Mitt. Anthrop. Gesell., Wien* 53 (1923): 26-27 by H. Obermaier.

270 ———. Entstehung und vorgeschichte Besiedlung des Fajumbekkens mit dem Mörissee. *Petermann's Mitt., Gotha* 77 (1931): 26-27.

271 **Bloch, A.** De l'origine des Egyptiens. *BSAP,* 5th ser., 4 (1903): 394-403.

Blom, R. See entry 1363.

272 **Bodichon, Eugène.** *Tableau Synoptique Représentant les Noms, les Egypte migrations, les Filiations, l'Origine, les Caractères Physiques et Moraux des Races de l'Afrique Septentrionale.* Nantes, 1894.

273 **Boehmer, R.M.** Orientalische Einfluss auf verzierten Messergriffen aus dem prädynastischen Ägypten. *Archäol. Mitt. Iran,* n.s., 7 (1974): 15-40.

274 ————. Das Rollsiegel im prädynastischen Ägypten. *Archäol. Anzeiger* 4 (1974): 495-514.

275 **Boghdady, Foad.** An archaic tomb at old Cairo. *ASAE* 32 (1932): 153-60.

Bollshakov, O.G. See entry 1430.

Boloyan, David S. See entry 1880.

276 **Bongrani, L. F.** Un vecchio lotto di antichità egiziane nel Museo delle origine le dell'Università di Roma. *Rivista Studi Orientali* 46 (1971): 119-27.

277 **Bonnet, Hans.** *Ein frühgeschichtliches Gräberfeld bei Abusir.* Vol. 4, *Veröffentlichungen der Ernst von Sieglin Expedition in Ägypten.* Leipzig, 1928.

Reviewed: *Ancient Egypt* 3 (1918): 122.

278 **Bonwick, James.** *Egyptian Belief and Modern Thought.* London, 1878.

279 **Borchardt, Ludwig.** <33> Ein neuer Königsname der ersten Dynastie. *SBAW* 48 (1897): 1054-58.

280 ————. Das Grab des Menes. *ZÄS* 36 (1898): 87-105.

281 ————. Königs Athothis asiatischer Feldzug. *Orientalische Studien Fritz Hommel zum 60sten Geburtstag. MVAG* 22 (1917): 342-45.

282 ————. Ein verzierter Stabteil aus vorgeschichtlicher Zeit. *ZÄS* 66 (1931): 12-14. [See also entry 445.]

283 **Boreaux, Charles.** <34> Les poteries décorées de l'Egypte prédynastique. *Rev. des Et. ethnogr. et sociol.* 1 (Paris, 1908): 35-52.

284 ————. *Etudes Nautique Egyptienne. L'Art de la Navigation en Egypte jusqu'a la Fin de l'Ancien Empire. MIFAO* 50 (1925).

Reviewed: *Ancient Egypt* 3 (1916): 90-91.
J. des Savants (1927): 385-93 by Commandants Carlini and Vivielle.

285 **Boscawen, William St.** The beginnings of Egyptian civilization: The explorations of Prof. Petrie at Coptos. *The Babylonian and Oriental society* 7 (1894): 234-39.

286 **Bosse-Griffiths, Kate.** A Prehistoric stone figure from Egypt. *Valcamonica Symposium, 1972: Actes du Symposium International sur les Religions de la Préhistoire* (Brescia, Italia, 1975): 317-22.

287 **Bosteaux-Paris, Charles.** A propos d'une faucille en silex trouvée en Egypte. *C.r. Assoc. Franç. pour l'Avancement des Sciences, Besançon, 1893,* 22 (Paris, 1893): part 1, p. 280. and part 2, p. 758.

288 ————. Les Egyptiens et les Phéneciennes auraient-ils eu des relations commerciales avec les peuple des gauloises marviennes au début de l'époque galatienne. *C.r. Assoc. Franç. pour l'Avancement des Sciences, Lille, 1909,* 38 (Paris, 1909): 874-77.

289 **Bothmer, Bernard V.** A predynastic Egyptian hippopotamus. *BMFA* 46 (1948): 64-69.

290 ————. A new fragment of an old palette. *JARCE* 8 (1969-70): 5-8.

291 **Boulain, J. A.** L'Egypte avant le pyramides. *Archeologia* 60 (1973): 15-19.

292 **Boule, M.** Fouilles en Egypte. *L'Anthropologie* 13 (1902): 414-15.

293 ————. Les monuments mégalithiques de la péninsule du Sinai. *L'Anthropologie* 26 (1915): 605.

294 ————. Le paléolithique égyptien. *L'Anthropologie* 26 (1915): 189-90 and 604.

295 ————. Synchronismes possible entre l'Europe et l'Egypte préhistoriques. *L'Anthropologie* 26 (1915): 604.

296 ———. Silex rostro-carénés d'Egypte. *L'Anthropologie* 29 (1918-19): 185-86.

297 ———. Ossements humains fossiles d'Egypte. *L'Anthropologie* 33 (1923): 442.

298 ———. Statuette préhistorique d'Egypte. *L'Anthropologie* 34 (1924): 605.

299 ———. Relations de la Crète minoenne avec l'Egypte et la Libye. *L'Anthropologie* 36 (1926): 182-83.

300 **Boulos, L.** The discovery of Medemia palm in the Nubian desert of Egypt. *Bot. Notiser* 121 (1968): 117-20.

301 **Bourguin, Jules.** Les premiers animaux domestiques . . . Les animaux domestiques dans l'antique Egypte. *Rapports faits à la Soc. Imp. d'Acclimatatio* 8 (Paris, 1860).

302 **Bouriant, Urbain.** Les tombeaux d'Hierakonpolis. *Etudes Archéologiques, Linguistiques et Historiques, Dédiées à ... C. Leemans.* (Leiden, 1885): 35-40.

303 **Bourriau, Janine.** *Umm el-Ga'ab: Pottery from the Nile Valley before the Arab Conquest.* [Exhibition organized by the Fitzwilliam Museum, Cambridge, 6 October to 11 December 1981. Cambridge, 1981.]

Reviewed: *JSSEA* 12 (1982): 91-92 by Jorge Ogdon.

304 **Bouysonnie,** Abbé **J.** Gravures sur rochers au Mont Sinai. *Revue Anthropologique* 34 (1924): 350-52.

305 **Bovier-Lapierre, Paul .** <37> La paléolithique stratifiée des environs du Caire. *L'Anthropologie* 35 (1925): 37-46.

306 ———. Nord d'Helouan (Egypte). *C.r. Congr. Intern. de Géogr., 1925,* 4 (Cairo, 1925): 268-82.

307 ———. Stations préhistoriques des environs du Caire. *C.r. Congr. Intern. de Géogr., 1925,* 4 (Cairo, 1925): 298-308.

308 ———. Les gisements paléolithiques de la plaine de l'Abassieh. *BIE* 8 (1926): 257-75.

309 ———. Schweinfurth et la préhistoire. *BSRGE* 14 (1926): 153-60.

310 ———. Les explorations de S.A.S. le Prince Kemal el Din Hussein: Contribution à la préhistoire du désert Libyque. *BIE* 10 (1929): 34-44.

311 ———. Récentes explorations de S.A.S. le Prince Kemal el Din Hussein dans le désert Libyque: Contribution à la préhistoire. *BIE* 12 (1930): 121-28.

312 ———. L'Egypte préhistorique. *Précis de l'histoire d'Egypte* 1 (1931): 1-50.

Reviewed: *Man* 33 (1933): 139 by G.D. Hornblower.

313 ———. La question chalossienne. *BSPF* 28 (1931): 203-208.

314 ———. La bourgade protohistorique de Méadi (sud du Caire). *CdE* 13-14 (1932): 203-208.

315 ———. Industries préhistoriques dans l'îsle d'Eléphantine et aux environs d'Assouan. *BIE* 16 (1934): 115-31.

316 ———. Une nouvelle station préhistorique (sébilienne) découverte à l'est du Delta par le lieutenant aviateur R. Grace. *BIE* 2 (1940): 289. [Arabic summary, p.303.]

Bradley, R.J. See entry 1941.

317 **Braidwood, Robert J.** *The Near East and the Foundations for Civilization: An Essay in the Appraisal of the General Evidence.* Eugene, Oregon, 1952.

Brandt, S. See entry 2383.

318 **Braunstein-Silvestre, Florence.** La Sahara à l'époque néolithique: Quelques problèmes d'Etude. *Assoc. Intern. pour l'Etude de la Préhistoire Egyptienne. Egypte avant l'Histoire* 1 (1980): 35-45.

319 ———. The predynastic of Egypt: An overview. *JSSEA* 11 (1981): 59-64.

320 **Breasted, James Henry.** <38> The origins of civilization. *The Scientific Monthly* 9 (1919): 289-316, 416-432; and 10 (1920): 87-209, 249-268.

321 ———. The predynastic union of Egypt. *BIFAO* 30 (1931): 709-724.

322 ———. The rise of man and modern research. *Ann. Rep., Smithsonian Institution* (Washington, 1932): 411-418.

323 ———. *The Oriental Institute.* Vol. 12, *University of Chicago Survey.* Chicago, 1933.

Bréaud, G. See entry 1092.

324 **Breccia, E.** Vestigia neolitiche nel nord del Delta. *Bull. Soc. Archéol. d'Alexandrie* 5 (1923): 132-57.

Reviewed: *Ancient Egypt* (1924): 56.

Breed, C.S. See entry 1363.

325 **Brentjes, Burchard.** *Fels und Höhlenbilder Afrikas.* Heidelberg, 1965. Transl. by Anthony Dent as *African Rock Art.* New York, 1969.

326 **Breuil, Henri.** Gravures rupestres du désert Libyque identiques à celles des anciens Bushmen. *L'Anthropologie* 36 (1926): 125-27.

327 ———. *L'Afrique Préhistoire. Cahiers d'Art* 5 (Paris, 1930).

———. See entry 1207.

328 **Briggs, L.C.** Living tribes of the Sahara and the problem of their prehistoric origin. *Actes de la IIIe Congr. de Prehist., Livingston, 1955* (London, 1957).

329 **Brinks, Jürgen.** Haus. *LdÄ* 2 (1975-): 1055-61.

330 **[British Museum.]** *A Guide to the Antiquities of the Stone Age in the Department of British and Mediaeval Antiquities.* London, 1902.

331 **Broca, Paul.** Sur l'origine des races d'Egypte et de leur civilization. *BSAP* 2 (1861): 550-55.

332 **Brothwell, Don R.** and **B.A. Chiarelli.** *Population Biology of the Ancient Egyptians.* London and New York, 1973.

Brotzen, F. See entry 210.

333 **Brovarski, Edward.** Naga-ed-Dër. *LdÄ* 4 (1975-): 296-317.

334 **Brown, Robert.** *The Races of Mankind: A Popular Description of the Characteristics, Manners, and Customs of the Principal Varieties of the Human Family.* 4 vols.. London, 1873-76.

335 **Brown, Robert Hanbury.** <40> *The Fayum and Lake Moeris.* London, 1893.

336 **Browne, A.J. Jukes.** On flint implements from Egypt. *JRAI* 7 (1878): 396-97.

337 **Brugsch, Heinrich Ferdinand Karl.** <42> *Geschichte Ägyptens unter den Pharaonen, nach dem Denkmälern Bearbeitet.* Leipzig, 1877. Transl. as *A History of Egypt under the Pharaohs, Derived Entirely from the Monuments,* 2 vols. (London, 1879) by H.D. Seymour, revised by M. Broderick (London, 1891).

338 ———. Ägyptische Beiträge zur Völkerkunde der ältesten Welt. *Deutsche Revue* 6, 4 (1881): 43-57.

339 ———. La table ethnique des anciens égyptiens. *RdE* 2 (1881-82): 322-35.

340 ———. Die altägyptische Völkertafel. *Verhandlungen des 5ten Orient. Congres* 2 (1882): 25-70.

341 ———. Die Negerstämme der Una Inschrift. *ZÄS* 20 (1882): 30-36.

342 ———. *Die Libysch-Kaukasischen Völkergruppen, an den Nordländern des afrikanischen*

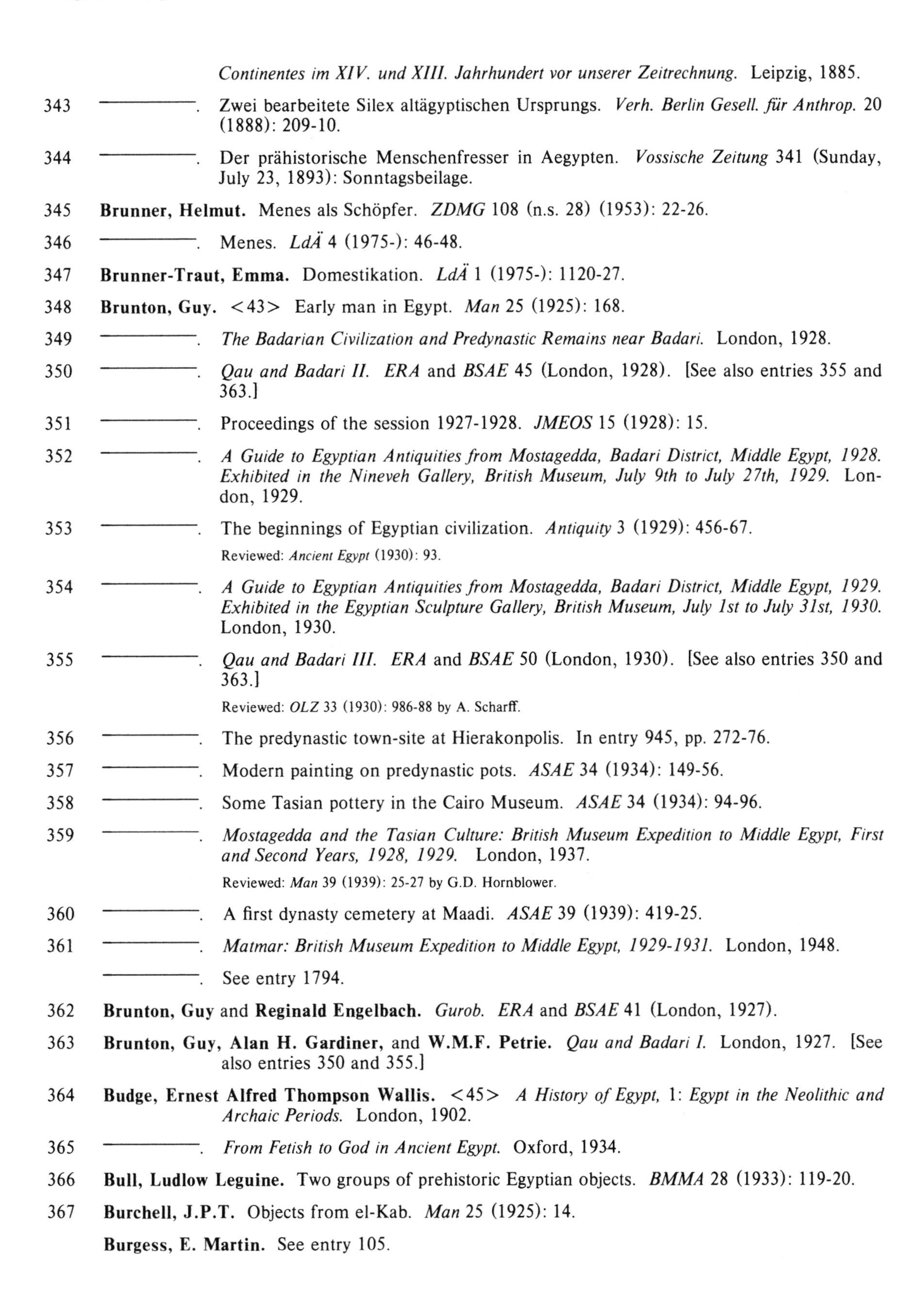

Continentes im XIV. und XIII. Jahrhundert vor unserer Zeitrechnung. Leipzig, 1885.

343 ————. Zwei bearbeitete Silex altägyptischen Ursprungs. *Verh. Berlin Gesell. für Anthrop.* 20 (1888): 209-10.

344 ————. Der prähistorische Menschenfresser in Aegypten. *Vossische Zeitung* 341 (Sunday, July 23, 1893): Sonntagsbeilage.

345 **Brunner, Helmut.** Menes als Schöpfer. *ZDMG* 108 (n.s. 28) (1953): 22-26.

346 ————. Menes. *LdÄ* 4 (1975-): 46-48.

347 **Brunner-Traut, Emma.** Domestikation. *LdÄ* 1 (1975-): 1120-27.

348 **Brunton, Guy.** <43> Early man in Egypt. *Man* 25 (1925): 168.

349 ————. *The Badarian Civilization and Predynastic Remains near Badari.* London, 1928.

350 ————. *Qau and Badari II. ERA* and *BSAE* 45 (London, 1928). [See also entries 355 and 363.]

351 ————. Proceedings of the session 1927-1928. *JMEOS* 15 (1928): 15.

352 ————. *A Guide to Egyptian Antiquities from Mostagedda, Badari District, Middle Egypt, 1928. Exhibited in the Nineveh Gallery, British Museum, July 9th to July 27th, 1929.* London, 1929.

353 ————. The beginnings of Egyptian civilization. *Antiquity* 3 (1929): 456-67.
Reviewed: *Ancient Egypt* (1930): 93.

354 ————. *A Guide to Egyptian Antiquities from Mostagedda, Badari District, Middle Egypt, 1929. Exhibited in the Egyptian Sculpture Gallery, British Museum, July 1st to July 31st, 1930.* London, 1930.

355 ————. *Qau and Badari III. ERA* and *BSAE* 50 (London, 1930). [See also entries 350 and 363.]
Reviewed: *OLZ* 33 (1930): 986-88 by A. Scharff.

356 ————. The predynastic town-site at Hierakonpolis. In entry 945, pp. 272-76.

357 ————. Modern painting on predynastic pots. *ASAE* 34 (1934): 149-56.

358 ————. Some Tasian pottery in the Cairo Museum. *ASAE* 34 (1934): 94-96.

359 ————. *Mostagedda and the Tasian Culture: British Museum Expedition to Middle Egypt, First and Second Years, 1928, 1929.* London, 1937.
Reviewed: *Man* 39 (1939): 25-27 by G.D. Hornblower.

360 ————. A first dynasty cemetery at Maadi. *ASAE* 39 (1939): 419-25.

361 ————. *Matmar: British Museum Expedition to Middle Egypt, 1929-1931.* London, 1948.

————. See entry 1794.

362 **Brunton, Guy** and **Reginald Engelbach.** *Gurob. ERA* and *BSAE* 41 (London, 1927).

363 **Brunton, Guy, Alan H. Gardiner,** and **W.M.F. Petrie.** *Qau and Badari I.* London, 1927. [See also entries 350 and 355.]

364 **Budge, Ernest Alfred Thompson Wallis.** <45> *A History of Egypt,* 1: *Egypt in the Neolithic and Archaic Periods.* London, 1902.

365 ————. *From Fetish to God in Ancient Egypt.* Oxford, 1934.

366 **Bull, Ludlow Leguine.** Two groups of prehistoric Egyptian objects. *BMMA* 28 (1933): 119-20.

367 **Burchell, J.P.T.** Objects from el-Kab. *Man* 25 (1925): 14.

Burgess, E. Martin. See entry 105.

368 **Burkitt, M.C.** *Prehistory: A Study of Early Cultures in Europe and the Mediterranean Basin.* Cambridge, 1921; second ed., 1925.

369 ————. Archaeological notes. *Man* 26 (1926): 10-13, 220-21.

————. See entry 1662.

Burleigh, R. See entry 165.

Burney, C.A. See entry 720.

370 **Burton, Richard Francis.** Flint flakes from Egypt. *JRAI* 7 (1878): 323-24.

371 ————. Stones and bones from Egypt and Midian. *JRAI* 8 (1879): 290-319.

372 **Burton-Brown, T.** *Studies in Third Millennium History.* London, 1946.

373 **Buschan, G.** Die Steinzeit und Bronzezeit in Ägypten. *Natur. und Offenbarung.* 37 (Münster, 1891): 106-11.

Buth, G.M. See Supplement entry 2489.

374 **Butler, B.H.** Skeletal remains from a Late Palaeolithic site near Esna, Upper Egypt. In entry 1339, pp. 176-83.

375 **de Buttafoco, D.** *Etude Historique sur l'Origine des Egyptiens.* Bastia, 1882.

376 ————. *Studio Storico Intorno alle Origini degli Egiziani.* Siena, 1883.

Butzer, E.K. See entry 416.

377 **Butzer, Karl W.** Late glacial and postglacial climatic variation in the Near East. *Erdkunde* 11 (1957): 21-25.

378 ————. Mediterranean pluvials and the general circulation of the Pleistocene. *Geografiska Annaler* 39 (Stockholm, 1957): 48-53.

379 ————. Quaternary stratigraphy and climate in the Near East. *Bonner Geogr. Abh.* 24 (Bonn, 1958).

380 ————. Studien zum vor- und frühgeschichtlichen Landschafts Wandel der Sahara: Das ökologische Problem der neolitischen Felsbilder der östlichen Sahara. *AAWLM, Math -Naturw. Kl.* 1 (1958): 1-49.

381 ————. Contributions to the Pleistocene geology of the Nile Valley. *Erdkunde* 13 (1959): 46-67.

382 ————. Environment and human ecology in Egypt during predynastic and early dynastic times. *BSGE* 32 (1959): 43-87.

383 ————. A minute predynastic flake industry from Hierakonpolis. *Archivo Intern. di Etnografia e Preistoria* 2 (Torino1959): 16-20.

384 ————. Die Naturlandschaft Ägyptens wahrend der Vorgeschichte und der dynastischen Zeit. *AAWLM, Math -Naturw. Kl.* 2 (1959).

385 ————. Some recent geological deposits in the Egyptian Nile Valley. *Geogr. J.* 125 (1959): 75-79.

386 ————. Archaeology and geology in ancient Egypt. *Science* 132 (1960): 1617-24.

387 ————. Remarks on the geography of settlement in the Nile Valley during Hellenistic times. *BSGE* 33 (1960): 5-36.

388 ————. Archaeologische Fundstellen Ober- und Mittelagyptens in ihrer geologischen Landschaft. *MDAIK* 1 (1960): 54-68.

389 ————. Pleistocene stratigraphy and prehistory in Egypt. *Quaternaria* 6 (1962): 456-65.

390 ————. Desert landforms at the Kurkur Oasis, Egypt. *Annals, Association of American Geographers* 55 (1965): 578-91.

391 ————. Archaeology and geology in ancient Egypt. In *New Roads to Yesteryear*, ed. by J.R. Caldwell (New York, 1966): 210-27.

392 ————. *Environment and Archaeology*. New York, 1966.

393 ————. Geologie und Paläogeographie archäologischer Fundstellen bei Sayala, (Unternubien). *DÖAW* 92 (1966): 89-98.

394 ————. Late Pleistocene sediments of the Kom Ombo Plain, Upper Egypt. *Alfred-Rust Festschrift Fundementa* 2 (Cologne, 1966): 213-27.

395 ————. Physical conditions in Eastern Europe, Western Asia and Egypt before the period of agriculture and urban settlement. *CAH*^{3}, vol. 1, pt. 1, 2 (1970, also in fasc. 1965): 35-69.

396 ————. Modern Egyptian pottery clays and Predynastic buff ware. *JNES* 33 (1974): 377-82.

397 ————. Bahr Jussuf. *LdÄ* 1 (1975-): 601.

398 ————. Birket Qarun. *LdÄ* 1 (1975-): 822-24.

399 ————. Bitterseen. *LdÄ* 1 (1975-): 824-25.

400 ————. Delta. *LdÄ* 1 (1975-): 1043-52.

401 ————. Dungul Oase. *LdÄ* 1 (1975-): 1153.

402 ————. Geographie. *LdÄ* 2 (1975-): 525-30.

403 ————. Klima. *LdÄ* 2 (1975-): 455-57.

404 ————. Kanal, Nil-Rotes Meer. *LdÄ* 3 (1975-): 312-13.

405 ————. Mareotis. *LdÄ* 3 (1975-): 188-90.

406 ————. Nil. *LdÄ* 4 (1975-): 480-83.

407 ————. Nilquellen. *LdÄ* 4 (1975-): 506-07.

408 ————. Nilmündungen. *LdÄ* 4 (1975-): 498.

409 ————. Ostwüste. *LdÄ* 4 (1975-): 637-38.

410 ————. Patterns of environmental change in the Near East during late Pleistocene and early Holocene times. In entry 2388, pp. 389-410.

411 ————. *Early Hydraulic Civilization in Egypt: A Study in Cultural Ecology*. Chicago, 1976.

412 ————. Perspectives on irrigation in pharaonic Egypt. In Denise Schmandt-Besserat (ed.), *Immortal Egypt: Invited Lectures on the Middle East at the University of Texas at Austin* (Malibu, California, 1978): 13-18.

413 ————. Pleistocene history of the Nile Valley in Egypt and Lower Nubia. In entry 2449, pp. 248-276.

414 ————. Civilizations: Organisms or systems? *American Scientist* 68 (1980): 517-23.

415 ————. Long-term Nile flood variation and political discontinuities in Pharaonic Egypt. In J.D. Clark and S. Brandt (eds.), *From Hunters to Farmers*. (Berkeley, 1982).

————. See entries 981, 1802 and 1880.

416 **Butzer, Karl W.** and **E.K. Butzer.** Treasures of Tutankhamun. *American Anthropologist* 79 (1977): 997-99.

417 **Butzer, Karl W.** and **C.L. Hansen.** On the Pleistocene evolution of the Nile Valley in southern Egypt. *The Canadian Geographer* 9, 2 (1965): 74-83.

418 ————. Upper Pleistocene stratigraphy in southern Egypt. In W.W. Bishop and J.D. Clark (eds.), *Background to Evolution in Africa*. (Chicago, 1967): 329-56.

419 ———. *Desert and River in Nubia: Geomorphology and Prehistoric Environments at the Aswan Reservoir.* Madison, Wisconsin, 1968.

420 ———. Late Pleistocene stratigraphy of the Kom Ombo Plain, Upper Egypt: A comparison with other recent studies near Esna-Edfu. *Bulletin, Association Sénégalaise pour l'Etude du Quaternaire* 34 (1972): 5-14.

C

421 **Calice, C.** [On the prehistory of Egyptian culture]. *Archaeologiai Ertesito* 40 (1923-26): 1-10.

422 **Callow, W.J., M.J. Baker,** and **D.H. Pritchard.** Haua Fteah series, Libya. *Radiocarbon* 5 (1963): 37.

423 ————. Wadi Gan, Libya. *Radiocarbon* 6 (1964): 27-28.

424 **Camps, G.** Mouvements de populations et civilisations préhistoriques et protohistoriques au Sahara depuis le Xe millénaires. *Revue d'Histoire et de Civilisation du Maghreb* 3 (1968): 7-11.

425 ————. *Les Civilisations Préhistoriques de l'Afrique du Nord et du Sahara.* Paris, 1974.

426 ————. Tableau chronologique de la préhistoire récente de l'Afrique; Deuxième synthèse des datations absolues obtenues par le carbone 14. *BSPF* 71 (1974): 261-78.

427 ————. *Dix Ans de Recherches Préhistoriques au Sahara (1965-1975).* Aix-en-Provence, 1975.

428 ————. Nouvelles remarques sur le néo-lithique du Sahara central et méridional. *Libyca* 23 (1975): 123-32.

429 ————. The prehistoric cultures of North Africa: Radiocarbon chronology. In entry 2388, pp. 181-92.

————. See entry 431.

430 **Camps, G., G. Delibrias** and **J. Thommeret.** Chronologie absolue et succession de civilisations préhistoriques dans le nord de l'Afrique. *Libyca* 16 (1968): 9-28.

431 **Camps-Fabrer, H.** and **G. Camps.** Perspectives et orientation de recherches sur le néolithiques saharien. *Revue de l'Occident Musulman* 11 (Aix-en-Provence, 1972): 21-30.

432 **Cantacusino, G.** Un rituel funéraire exceptionnel de l'époque néolithique en Europe et en Afrique septentrionale. *Dacia* 19 (Bucharest, 1975): 27-43.

433 **Capart, Jean.** <52> Note sur les origines de l'Egypte d'après les fouilles récentes. *Revue de l'Univ. de Bruxelles* 4 (1899): 105-39.

434 ————. Encore un mot au sujet de la décapitation dans l'Egypte ancienne. *OLZ* 3 (1900): 52.

435 ————. Conférence sur le préhistorique égyptienne. *BSAB* 20 (1901-2): 1-20.

436 ————. Les récentes acquisitions de la section égyptienne. *BSAB* 2 (1903): 25-29.

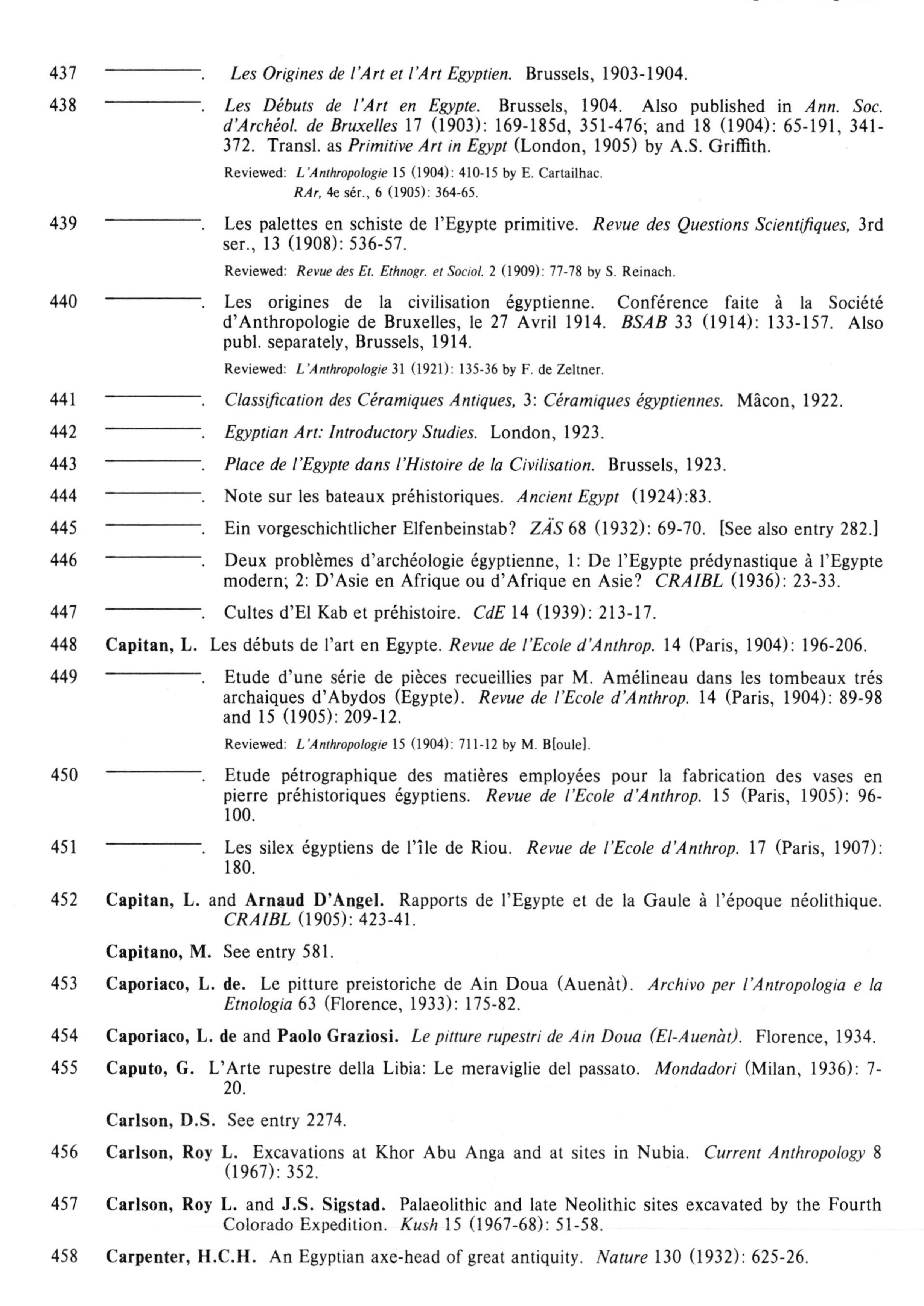

437 ———. *Les Origines de l'Art et l'Art Egyptien.* Brussels, 1903-1904.

438 ———. *Les Débuts de l'Art en Egypte.* Brussels, 1904. Also published in *Ann. Soc. d'Archéol. de Bruxelles* 17 (1903): 169-185d, 351-476; and 18 (1904): 65-191, 341-372. Transl. as *Primitive Art in Egypt* (London, 1905) by A.S. Griffith.

Reviewed: *L'Anthropologie* 15 (1904): 410-15 by E. Cartailhac.
RAr, 4e sér., 6 (1905): 364-65.

439 ———. Les palettes en schiste de l'Egypte primitive. *Revue des Questions Scientifiques,* 3rd ser., 13 (1908): 536-57.

Reviewed: *Revue des Et. Ethnogr. et Sociol.* 2 (1909): 77-78 by S. Reinach.

440 ———. Les origines de la civilisation égyptienne. Conférence faite à la Société d'Anthropologie de Bruxelles, le 27 Avril 1914. *BSAB* 33 (1914): 133-157. Also publ. separately, Brussels, 1914.

Reviewed: *L'Anthropologie* 31 (1921): 135-36 by F. de Zeltner.

441 ———. *Classification des Céramiques Antiques,* 3: *Céramiques égyptiennes.* Mâcon, 1922.

442 ———. *Egyptian Art: Introductory Studies.* London, 1923.

443 ———. *Place de l'Egypte dans l'Histoire de la Civilisation.* Brussels, 1923.

444 ———. Note sur les bateaux préhistoriques. *Ancient Egypt* (1924):83.

445 ———. Ein vorgeschichtlicher Elfenbeinstab? *ZÄS* 68 (1932): 69-70. [See also entry 282.]

446 ———. Deux problèmes d'archéologie égyptienne, 1: De l'Egypte prédynastique à l'Egypte modern; 2: D'Asie en Afrique ou d'Afrique en Asie? *CRAIBL* (1936): 23-33.

447 ———. Cultes d'El Kab et préhistoire. *CdE* 14 (1939): 213-17.

448 **Capitan, L.** Les débuts de l'art en Egypte. *Revue de l'Ecole d'Anthrop.* 14 (Paris, 1904): 196-206.

449 ———. Etude d'une série de pièces recueillies par M. Amélineau dans les tombeaux trés archaiques d'Abydos (Egypte). *Revue de l'Ecole d'Anthrop.* 14 (Paris, 1904): 89-98 and 15 (1905): 209-12.

Reviewed: *L'Anthropologie* 15 (1904): 711-12 by M. B[oule].

450 ———. Etude pétrographique des matières employées pour la fabrication des vases en pierre préhistoriques égyptiens. *Revue de l'Ecole d'Anthrop.* 15 (Paris, 1905): 96-100.

451 ———. Les silex égyptiens de l'île de Riou. *Revue de l'Ecole d'Anthrop.* 17 (Paris, 1907): 180.

452 **Capitan, L.** and **Arnaud D'Angel.** Rapports de l'Egypte et de la Gaule à l'époque néolithique. *CRAIBL* (1905): 423-41.

Capitano, M. See entry 581.

453 **Caporiaco, L. de.** Le pitture preistoriche de Ain Doua (Auenàt). *Archivo per l'Antropologia e la Etnologia* 63 (Florence, 1933): 175-82.

454 **Caporiaco, L. de** and **Paolo Graziosi.** *Le pitture rupestri de Ain Doua (El-Auenàt).* Florence, 1934.

455 **Caputo, G.** L'Arte rupestre della Libia: Le meraviglie del passato. *Mondadori* (Milan, 1936): 7-20.

Carlson, D.S. See entry 2274.

456 **Carlson, Roy L.** Excavations at Khor Abu Anga and at sites in Nubia. *Current Anthropology* 8 (1967): 352.

457 **Carlson, Roy L.** and **J.S. Sigstad.** Palaeolithic and late Neolithic sites excavated by the Fourth Colorado Expedition. *Kush* 15 (1967-68): 51-58.

458 **Carpenter, H.C.H.** An Egyptian axe-head of great antiquity. *Nature* 130 (1932): 625-26.

———. See entry 1942.

459 **Carriere, M.** *Die Anfänge der Kultur und das orientalische Alterthum in Religion, Dichtung und Kunst. Ein Beitrag zur Geschichte des menschlichen Geistes. Die Kunst im Zus. der Kulturentw.*, vol. 4. Leipzig, 1877.

460 **Cartailhac, Emile.** L'Age de la pierre en Egypte, d'après des découvertes de M. Fl. Petrie. [Discussion: M. Pommerol.] *C.r. Assoc. Franç. pour l'Avancement des Sciences* 21 (1892): 267.

461 ———. L'Age de la pierre en Afrique, 1: L'Egypte. Les découvertes de M. Flinders Petrie. *L'Anthropologie* 3 (1892): 405-25.

462 ———. The end of the stone age on the borders of the Mediterranean Basin. *BAAS, Report of the 64th Meeting, Oxford, 1894* (London, 1894): 783.

463 ———. Le temple de Koptos en l'Egypte préhistorique. *L'Anthropologie* 5 (1894): 683-86.

464 ———. Les palettes des dolmens aveyronnais et des tombes égyptiennes. *Bull. Soc. d'Archéol. du Midi de la France,* 2nd ser. (Toulouse, 1906): 473-77.

465 ———. Plaquette de schiste des dolmens aveyronnais analogues aux palettes égyptiennes. *C.r. Assoc. Franç. pour l'Avancement des Sciences* (Paris, 1906): 694-97.

466 ———. Silex taillés d'Egypte, une opinion inexacte. *L'Anthropologie* 17 (1906): 627-28.

467 ———. L'Age de la pierre égyptien dans le sahara français. *C.r. du Congr. Intern. d'Archéol. cl., 2e session* (Cairo, 1909): 199-200.

468 ———. Les palettes du Midi de la France et celles d'Egypte. *C.r. du Congr. Intern. d'Archéol. cl., 2e session* (Cairo, 1909): 193-95.

469 **Casey, Elizabeth T.** A prehistoric Egyptian vase. *Bull. of the School of Design of Rhode Island* 18 (1930): 8-10.

470 **Casini, Maria.** Manufatti litici egiziani a code di pesce. *Origini* 8 (Rome, 1974, publ. 1978): 203-28.

471 **Castillo y Quartiellers, R. del.** Recuerdo de un viaje Egipto. *Memoria Leida en la Real Academia del la Historie y Publicada en su Boletin.* (Madrid, 1908).

472 **Castillos, Juan Jose.** Fayum A and B settlements. *JEA* 59 (1973): 218.

473 ———. Further remarks on the Fayum A and B settlements. *JSSEA* 5, 2 (1974): 3-4.

474 ———. An analysis of the tombs in cemeteries 1300 and 1400-1500 at Armant. *JSSEA* 7, 2 (1977): 4-23.

475 ———. An analysis of the predynastic cemeteries E and U and the first dynasty cemetery S at Abydos. *JSSEA* 8, 3 (1978): 86-98.

476 ———. An analysis of the tombs in the predynastic cemeteries at Naqada. *JSSEA* 11 (1981): 97-106.

477 ———. *A Reappraisal of the Published Evidence on Egyptian Predynastic and Early Dynastic Cemeteries.* Toronto, 1982.

478 ———. *A Study of the Spatial Distribution of Large and Richly Endowed Tombs of the Egyptian Predynastic and Early Dynastic Cemeteries.* Toronto, 1982.

479 **Caton-Thompson, Gertrude.** Notes and catalogue of flint implements from Abydos and Helwan. *BSAE* (London, 1922).

480 ———. Preliminary report on Neolithic pottery and bone implements from the northern Fayum Desert, Egypt. *Man* 25 (1925): 153-56.

481 ———. The Neolithic industry of the northern Fayum Desert. *JRAI* 56 (1926): 309-23.

482 ———. Exploration in the northern Fayum. *Antiquity* 1 (1927): 326-48.

483 ———. The Fayum. *Antiquity* 2 (1928): 218-19.

484 ———. Neolithic pottery from the northern Fayum. *Ancient Egypt* 3 (1928): 70-89.

485 ———. Recent Excavations in the Fayum. *Man* 28 (1928): 109-13.

486 ———. The relation of palaeolithic man to the history and geology of the Nile Valley. *Man* 29 (1929): 132.

487 ———. Filling in a blank in Egypt's 'Prehistory'. *ILN* 4802 (1931): 424-26.

488 ———. Kharga Oasis. *Antiquity* 5 (1931): 221-26.

489 ———. Kharga Oasis: Royal Anthropological Institute's prehistoric research expedition to Kharga Oasis, Egypt; Preliminary outline of the second season's work. *Man* 31 (1931): 77-84.

490 ———. Prehistoric flints from Egypt. *Man* 31 (1931): 95.

491 ———. The Royal Anthropological Institute's prehistoric research expedition to Kharga Oasis, Egypt; The second season's discoveries (1931-1932). *Man* 32 (1932): 129-35.

492 ———. Mr. Beadnell's remarks on the prehistoric geography and underground waters of Kharga Oasis: Comments and replies. *Geogr. J.* 81 (1933): 134-39. [See also entry 213.]

493 ———. Note to subscribers to 'The Predynastic Research Committee of the Institute.' *Man* 33 (1933): 179-80.

494 ———. Recent discoveries in Kharga Oasis. *Report of the BAAS, 102nd Meeting, London, 1932* (London, 1933). Also in: *Proc. 1st Congr. Prehist. and Prdohist. Sci., London, 1932* (Oxford, 1934): 74.

495 ———. The camel in dynastic Egypt. *Man* 34 (1934): 21.

496 ———. The Aterian Industry: Its place and significance in the Palaeolithic world. *JRAI* 76 (1946): 87-130.

497 ———. The Levalloisian industries of Egypt. *Proc. Prehist. Soc.* 92 (1946): 57-120.
Reviewed: *L'Anthropologie* 51 (1947): 488-94 by R. Vanfrey.

498 ———. *Kharga Oasis in Prehistory; with a Physiographic Introduction by E.W. Gardner.* London, 1952.
Reviewed: *AJA* 57 (1953): 117-19 by W.C. Hayes.
Antiquaries J. 33 (1953): 84-85 by F.E. Zeuner.
Antiquity 27 (1953): 124-26 by C.B.M. McBurney.
CdE 28 (1953): 283-84 by Elizabeth della Santa.
Man 52 (1952): 151-52 by J.S.P. Bradford.
Man 53 (1953): 31 by C.E. Joel.

———. See also entry 855-57.

499 **Caton-Thompson, Gertrude** and **Elinor W. Gardner.** Early Egypt and the Caucasus. *Nature* 118 (1926): 463-64 and 624-25.

500 ———. Entry not used. [See entry 855.]

501 ———. Research in the Fayum. *Ancient Egypt* (1926): 1-4.

502 ———. Recent work on the problem of Lake Moeris. *Geogr. J.* 73 (1929): 20-60.
Reviewed: *L'Anthropologie* 39 (1929): 166-67 by M. Boule.

503 ———. The prehistoric geography of Kharga Oasis . *Geogr. J.* 80 (1932): 369-409.

504 ———. Kharga Expedition (1932-1933). *Man* 33 (1933): 179-80.

505 ———. *The Desert Fayum.* 2 vols. London, 1934.

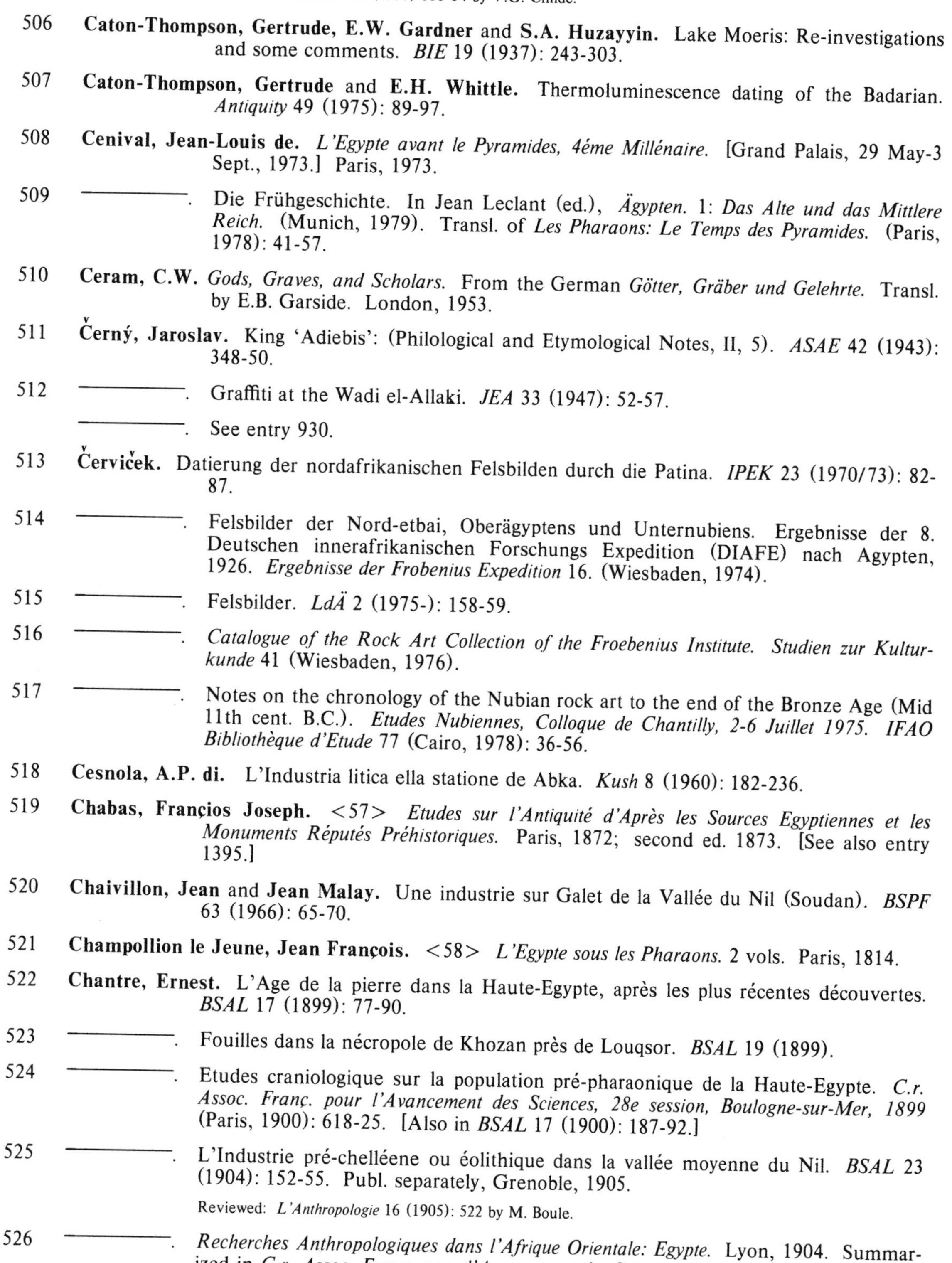

Reviewed: *L'Anthropologie* 46 (1936): 144-46 by S. Huzayyin.
Nature 136 (1935) 353-54 by V.G. Childe.

506 **Caton-Thompson, Gertrude, E.W. Gardner** and **S.A. Huzayyin.** Lake Moeris: Re-investigations and some comments. *BIE* 19 (1937): 243-303.

507 **Caton-Thompson, Gertrude** and **E.H. Whittle.** Thermoluminescence dating of the Badarian. *Antiquity* 49 (1975): 89-97.

508 **Cenival, Jean-Louis de.** *L'Egypte avant le Pyramides, 4éme Millénaire.* [Grand Palais, 29 May-3 Sept., 1973.] Paris, 1973.

509 ———. Die Frühgeschichte. In Jean Leclant (ed.), *Ägypten.* 1: *Das Alte und das Mittlere Reich.* (Munich, 1979). Transl. of *Les Pharaons: Le Temps des Pyramides.* (Paris, 1978): 41-57.

510 **Ceram, C.W.** *Gods, Graves, and Scholars.* From the German *Götter, Gräber und Gelehrte.* Transl. by E.B. Garside. London, 1953.

511 **Černý, Jaroslav.** King 'Adiebis': (Philological and Etymological Notes, II, 5). *ASAE* 42 (1943): 348-50.

512 ———. Graffiti at the Wadi el-Allaki. *JEA* 33 (1947): 52-57.

———. See entry 930.

513 **Červiček.** Datierung der nordafrikanischen Felsbilden durch die Patina. *IPEK* 23 (1970/73): 82-87.

514 ———. Felsbilder der Nord-etbai, Oberägyptens und Unternubiens. Ergebnisse der 8. Deutschen innerafrikanischen Forschungs Expedition (DIAFE) nach Agypten, 1926. *Ergebnisse der Frobenius Expedition* 16. (Wiesbaden, 1974).

515 ———. Felsbilder. *LdÄ* 2 (1975-): 158-59.

516 ———. *Catalogue of the Rock Art Collection of the Froebenius Institute. Studien zur Kulturkunde* 41 (Wiesbaden, 1976).

517 ———. Notes on the chronology of the Nubian rock art to the end of the Bronze Age (Mid 11th cent. B.C.). *Etudes Nubiennes, Colloque de Chantilly, 2-6 Juillet 1975. IFAO Bibliothèque d'Etude* 77 (Cairo, 1978): 36-56.

518 **Cesnola, A.P. di.** L'Industria litica ella statione de Abka. *Kush* 8 (1960): 182-236.

519 **Chabas, Françios Joseph.** <57> *Etudes sur l'Antiquité d'Après les Sources Egyptiennes et les Monuments Réputés Préhistoriques.* Paris, 1872; second ed. 1873. [See also entry 1395.]

520 **Chaivillon, Jean** and **Jean Malay.** Une industrie sur Galet de la Vallée du Nil (Soudan). *BSPF* 63 (1966): 65-70.

521 **Champollion le Jeune, Jean François.** <58> *L'Egypte sous les Pharaons.* 2 vols. Paris, 1814.

522 **Chantre, Ernest.** L'Age de la pierre dans la Haute-Egypte, après les plus récentes découvertes. *BSAL* 17 (1899): 77-90.

523 ———. Fouilles dans la nécropole de Khozan près de Louqsor. *BSAL* 19 (1899).

524 ———. Etudes craniologique sur la population pré-pharaonique de la Haute-Egypte. *C.r. Assoc. Franç. pour l'Avancement des Sciences, 28e session, Boulogne-sur-Mer, 1899* (Paris, 1900): 618-25. [Also in *BSAL* 17 (1900): 187-92.]

525 ———. L'Industrie pré-chelléene ou éolithique dans la vallée moyenne du Nil. *BSAL* 23 (1904): 152-55. Publ. separately, Grenoble, 1905.

Reviewed: *L'Anthropologie* 16 (1905): 522 by M. Boule.

526 ———. *Recherches Anthropologiques dans l'Afrique Orientale: Egypte.* Lyon, 1904. Summarized in *C.r. Assoc. Franç. pour l'Avancement des Sciences, 33e session, Grenoble, 1904*

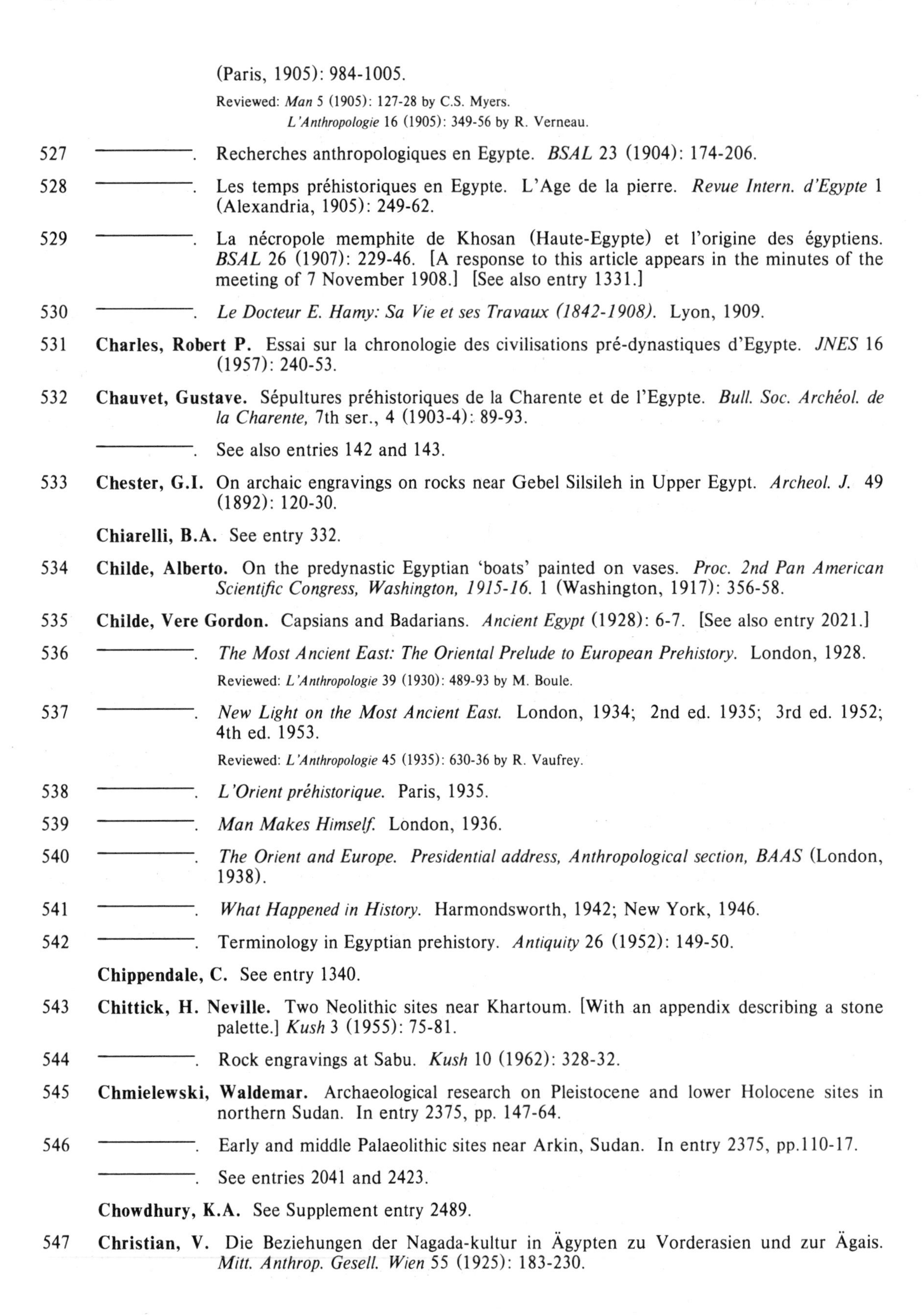

(Paris, 1905): 984-1005.

Reviewed: *Man* 5 (1905): 127-28 by C.S. Myers.
L'Anthropologie 16 (1905): 349-56 by R. Verneau.

527 ————. Recherches anthropologiques en Egypte. *BSAL* 23 (1904): 174-206.

528 ————. Les temps préhistoriques en Egypte. L'Age de la pierre. *Revue Intern. d'Egypte* 1 (Alexandria, 1905): 249-62.

529 ————. La nécropole memphite de Khosan (Haute-Egypte) et l'origine des égyptiens. *BSAL* 26 (1907): 229-46. [A response to this article appears in the minutes of the meeting of 7 November 1908.] [See also entry 1331.]

530 ————. *Le Docteur E. Hamy: Sa Vie et ses Travaux (1842-1908).* Lyon, 1909.

531 **Charles, Robert P.** Essai sur la chronologie des civilisations pré-dynastiques d'Egypte. *JNES* 16 (1957): 240-53.

532 **Chauvet, Gustave.** Sépultures préhistoriques de la Charente et de l'Egypte. *Bull. Soc. Archéol. de la Charente,* 7th ser., 4 (1903-4): 89-93.

————. See also entries 142 and 143.

533 **Chester, G.I.** On archaic engravings on rocks near Gebel Silsileh in Upper Egypt. *Archeol. J.* 49 (1892): 120-30.

Chiarelli, B.A. See entry 332.

534 **Childe, Alberto.** On the predynastic Egyptian 'boats' painted on vases. *Proc. 2nd Pan American Scientific Congress, Washington, 1915-16.* 1 (Washington, 1917): 356-58.

535 **Childe, Vere Gordon.** Capsians and Badarians. *Ancient Egypt* (1928): 6-7. [See also entry 2021.]

536 ————. *The Most Ancient East: The Oriental Prelude to European Prehistory.* London, 1928.

Reviewed: *L'Anthropologie* 39 (1930): 489-93 by M. Boule.

537 ————. *New Light on the Most Ancient East.* London, 1934; 2nd ed. 1935; 3rd ed. 1952; 4th ed. 1953.

Reviewed: *L'Anthropologie* 45 (1935): 630-36 by R. Vaufrey.

538 ————. *L'Orient préhistorique.* Paris, 1935.

539 ————. *Man Makes Himself.* London, 1936.

540 ————. *The Orient and Europe. Presidential address, Anthropological section, BAAS* (London, 1938).

541 ————. *What Happened in History.* Harmondsworth, 1942; New York, 1946.

542 ————. Terminology in Egyptian prehistory. *Antiquity* 26 (1952): 149-50.

Chippendale, C. See entry 1340.

543 **Chittick, H. Neville.** Two Neolithic sites near Khartoum. [With an appendix describing a stone palette.] *Kush* 3 (1955): 75-81.

544 ————. Rock engravings at Sabu. *Kush* 10 (1962): 328-32.

545 **Chmielewski, Waldemar.** Archaeological research on Pleistocene and lower Holocene sites in northern Sudan. In entry 2375, pp. 147-64.

546 ————. Early and middle Palaeolithic sites near Arkin, Sudan. In entry 2375, pp.110-17.

————. See entries 2041 and 2423.

Chowdhury, K.A. See Supplement entry 2489.

547 **Christian, V.** Die Beziehungen der Nagada-kultur in Ägypten zu Vorderasien und zur Ägais. *Mitt. Anthrop. Gesell. Wien* 55 (1925): 183-230.

548 **[Christiania Ethnografisk Museum.]** *Om en af H.M. Kongen til det Ethnografiske Musaeum Skjaenketaegyptisk Mumien af J. Lieblein... Christiania Videnskabs Forhandlinger* 5 (Christiania, 1890).

549 **Churcher, C.S.** Late Pleistocene vertebrates from archaeological sites in the Plain of Kom Ombo. *Royal Ontario Museum, Life Sciences Contributions* 82 (Toronto, 1972).

550 ———. Dakhla Oasis Project: Preliminary observations on the geology and vertebrate palaeontology of Northwestern Dakhla Oasis; A report on the 1979 fieldwork. *JSSEA* 10 (1980): 379-96.

551 **Churcher, C.S.** and **P. Smith.** Kom Ombo: Preliminary report on the fauna sites in Upper Egypt. *Science* 77 (1972): 259-61.

552 **Clark, J. Desmond.** *Atlas of African Prehistory.* Chicago, 1967.

553 ———. The prehistoric origins of African cultures. *J. African History* 5, 2 (1962): 161-83.

554 ———. A re-examination of the evidence for agricultural origins in the Nile Valley. *PPS* 37 (1971): 34-79.

555 ———. Conference overview. In entry 2388.

556 ———. Prehistoric populations and pressures favoring plant domestication in Africa. In J.R. Harlan, J.M.J. de Wet and A.B.L. Stemler (eds.), *Origins of African Plant Domestication.* (The Hague, 1976): 67-105.

———. See entries 8, 2382, 2383 and Supplement entry 2490.

557 **Clark, J. Desmond, J.L. Phillips,** and **P.S. Stanley.** Interpretations of prehistoric technology from ancient Egyptian and other sources, 1: Ancient Egyptian bows and arrows and their relevance for African prehistory. *Paleorient* 2, 2 (1974): 323-88.

Clarke, J.G.D. See entry 861.

558 **Clarke, H.** *The Early History of the Mediterranean Populations.* London, 1882.

559 **Clarke, Somers.** <65> El Kab and the great wall. *JEA* 7 (1921): 54-79.

———. See entry 2016.

560 **Clayton, P.A.** The western side of the Gilf Kebir. *Geogr. J.* 81 (1922): 254-59.

561 ———. A reconnaissance of the Gilf Kebir by the late Sir Robert Clayton East Clayton. *Geogr. J.* 18 (1933): 254.

562 ———. The south-western desert survey expedition, 1930-1931. *BSGE* 19 (1936): 241-65.

563 **Clédat, Jean.** Observations sur deux tableaux ethnographiques égyptiens. *Revue Mensuelle, Ecole d'Anthrop.* 9 (Paris, 1899): 297-300.

564 ———. Origines égyptiennes. *Rev. d'Ecole d'Anthrop.* (Paris, 1899): 201-206.

565 **Clère, J.J.** Un graffito du roi Djet dans le désert arabique. *ASAE* 38 (1938): 85-93. [See also entry 927.]

566 **Close, Angela E.** The lithic artifacts from Tamar Hat. *Libyca* 22 (1974): 58-66.

567 ———. The identification of style in lithic artifacts from North East Africa. *MIE* 61 (Cairo, 1977).

568 ———. Methods of analysis of lithic artifacts. In entry 2416, pp. 49-54.

569 ———. Stylistic analysis of the Wadi Kubbaniya assemblages. *Ibid.*, pp. 245-58.

———. See also entries 1340, 2384-85, 2416-17 and 2419.

570 **Close, Angela E.** and **Hanna Wieckowska.** Report on the site E-78-3. In entry 2416, pp. 77-118.

571 **Coghlan, H.H.** Notes on the prehistoric metallurgy of copper and bronze in the Old World. *Pitt Rivers Mus. Occas. Papers on Technology* 4 (London, 1951).

Reviewed: *Man* 52 (1952): 42-3 by H. Maryon.

Cohen, J. See entry 2269.

572 **Cohen, M.N.** *The Food Crisis in Prehistory: Overpopulation and the Origins of Agriculture.* New Haven, 1977.

573 **Cohen, P.** and **E. Service** (eds.). *Origins of the State: The Anthropology of Political Evolution.* Philadelphia, 1978.

574 **Cole, Sonia.** *The Prehistory of East Africa.* Harmondsworth, 1954.

575 **Collins, Robert O.** *Problems in African History.* Englewood Cliffs, New Jersey, 1968.

576 ———. Africa and Egypt. In entry 575, pp. 7-10.

577 **Commeaux, C.** La domestication des animaux dans l'Egypte ancienne. *Naturalia* 28 (Paris, 1956): 38-43.

Copeland, L. See entry 1081.

578 **Coppens, Y.** and **L. Balout.** Hominization: General problems. In J. Ki-Zerbo (ed.), *General History of Africa* 1: *Methodology and African Prehistory.* (London and Berkeley, 1981): 400-36.

579 **Cornevin, R.** *Histoire des Peuples de l'Afrique Noire.* Paris, 1963.

Corrain, Camillo. See entry 580.

580 **Corrain, Cleto, Camillo Corrain** and **M. Fabbri.** Una stazione del paleolitico superiore a nord-est de Tazerbo (Sahara libico). *Sibrium* 9 (1967-69): 11-12.

581 **Corrain, Cleto** and **M. Capitano.** Ricordi di escursioni scientifiche in Libia. *Atti e Memorie della Academia di Agricoltura, Scienze e Lettere di Verona,* 6th ser., 21 (1969-70): 49-60.

582 **Corrain, Cleto** and **M. Fabbri.** Oggetti di minore interesse, perloppiù levigatoi, provenienti da stazioni preistoriche della Tipolitania e del Fezzan. *Sibrium* 10 (1970): 441-43.

583 **Corrain, Cleto, M. Fabbri** and **P. Zampini.** Piccola stazione di arte rupestre nei pressi di Sebha, nel Fezzan. *Sibrium* 9 (1967-69): 79-81.

584 ———. Una stazione-officina litica nei pressi di Sebha (Fezzan). *Sibrium* 9 (1967-69): 3-9.

585 **Cottevielle-Giraudet, Rémy.** Gravures protohistoriques de la montagne thébaine. *BIFAO* 30 (1930): 545-52.

Reviewed: *Ancient Egypt* (1932): 83.

586 ———. Les races de l'Afrique du nord et la population oranaise. *Revue Anthropologique* 40 (1930): 136-54.

587 ———. L'Egypte avant l'histoire: Paléolithique —néolithique —âges du cuivre: Introduction à l'étude de l'Egypte pharaonique. *BIFAO* 33 (1933): 1-168.

588 ———. La préhistoire de l'Egypte. Etat actuel de la question. *XVe Congr. Inter. d'Anthrop. et d'Archéol. Préhist., Inst. Intern. d'Anthrop. Ve Session, Paris, 20-27 Septembre 1931* (Paris, 1933): 311-20.

589 **Courcelle-Seneuil, J.L.** L'Egypte préhistorique. *Revue de Géographie Commerciale* 40 (Bordeaux, 1914): 24-31.

590 **Courtet de l'Isle, Victor.** Etude sur les anciennes races de l'Egypte. *Bull. Soc. Ethnogr.* 1 (Paris, 1847): 5.

591 ———. Etude sur les ancienne races de l'Egypte et de l'Ethiopie. *Nouvelles Annales des Voyages* 113 (Paris, 1847): 326-40; and 114 (Paris, 1848): 299-318.

592 **Covington, Lorenzo Dow.** Mastaba mount excavations. *ASAE* 6 (1905): 193-218.

593 **Cowper, Henry Swainson.** <70> On a series of small worked flints from Hilwan, Egypt. *Man*

11 (1911): 6-11.

594 **Crompton, Winifred Mary.** <71> A carved slate palette in the Manchester Museum. *JEA* 5 (1918): 57-60.

595 **Cullimore, Isaac.** <73> Pharaoh and his princes; or, the dynastic changes in the ancient Egyptian goverment, as its five Περιεθνοι or states, successively took the form of a pentarchy, tetrarchy, dyarchy, monarchy, and dodekarchy. In answer to the unscriptural and unhistorical hypothesis of the thirty dynasties of the historian Manetho, representing a consecutive monarchy, and the theories founded on this basis. *Original Papers of the Syro-Egyptian Society* 1, 1 (London, 1845): 1-13.

596 **Currelly, C.T.** A sequence of Egyptian stone implements. *BAAS* 28 (1908): 848.

597 ———. *Catalogue Générale des Antiquités Egyptiennes du Musée du Caire, nos. 63001-64906: Stone Implements.* Cairo, 1913.

———. See entry 120.

598 **Cuvillier, J.** L'Egypte et la préhistoire. *La Bourse Egyptienne* (Cairo, 24 Octobre 1932).

D

599 **Dammann, C.** and **F.W. Dammann.** *Ethnologischer Atlas sämmtlicher Menschenrassen in Photographien.* Hamburg, 1876.

Dammann, F.W. See entry 599.

600 **Daniel, Glyn E.** *A Hundred Years of Archaeology.* London, 1950.

601 ———. *The First Civilizations: The Archaeology of their Origins.* New York and London, 1968.

602 ———. *A Hundred and Fifty Years of Archaeology.* Cambridge, Mass., 1976.

603 **Daressy, Georges.** <76> Outils en silex, trouvés en Egypte. *BIE,* 3rd ser., 5 (1894): 61-62.

604 ———. Une édifice archaique à Nezlet Batran. *ASAE* 6 (1905): 99-106.

605 ———. Qaret el-Gindi. *ASAE* 11 (1910): 169-172.

606 ———. La pierre de Palerme et la chronologie de l'ancien empire. *BIFAO* 12 (1916): 161-214.

Reviewed: *Ancient Egypt* (1916): 182-84.

607 ———. Casse-tête préhistorique en bois de Gebelien. *ASAE* 2 (1922): 17-32.

Reviewed: *Ancient Egypt* (1925): 119.

608 ———. Sur trois haches en mineral de fer. *ASAE* 22 (1922): 157-66.

609 **Dart, Raymond A.** Population fluctuation over 7000 years in Egypt. *Trans. Royal Soc. South Africa* 27 (1939): 95-145.

610 ———. Cultural diffusion from, in and to Africa. In entry 705, pp. 160-174.

611 **Davesiès, Lucien.** Les différentes races des habitants de l'Egypte. *Revue Universelle* (1899).

612 **Davis, Whitney M.** The origins of register composition in predynastic Egyptian art. *JAOS* 96 (1976): 404-18.

613 ———. Toward a dating of prehistoric Nile Valley rock drawings. *JSSEA* 8, 1 (December, 1977): 25-34.

614 ———. Dating prehistoric rock-drawings in Upper Egypt and Nubia. *Current Anthropology* 19 (1978): 216-17.

615 ———. More on the prehistoric rock-drawings. *JSSEA* 8, 3 (May, 1978): 84-85.

616 ———. Sources for the study of rock art in the Nile Valley. *GM* 32 (1979): 59-74.

617 ———. The foreign relations of Pre-Dynastic Egypt, 1: Egypt and Palestine in the Predynastic Period. *JSSEA* 11 (1981): 21-27.

———. See also Supplement entry 2491.

618 **Davison, Dorothy.** *The Story of Prehistoric Civilizations.* London, 1951.

Davy, G. See entry 1472.

619 **Dawkins, Boyd.** On the hilt of the Neolithic axe. *JMEOS* 13 (1927): 9.

620 ———. Note on teeth, bones and flint implements (found in Egypt and Lebanon). In entry 623, pp. 300-01.

621 **Dawson, John W.** Prehistoric man in Egypt and Syria. *The Egyptian Gazette* (Cairo, May 20, 1884): 2.

622 ———. Rough-notes of a naturalist's visit to Egypt. *The Leisure Hour* 33 (1884): 174-90.

623 ———. Notes on prehistoric man in Egypt and the Lebanon. Being a paper read before a meeting of the Victoria Institute, May 6, 1884. *J. Victoria Institute* 18 (1885): 287-301. [See entry 620.]

624 ———. *Egypt and Syria: Their Physical Features in Relation to Bible History.* London, 1887.

625 ———. Prehistoric times in Egypt and Palestine. *N. American Review* 154 (1892): 672-83 and (1893): 69-83.

626 **Dawson, Warren Royal.** <79> *Who Was Who in Egyptology.* London, 1951. 2nd ed. revised by Eric P. Uphill, London, 1972.

627 **Debono, Fernand.** Hélouan – El Omari: Fouilles du Service des Antiquités 1943-1945. *CdE* 21 (1945): 50-54.

628 ———. Pics en pierre de Sérabit el-Khadim (Sinai) et d'Egypte. *ASAE* 46 (1947): 165-85.

629 ———. El Omari (près d'Hélouan), exposé sommaire sur les campagnes des fouilles, 1943-1944 et 1948. *ASAE* 48 (1948): 561-69.

630 ———. Le paléolithique final et le mésolithique à Hélouan. *ASAE* 48 (1948): 629-37.

631 ———. Héliopolis – Trouvailles prédynastiques. *CdE* 25 (1950): 233-37.

632 ———. La nécropole prédynastique d'Héliopolis (fouilles de 1950). *ASAE* 52 (1950): 625-52.

633 ———. Expédition archéologique royale au campagne 1949. *ASAE* 51 (1951): 59-110.

634 ———. La civilisation prédynastique d'El Omari (nord d'Hélouan). *BIE* 37 (1956): 329-39.

635 ———. Le sentiment religieux à l'époque préhistorique en Egypte. *CHE* 11 (1969): 1-13.

636 ———. Etudes des dépôts de silex. In *Graffiti de La Montagne Thébaine* 1, 2 (Cairo,1971): 32-50.

637 ———. Prospection préhistorique (Campagne 1972-73). *Ibid.,* 1, 4.

638 ———. Recherches préhistoriques dans la région d'Esna. *BIFAO* 69 (1971): 245-51.

639 ———. Thèbes préhistorique, ses survivances à l'époque pharaonique d'après les découvertes recentes. *Actes du XIXe Congrès Intern. des Orient* 1 (Paris, 1975): 34-37

640 ———. L'homme oldowaien en Egypte. *BIE* 46 (1975). [Not seen.]

641 ———. Survivances préhistorique de l'usage de silex à l'époque pharaonique. *BIE 47* (1976).

642 ———. Die Vorgeschichte. In Jean Leclant (ed.), *Ägypten,* 1: *Das Alte und das Mittleren*

Reich. (Munich, 1979): 29-40. Transl. of *Les Pharaons: Le Temps des Pyramides les Préhistoire.* Paris, 1978.

643 ————. Prehistory in the Nile Valley. In J. Ki-Zerbo (ed.), *General History of Africa,* 1: *Methodology and African Prehistory.* (London and Berkeley, 1981): 634-55.

644 **Decker, Wolfgang.** Gebel el-Araq. *LdÄ* 2 (1975-): 434.

645 **Decorse, J.** Le tatouage, les mutilations ethniques et la parure chez les populations Soudan. *L'Anthropologie* 16 (1905): 129-47.

646 **Defontaines, P.** Apparition du genre de vie littoral aux temps préhistoriques. *La Géographie* 42 (Paris, 1924): 232-33.

647 **Delafosse, Maurice.** Sur des traces probables de civilisation égyptienne à la Côte d'Ivoire. *L'Anthropologie* 11 (1900): 431-51, 543-68, and 677-90.

648 **Delanoue, J.** Ateliers de fabrication d'outils en pierre dans la Haute-Egypt. *C.r. du Congr. Intern. d'Anthrop. et d'Archéol. Préhist., 6e Session, 1872* (Brussels, 1873): 313-18.

Delaporte, L. See entry 1146.

Delibrias, G. See entry 430.

649 **Delibrias, G., M.T. Guillier** and **J. Labeyrie.** Tejerhi, Fezzan. *Radiocarbon* 6 (1964): 242.

650 **Demoule, J.-P.** Domestication des animaux: les précisions du carbon-14. *La Recherche* 34 (1973): 498-500.

651 **Denon, Dominique Vivant.** <83> *Voyages dans la Basse et la Haute Egypte pendant les Campaigns de Bonaparte en 1798 et 1799.* Paris, 1802. Transl. as *Travels in Upper and Lower Egypt, During the Campaigns of General Bonaparte...* and with an historical account by E.A. Kendall. London, 1803.

Denny, Alice. See entry 1946.

652 **Derricourt, Robin M.** Radiocarbon chronology for Egypt and North Africa. *JNES* 30 (1971): 271-292.

653 **Derry, Douglas E.** Notes on predynastic Egyptian tibiae. *J. Anatomy and Physiology* 41 (1907): 123-30.

654 ————. Crania from Merimde, 1931-1932. In entry 1134, pp. 60-61.

655 ————. Note on the human remains at Merimde. In entry 1134, p. 197.

656 ————. Preliminary note on human remains from a neolithic settlement at Merimde-Benisalame. In entry 1136, pp. 53-60.

657 ————. Preliminary note on the human remains from the royal excavations at Helwan. In entry 1973, pp. 249-51.

658 ————. The Dynastic Race in Egypt. *JEA* 42 (1956): 80-85.

————. See entries 1538 and 1913.

659 **Desor, Edouard.** Notice sur les silex préhistoriques des banks du Nil. *Bull. Soc. des Sciences Naturelle de Neuchatel.* 12 (1880): 435-38.

660 **Desroches-Noblecourt, C.** *Le Style Egyptien.* Paris, 1946.

661 **Diagne, P.** History and linguistics. In J. Ki-Zerbo (ed.), *General History of Africa,* 1: *Methodology and African Prehistory.* (Berkeley and London, 1981): 233-60.

Dimbleby, G.W. See entries 2263a and 2265.

el-Dine, [Prince] **Kemal.** See entry 1207.

662 ————. Entry not used.

663 **Dingemans, Guy.** Races et biologie en Egypte. *CHE* 9 (1957): 8-10.

664 **Diop, Cheikh Anta.** *Nations Négres et Cultures. De l'Antiquité Négro-Egyptienne aux Problèmes Culturels de l'Afrique noire d'Aujourd'hui.* Paris, 1955; 2nd ed. Paris, 1964. First ed. transl. as: *Negro Nations and Culture* by Mercer Cook, New York, 1974. [Excerpts from pp. 19-23, 31, 210-12, 240-44, 246, and 253 of 1st ed., and pp. 19- 20 of 2nd ed., in entry 575, pp. 10-16 and 19-20. Transl. by Nell Painter and R.O. Collins.]

665 ———. *Afrique Noire Précoloniale: Etude Comparée des Système Politique et Sociaux de l'Europe et de l'Afrique Noire, de l'Antiquité à la Formation des Etats Modernes.* Paris, 1960.

666 ———. Historie primitive de l'Humanité: Evolution du monde noire. *Bull. de l'Inst. Fr. d'Afrique Noire* 24 (Dakar, 1962): 449-541.

667 ———. Résponses à quelques critiques. *Bull. de l'Inst. Fr. d'Afrique Noire* 24 (Dakar, 1962): 449-541.

668 ———. *Antériorité des Civilisations Négres: Mythe ou Vérité.* Paris, 1967.

———. See also **Obenga** entry 1631 for comments.

669 **Dixon, D.M.** A note on cereals in ancient Egypt. In entry 2263a, pp. 131-42.

670 **Dixon, Roland.** *The Racial History of Man.* New York, 1923.

671 **Dollfus, Gustave Frederic.** Die prähistoriche Geologie im Orient (Syria und Ägypten). *Petermann's Mitt., Gotha* 57, 2 (1911): 17.

672 **Dolukhanov, P.M.** [The natural conditions and prehistoric culture of the Near and Middle East in the late Pleistocene and Holocene.] *Patma Banasirakan Handes, Istoriko-Filologicheskiy Zhurnal* 62 (Preven, 1973): 174-78. [In Russian].

673 **Donadoni, Sergio.** Remarks about Egyptian connections of the Saharan rock shelter art. In entry 841, pp. 85-90.

674 **Donahue, V.A.** A bibliography of Elise Jenny Baumgartel. *JEA* 63 (1977): 48-51.

675 **Dothan, M.** High loop-handled cups and the relations between Mesopotamia, Palestine, and Egypt. *PEQ* 83 (1953): 132-37.

676 **Drake, St. Clair.** *Détruire le Mythe Chamitique devoir des Hommes Cultivés.* Paris, 1960.

Drappier, D. See entry 2291.

677 **Dreyer, Günter.** Ein frühdynastische Königsfigürchen aus Elephantine. *MDAIK* 37 (1981): 123-25. (=Festschr. Habachi).

678 **Drioton, Etienne Marie-Felix** <88> and **Jacques Vandier.** *Les Peuples de l'Orient Mediterranéen, 2: L'Egypte.* Paris, 1938; 2nd ed. 1946; 3rd ed. 1953; 4th ed. 1962. Publ. in Arabic (Cairo, 1952).

679 **Drobniewicz, B.** Deir el Bahari, Site 20 (Neolithic workshop site). *Recherches Archéologiques* (Krakow, 1975): 60-61.

———. See entry 884.

680 **Dumichen, Johannes.** <92> Geshichte des alten Ägyptens. In Wilhelm Oncken (ed.), *Allgemeine Geschichte* 1 (Berlin, 1878).

681 **Dunbar, J.H.** Some Nubian rock pictures. *SNR* 17 (1934): 139-67.

682 ———. Some Nubian rock pictures. *SNR* 18 (1935): 303-308.

Reviewed: *Amer. Anthrop.* 38 (1936): 123-24 by A.E. Robinson.

683 ———. *The Rock Pictures of Lower Nubia.* Cairo, 1941.

Dunham, Dows. See entry 1355.

684 **Duprat, Pierre Pascal.** *Essai Historique sur les Races Anciennes et Modernes de l'Afrique Septentrionale, leurs Origins, leurs Mouvements, et leurs Transformations.* Paris, 1845.

685 **Dürst, Ulrich.** *Die Rinder von Babylonien, Assyrien und Aegypten.* Berlin, 1899.

686 **Dürst, J.U.** and **C. Gaillard.** Studien über die Geschichte des ägyptisches Hausschafer. *RecTrav* 24 (1902): 44ff.

687 **Dzierzykray-Rogalski, T.** Etudes préliminaire des ossements humains des IVe-IIIe millenaires av. J.-C. à Kadero (Soudan). *Etudes Nubiennes, Colloque de Chantilly, 2-6 Juillet, 1975. IFAO Bibliothèque d'Etude* 77 (Cairo, 1978): 87-90.

688 ————. Neolithic skeletons from Kadero, Sudan. *Current Anthropology* 18 (1977): 585-86.

E

689 **Ebers, Georg Moritz.** <94> *Cicerone durch das alte und neue Ägypten.* 2 vols. Stuttgart and Leipzig, 1886.

690 ———————. Über die Feuersteinmesser in Ägypten. *ZÄS* 9 (1871): 17-22.

691 ———————. *Ägypten und die Bücher Moses.* Leipzig, 1868. [Vol. 1; no others publ.]

692 **Echegaray, J.G.** Origines del Neolitico Sirio-Palestino. *Cuadernos de Arquelogia* 6 (Bilbao, 1978).

693 **Ed., J.H.** Notes sur la chronométrie préhistorique. *Revue d'Egypte* 2 (Cairo, 1895):102-22.

694 **Edgerton, William F.** Ancient Egyptian ships and shipping. *AJSL* 39 (1922-23): 109-35.

695 **Edwards, I.E.S.** *The Pyramids of Egypt.* 1st ed. London, 1947; rev. ed. London, 1961; 3rd. ed. New York, 1972; Arabic ed. Cairo, 1956.

696 ———————. Some early dynastic contributions to Egyptian architecture. *JEA* 35 (1949): 123-28.

697 ———————. An Egyptian bestiary of 5000 years ago. *ILN* (Dec. 17, 1955): 1061.

698 ———————. The early dynastic period in Egypt. CAH^2, vol. 1, 11; CAH^3, vol. 1, pt. 2, 11 pp. 1-70. (Cambridge, 1965 and 1970; and in fasc. 1964).

699 ———————. Absolute dating from Egyptian records and comparison with carbon-14 dating. *Phil. Trans. Roy. Soc.* 269 (1970): 11-18.

700 **Eickstedt, E.V.** Völkerbiologische Problem der Sahara. *Beiträge zur Kolonialforschung, Tagungsband* 1 (Berlin, 1943).

701 ———————. Das Hamiten Problem. *Homo: Inter. Zeits. für die Vergleichende Forschung am Menschen* 1 (Stuttgart, 1949).

702 **Eiwanger, Josef.** Erster Vorbericht über die Wiederaufnahme der Grabungen in der neolitischen Siedlung Merimde-Benisalame. *MDAIK* 34 (1978): 33-42.

703 ———————. Merimde-Beni-Salame. *LdÄ* 4 (1975): 94-96.

Elachi, C. See entry 1363.

704 **Elkin, A.P.** Elliot Smith and the diffusion of culture. In entry 705, pp. 139-59.

705 **Elkin, A.P.** and **N.M.G. Macintosh** (eds). *Grafton Elliot Smith: The Man and His Work.* Sydney, 1974.

706 **Ellis, L.B.** On the meaning of . *Ancient Egypt* (1922): 77.

Elmendorf, J. See entry 1340.

707 **Emery, Walter Bryan.** *Excavations at Saqqara: The Tomb of Hemaka, I.* [With the collaboration of Zaki Yusef Saad.] Cairo, 1938.

708 ————. A preliminary report on the architecture of the tomb of Nebetka. *ASAE* 38 (1938): 455-59.

709 ————. The tomb of the first pharaoh? A great discovery believed to be the burial-place of the pharaoh Aha. *ILN* 192 (1938): 247-49.

710 ————. An ancient Egyptian meal preserved for 5000 years: The Saqqara find. *ILN* 194 (1939): 51.

711 ————. *Excavations at Saqqara: Hor-Aha.* [With the collaboration of Zaki Yusef Saad.] Cairo, 1939.

712 ————. A preliminary report on the first dynasty copper treasure from North Saqqara. *ASAE* 39 (1939): 427-37.

713 ————. A cylinder seal of the Uruk Period. *ASAE* 45 (1947): 147-50.

714 ————. New light on first dynasty Egypt. *ILN* 18 (1947): 91.

715 ————. *Excavations at Saqqara: The Great Tombs of the First Dynasty.* Vol. 1. Cairo, 1949.

716 ————. *Saqqara and the Dynastic Race.* [Inaugural lecture delivered at University College, London, 28 February 1952.] London, 1952.

717 ————. An Egyptian royal tomb 1500 years before Tutankhamun: A major discovery in the archaic cemetery of North Saqqara. *ILN* 222 (1953): 839-43.

718 ————. Excavating the prototype of the pyramid: the discovery of an immense Egyptian tomb of 5000 years ago, which may be that of the Pharaoh Ka-a. *ILN* 224 (1954): 803-805.

719 ————. Excavations at Saqqara, 1953 and 1954. *Archaeological Newsletter* 5, 3 (1954): 49-51.

720 ————. *Excavations at Saqqara: Great Tombs of the First Dynasty.* Vol. 2. [With the collaboration of T.G.H. James, A. Klasens, R. Anderson, C.A. Burney.] London, 1954.

Reviewed: *CdE* 63 (1957): 48-50 by Pierre Gilbert.

721 ————. A 5000-year-old royal tomb, probably that of Udimu. *ILN* 226 (1955): 500-503.

722 ————. Fouilles à Saqqarah-Nord. *RC* (spéc. no., Les grandes découvertes archéologiques de 1954), 33 (1955): 12-17.

723 ————. Royal tombs at Saqqara. *Archaeology* 8 (1955): 2-9.

724 ————. An Egyptian queen's tomb of 5000 years ago: Her-neit's jewels. *ILN* 228 (1956): 646-48.

725 ————. The tombs of the first pharaohs. *Scientific American* 197 (1957): 106-16.

726 ————. *Excavations at Saqqara: Great tombs of the first Dynasty.* Vol. 3. [With the collaboration of A. Klasens.] London, 1958.

727 ————. *Archaic Egypt.* Harmondsworth, 1961. Transl. into German as *Ägypten: Geschichte und Kultur der Frühzeit, 3200-2800 v. Chr.,* (Munich, 1964) by Paul Baudisch.

Engl. ed. reviewed: *AJA* 67 (1963): 85-87 by W.K. Simpson.
Antiquity 36 (1962): 229-30 by Cyril Aldred.
Archaeology 15 (1962): 284 by Wm. St. Smith.
RdE 14 (1962): 113-18 by J.-Ph. Lauer.

728 ————. A funerary repast in an Egyptian tomb of the archaic period. *Scholae Adriani de Buck Memoriae dictatae* 1 (Leiden, 1962).

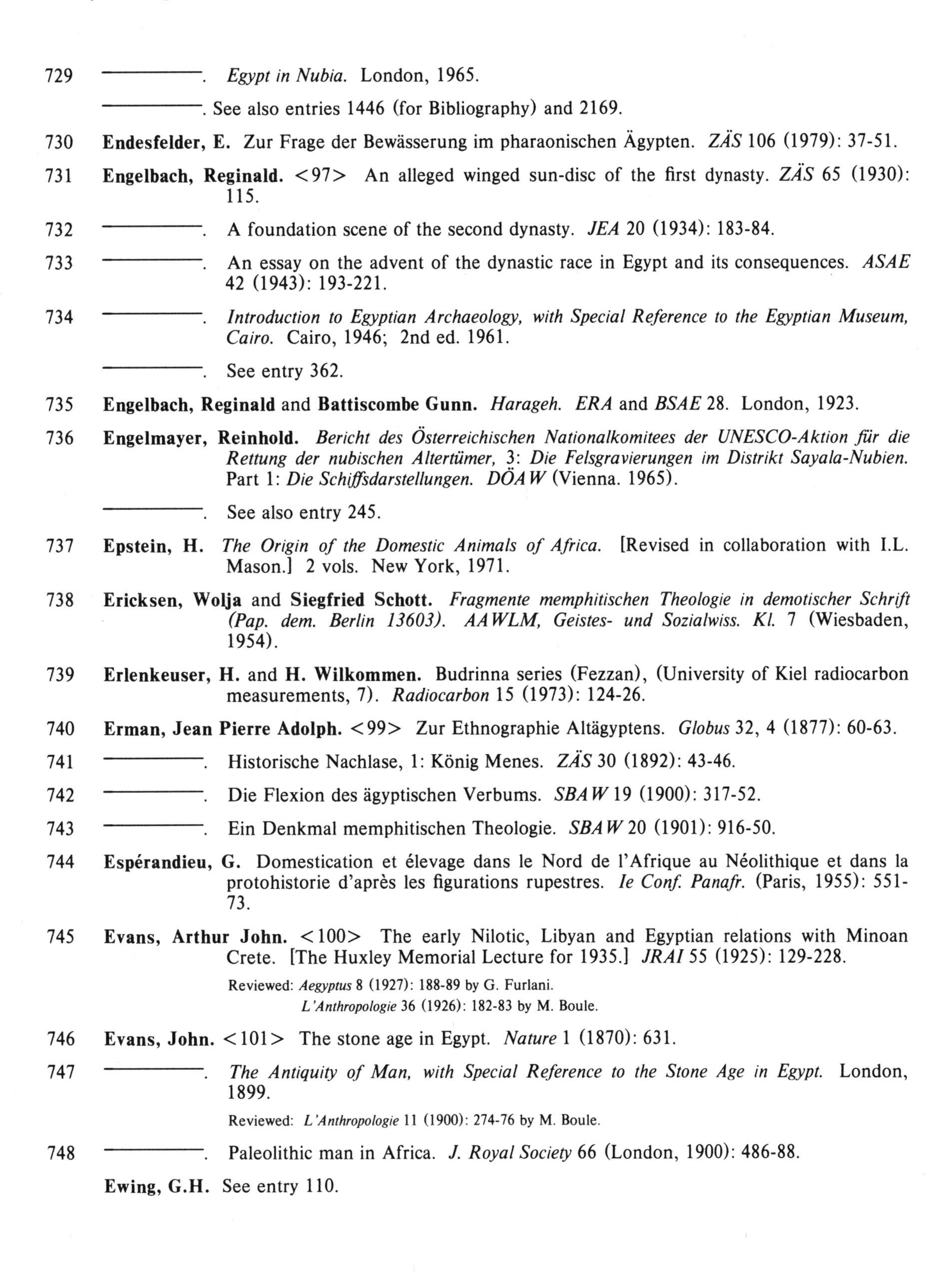

729 ———. *Egypt in Nubia.* London, 1965.

———. See also entries 1446 (for Bibliography) and 2169.

730 **Endesfelder, E.** Zur Frage der Bewässerung im pharaonischen Ägypten. *ZÄS* 106 (1979): 37-51.

731 **Engelbach, Reginald.** <97> An alleged winged sun-disc of the first dynasty. *ZÄS* 65 (1930): 115.

732 ———. A foundation scene of the second dynasty. *JEA* 20 (1934): 183-84.

733 ———. An essay on the advent of the dynastic race in Egypt and its consequences. *ASAE* 42 (1943): 193-221.

734 ———. *Introduction to Egyptian Archaeology, with Special Reference to the Egyptian Museum, Cairo.* Cairo, 1946; 2nd ed. 1961.

———. See entry 362.

735 **Engelbach, Reginald** and **Battiscombe Gunn.** *Harageh. ERA* and *BSAE* 28. London, 1923.

736 **Engelmayer, Reinhold.** *Bericht des Österreichischen Nationalkomitees der UNESCO-Aktion für die Rettung der nubischen Altertümer,* 3: *Die Felsgravierungen im Distrikt Sayala-Nubien.* Part 1: *Die Schiffsdarstellungen. DÖAW* (Vienna. 1965).

———. See also entry 245.

737 **Epstein, H.** *The Origin of the Domestic Animals of Africa.* [Revised in collaboration with I.L. Mason.] 2 vols. New York, 1971.

738 **Ericksen, Wolja** and **Siegfried Schott.** *Fragmente memphitischen Theologie in demotischer Schrift (Pap. dem. Berlin 13603). AAWLM, Geistes- und Sozialwiss. Kl.* 7 (Wiesbaden, 1954).

739 **Erlenkeuser, H.** and **H. Wilkommen.** Budrinna series (Fezzan), (University of Kiel radiocarbon measurements, 7). *Radiocarbon* 15 (1973): 124-26.

740 **Erman, Jean Pierre Adolph.** <99> Zur Ethnographie Altägyptens. *Globus* 32, 4 (1877): 60-63.

741 ———. Historische Nachlase, 1: König Menes. *ZÄS* 30 (1892): 43-46.

742 ———. Die Flexion des ägyptischen Verbums. *SBAW* 19 (1900): 317-52.

743 ———. Ein Denkmal memphitischen Theologie. *SBAW* 20 (1901): 916-50.

744 **Espérandieu, G.** Domestication et élevage dans le Nord de l'Afrique au Néolithique et dans la protohistorie d'après les figurations rupestres. *Ie Conf. Panafr.* (Paris, 1955): 551-73.

745 **Evans, Arthur John.** <100> The early Nilotic, Libyan and Egyptian relations with Minoan Crete. [The Huxley Memorial Lecture for 1935.] *JRAI* 55 (1925): 129-228.

Reviewed: *Aegyptus* 8 (1927): 188-89 by G. Furlani.
L'Anthropologie 36 (1926): 182-83 by M. Boule.

746 **Evans, John.** <101> The stone age in Egypt. *Nature* 1 (1870): 631.

747 ———. *The Antiquity of Man, with Special Reference to the Stone Age in Egypt.* London, 1899.

Reviewed: *L'Anthropologie* 11 (1900): 274-76 by M. Boule.

748 ———. Paleolithic man in Africa. *J. Royal Society* 66 (London, 1900): 486-88.

Ewing, G.H. See entry 110.

F

749 **Fabbri, M.** Incisioni su gusci di uova di struzzo a Sliten (Tripolitania). *Bollettino del Centro Camuno di Studi Preistorici* 10 (1973): 232-33.

———. See entries 580, 582-84.

750 **Fabbro, A. del.** Stazione litica all'aperto nei pressi dell'Uadi Ar Ribat (Tripolitania). *La Arti* 5 (1968): 93-97.

751 **Fairman, H.W.** The myth of Horus at Edfu, I. *JEA* 21 (1935): 26-36.

752 ———. Town planning in pharaonic Egypt. *Town Planning Review* 20 (1949): 33-51.

———. See entries 264 and 1560.

753 **Fairservis, Walter A., Jr.** Preliminary report on the first two seasons at Hierakonpolis. *JARCE* 9 (1971): 7-27 and 67-99.

754 ———. *Preliminary Report on Excavations at Hierakonpolis: The Season January to March, 1978: The Work on the Kom el Ahmar and the 'Fort'.* New York, 1980. (mimeographed).

———. See Supplement entry 2492.

Falk, Richard H. See entry 2205.

755 **Farina, Giulio.** <102> Su alcune leggende intorno alle invasioni semitiche nell'Egitto predinastico. *Rivista di Anthrop.* 27 (Rome, 1925): 1-18.

756 **Fattovich, R.** Two predynastic decorated vases from Hammamiya (Upper Egypt). *Oriens Antiquus* 17, 3 (1978): 199-202.

757 ———. Trends in the study of predynastic social structure. In entry 1898, pp. 215-20.

758 **Faulkenburger, F.** *Craniologie Egyptienne: Etude Comparée sur 1787 Crânes Egyptiens depuis des Temps Prédynastiques jusqu'a nos Jours.* Mainz, 1946.

759 ———. La composition raciale de l'ancienne Egypte. *L'Anthropologie* 51 (1947): 239-50.

760 ———. Das Rassenproblem in Ägypten: Eine kraniologische Studie. *Homo* 1 (1950): 56-64.

761 **Faulkner, R.O.** The 'Cannibal Hymn' from the Pyramid Texts. *JEA* 10 (1924): 97-103.

Faure, H. See entries 1988 and 2449.

762 **Favenc, B.** Silex taillés provenant du désert Arabique (Egypte). *C.r. Assoc. Franc. pour*

l'Avancement des Sciences, 31e session, Montauban 1 (Paris, 1902): 256-57.

763 ———. Note sur le paleolithique égyptien. *Ibid.* 2 (Paris, 1903): 860-62.

764 **Fawcett, Cicely D.** and **Alice Lee.** A second study of the variation and correlation of the human skull, with special reference to the Naqada crania. *Biometrika* 1, 4 (1901-2): 408-67.

765 **Fazzini, Richard.** *Images for Eternity: Egyptian Art from Berkeley and Brooklyn.* New York, 1975.

766 **Ferring, C. Reid.** The Aterian in North African prehistory. In entry 2388, pp. 113-26.

767 **Finegan, Jack.** *Archaeological History of the Ancient Middle East.* Boulder, Colorado and Folkstone, England, 1979.

768 **Finkenstaedt, Elizabeth.** The internal chronology of Egyptian predynastic black-topped ware. [Summary of paper presented to 75th Gen. Meeting of AIA Dec., 1973 in St. Louis.] *AJA* 78, 2 (1974): 165.

769 ———. The chronology of Egyptian predynastic black-topped ware. *ZÄS* 103 (1976): 5-8.

770 ———. Regional painting style in predynastic Egypt. *ZÄS* 107 (1980): 116-20.

771 ———. Egyptian ivory tusks and tubes. *ZÄS* 106 (1979): 51-59.

772 **Firth, Cecil M.** *<104> The Archaeological Survey of Nubia: Report for 1908-1909.* Cairo, 1912.

773 ———. *The Archaeological Survey of Nubia: Report for 1909-1910.* Cairo, 1915.

774 ———. *The Archaeological Survey of Nubia: Report for 1910-1911.* Cairo, 1927.

775 **Fischer, Henry George.** A fragment of a late predynastic Egyptian relief from the eastern Delta. *Artibus Asiae* 21 (1958): 64-88.

776 ———. An Egyptian royal stela of the second dynasty. *Artibus Asiae* 24 (1961): 45-56.

777 ———. A first dynasty bowl inscribed with the group *Ht.* *CdE* 36 (1961): 19-22.

778 ———. *Dendara in the Third Millennium B.C. down to the Theban Domination.* New York, 1969.

779 ———. Koptos. *LdÄ* 3 (1975-): 737-40.

780 **Fischer, H.** *Die Geburt der Hochkultur in Ägypten und Mesopotamien. Die primäre Entwurf des menschlischen Dramas.* Frankfurt, 1981.

Fischietti, I. See entry 1499.

781 **Fitzgerald, G.M.** Stone age sites recently investigated. *PEQ* 62 (1930): 85-90.

Reviewed: *Ancient Egypt* (1930): 94.

782 **Fleay, F.G.** *Egyptian Chronology: An Attempt to Conciliate the Ancient Schemes and to Educe a Rational System.* London, 1899.

Fleming, S.J. See entry 1671.

783 **Flight, C.** A survey of recent results in the radiocarbon chronology of Northern and Western Africa. *J. African History* 14 (1973): 531-54.

784 **Forbes, H.O.** On a collection of stone implements in the Mayer Museum, made by H.W. Seton-Karr, in mines of the ancient Egyptians discovered by him on the plateaux of the Nile Valley. *Bull. Liverpool Museum* 2 (1900): 77-115.

Reviewed: *L'Anthropologie* 11 (1900): 615-17 by M. Boule.
Geol. Mag. 7 (1900): 326-29 by T.R.J.

785 ———. The age of the surface flint implements of Egypt and Somalialand. *Bull. Liverpool Museum* 3 (1901): 48-61.

Reviewed: *L'Anthropologie* 13 (1902): 109-10.
Archaeological Report EEF (1900-1901): 44-45.

786 **Forde-Johnston, J.L.** *Neolithic Cultures of North Africa. Liverpool Univ. Monographs in Archaeology and Oriental Studies.* (Liverpool, 1966).

787 **Forni, G.** Arte preistorica e struttura, analogua, individualita delle culture. Considerazioi sull'origine ed evoluzione del genere di vita pastorale nel Sahara preistorico, en base all'interpretazione delle raffigurazioni rupestri dell'Acasus. *Valcamonica Symposium, 1968: Actes du Symposium International d'Art Préhistorique* 1 (Valcamonica, 1970): 357-67.

788 **Forrer, R.** *Achmim-Studie, Über Steinzeit Hockergräber zu Akhmim, Nagada, etc., in Ober-Ägypten und uber-europäische Parallelfunde.* Strasbourg, 1901.

Reviewed: *Sphinx* 6 (1903): 314 by K. Piehl.

789 ———. Die Ägyptischen, Kretischen, Phönikischen, etc. Gewichte und Masse der Europäischen Kupfer-bronze und Eisenzeit. *Jahrb. d. Gesellsch. f. Lothringische Gesch. und Altertumsk* 18 (Metz, 1906): 1-177.

790 **Forster, Charles.** *The One Primeval Language Traced Experimentally through Ancient Inscriptions.* 1: *The Voice of Israel from the Rocks of Sinai, or the Sinaitic Inscriptions...;* 2: *The Monuments of Egypt, and the Vestiges of Patriarchial Traditions;* 3: *The Monuments of Assyria, Babylonia, and Persia.* 3 vols. London, 1851-1854.

791 **Foucart, Georges.** <107> Les monuments commemoratifs du Sed à Hierakonpolis. *Sphinx* 5 (1901): 102-9.

792 ———. Sur la décoration des vases de la période dite Naggadeh. *CRAIBL* (1905): 257-78.

793 ———. [Current prehistoric studies.] *Sphinx* 18 (1914-1915): 51-53.

794 **Fouquet, Daniel Marie.** <107> *Recherches sur les Origines de l'Egypte: L'Age de la pierre et des metaux.* Paris, 1896.

795 ———. Recherche sur les crânes de l'époque de la pierre taillée en Egypte. In entry 1476, pp. 269-380.

796 **Fourdrignier, Edouard.** Silex taillés de l'époque mousterienne provenant d'Egypte. *BSAP,* 4th ser., 9 (1898): 388.

797 **Fourmont, Etienne.** <108> *Réflexions Critiques sur l'Origine, l'Histoire et la Succession des Anciens Peuples Chaldéens, Hebreux, Phéniciens, Egyptiens, Grecs, etc., jusqu'au Temps de Cyrus.* Paris, 1735; 2nd ed. 1747.

798 **Fournier, E.** Les silex égyptiens de l'île de Riou. *L'Homme Préhistorique* 5 (Paris, 1907): 374-75.

799 ———. Sur les prétendus silex égyptiens de l'île Riou. *Bull. Soc. Archéol. de Provence* 1 (1904-1907). Also published separately, Marseille, 1907.

800 **Fourtau, R.** Note sur le paléolithique en Egypte. *BIE,* 3th ser., 8 (1897): 227-34.

801 **Franchet, L.** Sur un procédé préhistorique employé par les indigènes du Fayoum, pour la fabrication des poteries, sans l'aide de four: Contribution à la palethnologie égyptiens. *C.r. Assoc. Franç. pour l'Avancement des Sciences 43e Session, Le Havre, 1914* (Paris, 1915): 151.

802 ———. L'Outillage en pierre de l'époque énéolithique et du commencement de l'âge de bronze à Thèbes. *Ibid.* p. 151.

803 ———. La céramique du désert Libyque. *Revue Scient. Illust.* (Paris, 11 Decembre 1926).

804 **Frankfort, Henri.** <108> *Studies in Early Pottery of the Near East,* 1: *Mesopotamia, Syria, and Egypt, and their Earliest Interrelations. Occas. Paper, RAI* 6 (London, 1924).

Reviewed: *Ancient Egypt* (1925): 125-27.
JEA 9 (1924): 338-39.
Man 25 (1925): 13-14 by W.M.F. Petrie.

805 ———. *Studies in early pottery of the Near East,* 2: *Asia, Europe, and the Aegean, and their earliest interrelations. Occas. Paper, RAI* 8 (London, 1927).

Reviewed: *Ancient Egypt* (1927): 52-56.

806 ———. The cemeteries of Abydos: Work of the season 1925-1926. *JEA* 14 (1930): 214-15.

807 ———. *Cylinder Seals.* London, 1939.

808 ———. The origin of monumental architecture in Egypt. *AJSL* 58 (1941): 329-58.

809 ———. *Ancient Egyptian Religion: An Interpretation.* New York, 1948.

810 ———. *Kingship and the Gods: A Study of Ancient Near Eastern Religion as the Integration of Society and Nature.* Chicago, 1948. Also publ. in French as *La Royauté et les Dieux.* (Paris, 1951).

811 ———. The ancient Egyptians and the Hamites. *Man* 49 (1949): 95-96. [See entry 1853.]

812 ———. *The Birth of Civilization in the Near East.* London and Bloomington, Indiana, 1951; repr. 1956.

813 ———. The African foundation of ancient Egyptian civilization. *Atti del I Congres Internazionale di Preistoria et Protostoria Mediterranea, Firenza-Napoli-Roma, 1950* (Florence, 1952): 115-17.

814 **Franzen, J.** Entstehung und Alter der Höhle von Haua Fteah (Cyrenaica). *Natur. und Museum* 102 (1972): 37-49.

815 **Freier, E.** Vier Siegel der Früzeit im Leipziger Museum. *ZÄS* 107 (1980): 52-56.

816 **Frey, J.** *Les Egyptiens Préhistoriques Identifés avec les Annamites d'après les Inscriptions Hiéroglyphiques.* Paris, 1905.

817 **Friedel, C.** Sur des materières grasses trouvées dans les tombes égyptiens d'Abydos. *CrASP* 124 (1897): 648-53.

818 **Fritsch, G.** Vergleichende Betrachtung über die ältesten ägyptischen Darstellung von Volkstypen. *Naturwissenschaftliche Wochenschrift,* n.f. 3, 19 (Jena, 1904): 673-82.

819 **Frobenius, Leo.** *Kulturgeschichte Afrikas: Prolegomena zu einer historischen Gestaltlehre.* Zurich, 1933.

820 ———. Die Ergebnisse der deutschen (Inner-afrikanischen) Forschungs-Expedition in die libysche Wüste und den anglo-ägyptischen Sudan 1933. *Beiblatt 4. Zu den Mitteil. des Forschungs-Inst. für Kulturmorphologie.* (Frankfort, 1934).

821 ———. Prehistoric art in the Libyan desert. *Nature* 133 (1934): 20.

822 ———. L'art rupestre du Fezzan. In E. Haberland (ed.), *Leo Frobenius: Une Anthologie* (Wiesbaden, 1973): 93-103.

823 ———. Rock art of the Fezzan. *Studien zur Kulturkunde* 32 (1973): 83-92.

824 **Frobenius, Leo** and **D.C. Fox.** *Prehistoric Rock Pictures in Europe and Africa. From Material in the Archives of the Research Institute for the Morphology of Civilizations, Frankfort-on-Mainz.* New York, 1937.

Fry, E.I. See entry 2389.

825 **Fumagalli, Savina.** Il cranio della necropole neolitica di Gebelen (Alto Egitto), Nota Ia. *Atti della Accademia delle Scienze di Torino* 86 (1952).

826 ———. Il cranio della necropoli neolitica de Gebelen (Alto Egitto), Nota Seconda. *Atti della Societa Italiana di Scienze Naturale et del Museo Civico di Storia Naturale in Milano* 91 (1952): 55-94.

827 ———. Struttura dei tessuti dentari nei neolitici Egiziani di Gebelen (Alto Egitto). *Atti della Accademia della Scienze di Torino* 86 (1952).

828 ———. Saggio di suppellittile etnografica neolitica della necropoli di Gebelen. *Atti del Congresso di Studi Etnografici Haliani, 1952* (Naples, 1953): 369-82.

G

829 **Gaballa, G.A.** *Narrative in Egyptian Art.* Mainz, 1976.

830 **Gabra, Sami.** Fouilles du Service des Antiquités à Deir Tasa. *ASAE* 30 (1930): 147-58.

831 **Gabriel, B.** Steinplätze: Feuerstellen neolithischer Nomaden in der Sahara. *Libyca* 21 (1973): 151-68.

832 **Gadd, C.J.** *Ideas of Divine Rule in the Ancient East.* [The Schweich Lecture of the British Academy, 1941.] London, 1948.

833 **Gaillard, Claude.** <110> Contribution à l'étude de la faune préhistorique de l'Egypte. *Archives Mus. d'Hist. Nat. de Lyon* 14 (Lyon, 1934).

Reviewed: *L'Anthropologie* 45 (1935): 142-43 by R. Vaufrey.

———. See entry 1332.

834 **Gaillardot**, Dr. M. Arcelin et les silex taillés en Egypte. *BIE,* 1st ser., 12 (1872-1873): 68-71.

835 ———. Sur une question de priorité soulevée au sujet des premières découvertes relative aux instruments de silex de l'époque préhistorique. *BIE,* 1st ser., 12 (1872-1873): 80-84.

836 ———. Communication de deux lettres de Sir John Lubbock et de M. Arcelin au sujet des instruments de silex. Quelques réflexions sur les traces de l'époque de la pierre taillée en Egypte à propos des découvertes de M. Schliemann en Egypte. *BIE,* 1st ser., 13 (1874-1875): 57-59.

837 **Galassi, Giuseppe.** <110> *Tehenu e le Origini Mediterranea della Civiltà egizia.* Rome, 1942.

838 ———. Preistoria e protostoria mediterranea. L'arte del più antico Egitto nel Museo di Torino. *Estrata della 'Rivista dell'Instituto nazionale d'Archéologia e storia dell'arte,'* n.s., A, 4 (1955).

Gallagher, John. See entry 1946.

839 **Galloway, William B.** *Dissertations on the Philosophy of the Creation and the First Ten Chapters of Genesis, Allegorized in Mythology; Containing Expositions of the Ancient Cosmogenies and Theogenies, the Invention of Hieroglyphics and of the Ancient Hebrew Language and Alphabet; Being Contributions to the Evidence of Natural and Revealed Religion.* Edinburgh and London, 1885.

840 **Gandolphe**, Dr. and **G.E. Smith.** A propos de la prétendue découverte de la syphilis chez les Egyptiens préhistoriques. *BSAL* 28 (1909): 73-86. [See also entry 1330.]

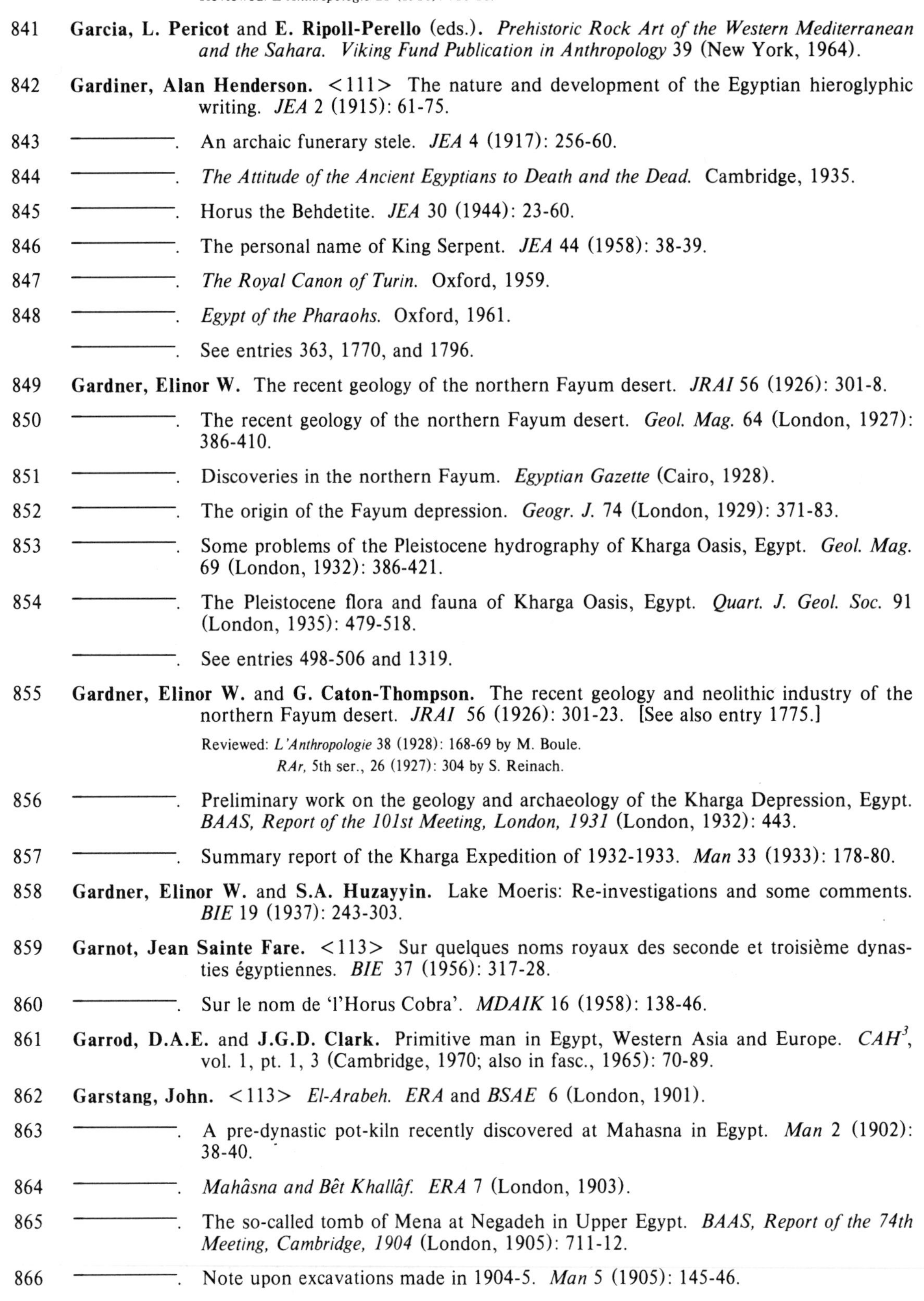

Reviewed: *L'Anthropologie* 21 (1910): 716-18.

841 **Garcia, L. Pericot** and **E. Ripoll-Perello** (eds.). *Prehistoric Rock Art of the Western Mediterranean and the Sahara. Viking Fund Publication in Anthropology* 39 (New York, 1964).

842 **Gardiner, Alan Henderson.** <111> The nature and development of the Egyptian hieroglyphic writing. *JEA* 2 (1915): 61-75.

843 ————. An archaic funerary stele. *JEA* 4 (1917): 256-60.

844 ————. *The Attitude of the Ancient Egyptians to Death and the Dead.* Cambridge, 1935.

845 ————. Horus the Behdetite. *JEA* 30 (1944): 23-60.

846 ————. The personal name of King Serpent. *JEA* 44 (1958): 38-39.

847 ————. *The Royal Canon of Turin.* Oxford, 1959.

848 ————. *Egypt of the Pharaohs.* Oxford, 1961.

————. See entries 363, 1770, and 1796.

849 **Gardner, Elinor W.** The recent geology of the northern Fayum desert. *JRAI* 56 (1926): 301-8.

850 ————. The recent geology of the northern Fayum desert. *Geol. Mag.* 64 (London, 1927): 386-410.

851 ————. Discoveries in the northern Fayum. *Egyptian Gazette* (Cairo, 1928).

852 ————. The origin of the Fayum depression. *Geogr. J.* 74 (London, 1929): 371-83.

853 ————. Some problems of the Pleistocene hydrography of Kharga Oasis, Egypt. *Geol. Mag.* 69 (London, 1932): 386-421.

854 ————. The Pleistocene flora and fauna of Kharga Oasis, Egypt. *Quart. J. Geol. Soc.* 91 (London, 1935): 479-518.

————. See entries 498-506 and 1319.

855 **Gardner, Elinor W.** and **G. Caton-Thompson.** The recent geology and neolithic industry of the northern Fayum desert. *JRAI* 56 (1926): 301-23. [See also entry 1775.]

Reviewed: *L'Anthropologie* 38 (1928): 168-69 by M. Boule.
RAr, 5th ser., 26 (1927): 304 by S. Reinach.

856 ————. Preliminary work on the geology and archaeology of the Kharga Depression, Egypt. *BAAS, Report of the 101st Meeting, London, 1931* (London, 1932): 443.

857 ————. Summary report of the Kharga Expedition of 1932-1933. *Man* 33 (1933): 178-80.

858 **Gardner, Elinor W.** and **S.A. Huzayyin.** Lake Moeris: Re-investigations and some comments. *BIE* 19 (1937): 243-303.

859 **Garnot, Jean Sainte Fare.** <113> Sur quelques noms royaux des seconde et troisième dynasties égyptiennes. *BIE* 37 (1956): 317-28.

860 ————. Sur le nom de 'l'Horus Cobra'. *MDAIK* 16 (1958): 138-46.

861 **Garrod, D.A.E.** and **J.G.D. Clark.** Primitive man in Egypt, Western Asia and Europe. CAH^3, vol. 1, pt. 1, 3 (Cambridge, 1970; also in fasc., 1965): 70-89.

862 **Garstang, John.** <113> *El-Arabeh. ERA* and *BSAE* 6 (London, 1901).

863 ————. A pre-dynastic pot-kiln recently discovered at Mahasna in Egypt. *Man* 2 (1902): 38-40.

864 ————. *Mahâsna and Bêt Khallâf. ERA* 7 (London, 1903).

865 ————. The so-called tomb of Mena at Negadeh in Upper Egypt. *BAAS, Report of the 74th Meeting, Cambridge, 1904* (London, 1905): 711-12.

866 ————. Note upon excavations made in 1904-5. *Man* 5 (1905): 145-46.

867 ————. The tablet of Mena. *ZÄS* 42 (1905): 61-65.

868 ————. Excavations at Hierakonpolis, at Esna and in Nubia. *ASAE* 7 (1907): 132-38.

869 **Gautier, Achilles.** Mammalian remains of the northern Sudan and southern Egypt. In entry 2415, pp. 80-99.

————. See entries 1340, 1341, 2385 and 2422.

870 **Gautier, Achilles, Peter Ballman** and **Willem Van Meer.** Mollusks, fish, birds and mammals from the Late Palaeolithic sites in Wadi Kubbaniya. In entry 2416, pp. 281-94.

871 **Gauthier, Henri Louis Marie Alexandre.** <114> *Le Livre des Rois d'Egypte,* 1: *Des Origines à la Fin de la XIIe Dynastie. MIFAO* 17 (Cairo, 1907).

872 ————. Quatre fragments nouveaux de la pierre de Palerme au Musée du Caire. *CRAIBL* (1914): 489-96.

873 **Geiger, Lazarus.** *Contributions to the History of the Development of the Human Race. Lectures and Dissertations.* Transl. from the 2nd German edition by David Asher. London, 1880.

874 **George, Beatte.** Frühe keramik aus Aegypten. *B. Medelhavsmuseet* 10 (Stockholm, 1975).

875 **Germain, Louis.** Les origines de la civilisation précolombienne et les théories d'Elliot Smith. *L'Anthropologie* 32 (1922): 93-126. [See also entry 2159.]

876 ————. La préhistoire orientale et l'oeuvre de Jacques de Morgan. *L'Anthropologie* 38 (1928): 317-45.

877 **Ghoneim, Wafik.** *Die ökonomische Bedeutung des Rindes im alten Ägypten. Habelts Dissertationsdrucke, Reihe Ägyptologie* 3 (Bonn, 1977).

878 **Giegegack, Robert F.** *Late Pleistocene History of the Nile Valley in Egyptian Nubia.* Unpubl. Ph.D. diss., Yale Univ., New Haven, 1968.

Gijselings, G. See entries 2290-2294.

879 **Gilbert, P.** Fauves au long cou communs à l'art égyptien et à l'art sumérien archaiques. *CdE* 43 (1947): 38-41.

880 **Gilbey, B.E.** and **M. Lubrau.** The ABO and Rh blood group antigens in pre-dynastic Egyptian mummies. *Man* 53 (1953): 23.

881 **Gilead, D.** [Prehistoric finds in the Negev and Sinai.] *Mitekufat Haeven* 11 (Jerusalem, 1973): 36-42. [In Hebrew]

882 ————. Handaxe industries in Israel and the Near East. *World Archaeology* 2 (1970): 1-11.

883 **Ginter, B.** Deir el-Bahari, Site 21b (Flint workshops from various periods of the Palaeolithic and Neolithic ages). *Recherches Archéologiques* (Krakow, 1975): 61-66.

884 **Ginter, Boleslaw, Janusz K. Koslowski** and **B. Drobniewicz.** Silex industrien von el-Tärif. *AV* 26 (Mainz, 1979). Transl. from Polish by P. Lenz.

885 **Ginter, Boleslaw, Janusz K. Kozlowski** and **Joachim Sliwa.** Excavation report on the prehistoric and predynastic settlement in el-Tarif 1978. *MDAIK* 35 (1979): 87-102.

886 **Giuffrida-Ruggeri, Vincenzo.** Were the pre-dynastic Egyptians Libyans or Ethiopians. *Man* 15 (1915): 51-56. [See also entry 2163.]

Reviewed: *L'Anthropologie* 29 (1918): 127-28 by M. Boule.

887 ————. A few notes on the neolithic Egyptians and the Ethiopians. *BAAS, Report of the 80th meeting, Manchester, 1915* (London, 1916): 670-71.

Reviewed: *Man* 16 (1916): 87-90.

888 ————. The Mokattam skull. *Cairo Science J.* 9 (1917): 25-26.

889 ————. Appunti di etnologia egiziana. *Aegyptus* 2 (1921): 179-89.

890 ————. The actual state of the question of the most ancient Egyptian populations. *Harvard African Studies,* 3: *Varia Africana* (Cambridge, Mass., 1922): 3-7.

891 **Glanville, Stephen Randolph Kingdom.** <116> Egyptian theriomorphic vessels in the British Museum. *JEA* 12 (1926): 52-69.

892 ————. 'Badarian' antiquities from Egypt. *British Museum Quart.* 46 (1930): 103-4.

893 ————. An archaic statuette from Abydos. *JEA* 17 (1931): 65-66.

Glass, J. See entry 53.

Gliddon, George Robins. <117> See entry 1627.

894 **Gobert, E.G.** Pièces préhistoriques recueillies à Tejerhi. In P. Bellair, et al., *Mission au Fezzan, 1940* (Tunis, 1953): 17-19.

895 **Gobineau, Arthur de.** Extrait d'une lettre à M. Alf. Maury (On the different races of men in Egypt). *Bull. Soc. Géogr.,* 4th ser., (1856): 202.

896 ————. *Essai sur l'Inégalité des Races Humaines.* Paris, 1884. Transl. by Adrian Collins as *The Inequality of Human Races.* London, 1915.

897 **Godron, Gérard.** A propos du nom royal [hieroglyphs]. *ASAE* 49 (1949): 217-21.

898 ————. Note complémentaire à l'article sur la lecture du nom royal [hieroglyphs]. *ASAE* 49 (1949): 547.

899 ————. Deux notes d'épigraphie thinite. *RdE* 8 (1951): 91-100.

900 ————. Quel est le lieu de provenance de la 'Pierre de Palerme'? *CdE* 53 (1952): 17-22.

901 ————. Notes d'épigraphie thinite. *ASAE* 58 (1957): 191-206.

902 ————. Etudes sur l'époque archaic. *BIFAO* 57 (1958): 143-55.

903 **Godwin, H.** and **E.H. Willis.** Wadi Ganima, Libya. *Radiocarbon* 4 (1962): 69.

904 **Goedicke, Hans.** The pharaoh Ny-Swtḥ. *ZÄS* 81 (1956): 18-24.

905 ————. King Ḥwḏf3? *JEA* 42 (1956): 50-53.

Goldberg, P. See entry 1040.

906 **Golénischeff, Vladimir Samionovich.** <118> Une excursion à Bérénice. *RecTrav* 13 (1890): 75-99.

907 **Gomaà, Farouk.** El-Gerzeh. *LdÄ* 2 (1975-): 556.

908 **Gophna, R.** 'En-Besor: An Egyptian first dynasty staging post in the northern Negev. *Expedition* 20 (1978): 4-7.

Gould, S.J. See Supplement entry 2493.

909 **Grant, J.A.** The climate of Egypt in geological, prehistoric and ancient historic times. *J. Vict. Institute* 32 (1900): 87-105.

Gratta, T. del. See entry 1499.

910 **Graziosi, P.** Il Fezzan preistorico. *L'Illustrazione Italiana* 3 (Milan, 1934): 90-91.

911 ————. Le pitture rupestre di El Auenat in Libia. *Pan* (Milan, 1934): 264-374.

912 ————. Realazione preliminaire delle ricerche compiute nel Fezzan dalla missione preistorica della Reale Società Geografica Italiana (aprile-maggio 1933). *BSGE,* 6th ser., 11 (1934): 107-26.

913 ————. Préhistoire. *Le Sahara Italien: Guide Official de la Section Italienne. Exposition du Sahara. Ministère des Colonies.* (Rome, 1934): 37-42.

914 ————. *Arte Preistorica nell Libia. La Scena Illustrata.* Florence, 1936.

915 ———. Rupi graffite e dipinte dell Libia. *Sapere, Aumdidinale di Divulgazione di Scienza Tecnica e Arte Applicata* 6 (Milano, 1937): 197-99.

916 ———. I graffite rupestri della Libia. *L'Italia d'Oltremare* 20 (1938): 316-20.

917 ———. Missione preistorica nel Fezzan compiuta nel marzo-aprile 1938, XVI. *La Ricerca Scientifica,* 2nd ser., 9 (1938): 613-14.

918 ———. Leo Frobenius e la sua esplorazione fezzanese. *AAI* 3 (1940): 463-68.

919 ———. The rock carvings of Wadi Al-Khail in Tripolitania. *Rivista de Scienze Preistoriche* 11 (1956): 234-39.

920 ———. *Arte preistorica del Sahara Libico. Roma - Palazzo di Venezia, 16 marzo - 12 aprile 1960.* Rome, 1960.

921 ———. L'art paléolithique de la 'province méditerranéene' et ses influences dans les temps post- paléolithiques. *Viking Fund Publ. in Anthropology* 39 (1964): 35-46.

922 ———. Le incisioni rupestre dell'Udei El Chel in Tripolitania. *La Arti* 5 (1968): 9-36.

923 ———. Recente missione per lo studio dell'arte rupestre nel Fezzan. *Valcamonia Symposium. Actes du Symposium International d'Art Préhistorique* 1 (Valcamonia, 1970): 329-43.

924 ———. The therianthropic figures of Fezzan and their meaning. *Bollettino del Centro Camuno di Studi Preistorici* 9 (1972): 161.

———. See entries 454 and 1499.

925 **Grdseloff, Bernhard.** <122> Notes sur deux monuments inédits de l'ancien empire. *ASAE* 44 (1944): 107-25.

926 ———. Notes d'epigraphie archaique, 1: La tablette de Nagada et le roi Menes. *ASAE* 44 (1944): 279-82. [See also entry 2328.]

927 ———. Notes d'epigraphie archaique, 2: Le nom du roi ['Serpent']. *ASAE* 44 (1944): 282-84. [See also entry 565.]

928 ———. Notes d'epigraphie archaique, 3: Le nom du roi [nswt-bity] de l'Horus Smr-ẖt. *ASAE* 44 (1944): 284-88.

929 ———. Notes d'epigraphie archaique, 4: Le roi Wenig de la IIe dynastie. *ASAE* 44 (1944): 288-92.

930 ———. Notes d'epigraphie archaique, 5: La fin de la second dynastie ou la 'Periode Sethienne', [with a note by J. Černý.] *ASAE* 44 (1944): 293-302.

931 **Green, Frederick William.** <124> Prehistoric drawings at el-Kab. *PSBA* 25 (1903): 371-72.

932 ———. *Prehistoric wall-painting in Egypt. BSAE* (London, 1950).

———. See entry 1851.

933 **Greene, W.** On an early dynastic vase in the Fitzwilliam Museum. In *Essays and Studies Presented to William Ridgeway.* (Cambridge, 1913): 266-68.

Greene, D.L. See entry 110.

934 **Greene, D.L.** and **L. Scott.** An evolutionary interpretation of congenital frontal sinus absence in the Wadi Halfa Mousterian population. *Man* 8 (1973): 471-74.

935 **Greene, John C.** *The Death of Adam: Evolution and its Impact on Western Thought.* Ames, Iowa, 1959.

936 **Greenly, E.** Post-glacial time and ancient Egypt. *Geol. Mag.,* n.s., 6 (1909): 537-38.

937 **Greenwood, P.H.** Fish remains. In entry 2388, pp. 100-109.

938 **Greg, R.P.** Neolithic flint implements of the Nile Valley and Egypt. *JRAI* 10 (1880): 424-29.

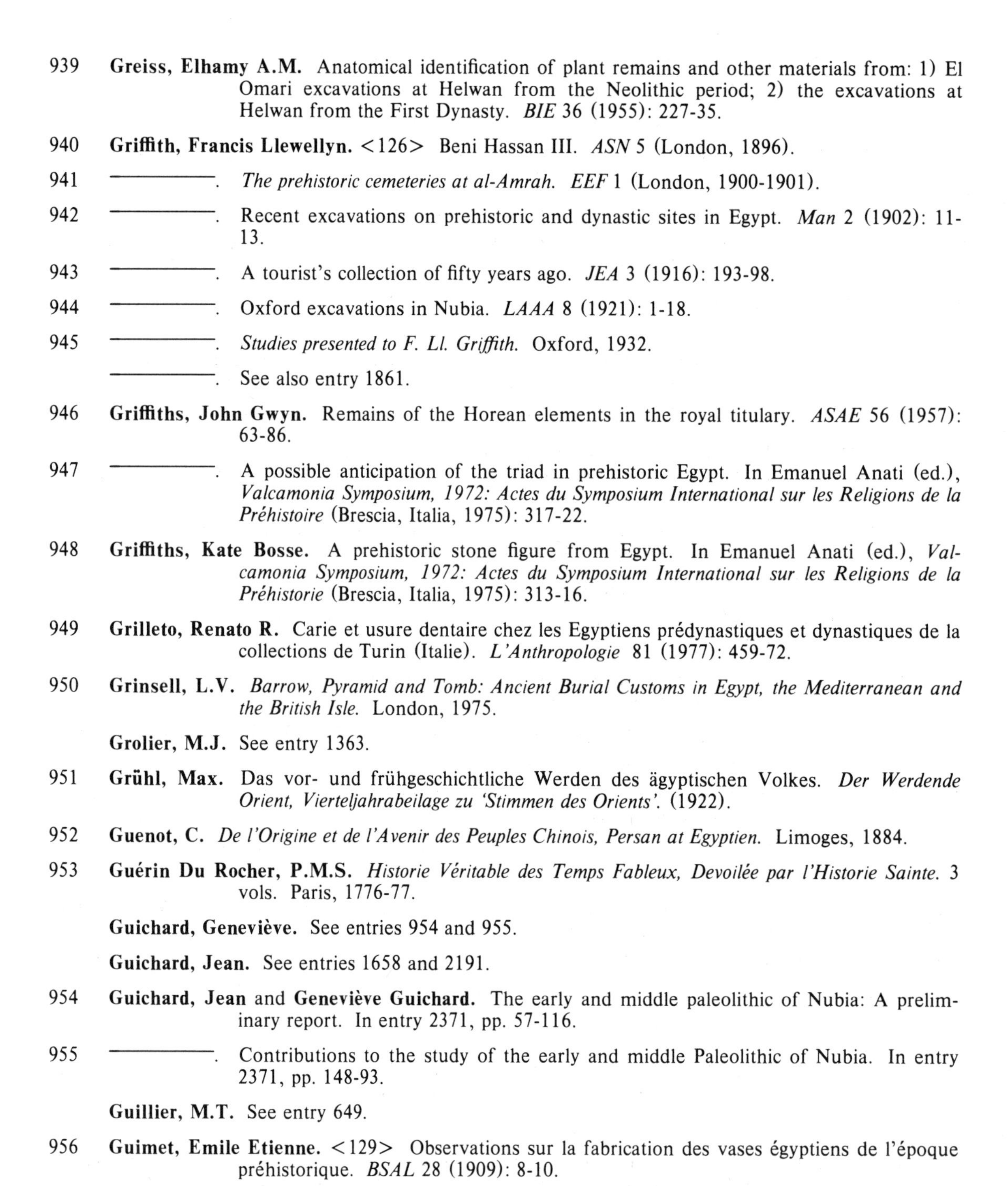

939 **Greiss, Elhamy A.M.** Anatomical identification of plant remains and other materials from: 1) El Omari excavations at Helwan from the Neolithic period; 2) the excavations at Helwan from the First Dynasty. *BIE* 36 (1955): 227-35.

940 **Griffith, Francis Llewellyn.** <126> Beni Hassan III. *ASN* 5 (London, 1896).

941 ————. *The prehistoric cemeteries at al-Amrah. EEF* 1 (London, 1900-1901).

942 ————. Recent excavations on prehistoric and dynastic sites in Egypt. *Man* 2 (1902): 11-13.

943 ————. A tourist's collection of fifty years ago. *JEA* 3 (1916): 193-98.

944 ————. Oxford excavations in Nubia. *LAAA* 8 (1921): 1-18.

945 ————. *Studies presented to F. Ll. Griffith.* Oxford, 1932.

————. See also entry 1861.

946 **Griffiths, John Gwyn.** Remains of the Horean elements in the royal titulary. *ASAE* 56 (1957): 63-86.

947 ————. A possible anticipation of the triad in prehistoric Egypt. In Emanuel Anati (ed.), *Valcamonia Symposium, 1972: Actes du Symposium International sur les Religions de la Préhistoire* (Brescia, Italia, 1975): 317-22.

948 **Griffiths, Kate Bosse.** A prehistoric stone figure from Egypt. In Emanuel Anati (ed.), *Valcamonia Symposium, 1972: Actes du Symposium International sur les Religions de la Préhistorie* (Brescia, Italia, 1975): 313-16.

949 **Grilleto, Renato R.** Carie et usure dentaire chez les Egyptiens prédynastiques et dynastiques de la collections de Turin (Italie). *L'Anthropologie* 81 (1977): 459-72.

950 **Grinsell, L.V.** *Barrow, Pyramid and Tomb: Ancient Burial Customs in Egypt, the Mediterranean and the British Isle.* London, 1975.

Grolier, M.J. See entry 1363.

951 **Grühl, Max.** Das vor- und frühgeschichtliche Werden des ägyptischen Volkes. *Der Werdende Orient, Vierteljahrabeilage zu 'Stimmen des Orients'.* (1922).

952 **Guenot, C.** *De l'Origine et de l'Avenir des Peuples Chinois, Persan at Egyptien.* Limoges, 1884.

953 **Guérin Du Rocher, P.M.S.** *Historie Véritable des Temps Fableux, Devoilée par l'Historie Sainte.* 3 vols. Paris, 1776-77.

Guichard, Geneviève. See entries 954 and 955.

Guichard, Jean. See entries 1658 and 2191.

954 **Guichard, Jean** and **Geneviève Guichard.** The early and middle paleolithic of Nubia: A preliminary report. In entry 2371, pp. 57-116.

955 ————. Contributions to the study of the early and middle Paleolithic of Nubia. In entry 2371, pp. 148-93.

Guillier, M.T. See entry 649.

956 **Guimet, Emile Etienne.** <129> Observations sur la fabrication des vases égyptiens de l'époque préhistorique. *BSAL* 28 (1909): 8-10.

Guinet, P. See entry 2269.

Gunn, B. See entry 735.

H

Haas, Herbert. See entries 2418 and 2419.

957 **Habachi, Labib.** A first dynasty cemetery at Abydos. *ASAE* 39 (1939): 767-81.

958 **el-Hadidi, M. Nabil.** The predynastic flora of the Hierakonpolis region. In entry 1062, pp. 93-101.

959 ———. Plant remains from Late Palaeolithic sites in Wadi Kubbaniya. In entry 2416, pp. 295-98.

———. See also entries 2385 and 2419.

Haesaerts, P. See entry 1021.

960 **Hall, Henry Reginald Holland.** <131> Note on the early use of iron in Egypt. *Man* 3 (1903): 147-49.

961 ———. The early occurrence of iron in Egypt. *Man* 5 (1905): 69-71.

962 ———. Palaeolithic implements from the Thebaid. *Man* 5 (1905): 35-37.

963 ———. The discoveries at Tell el-'Obeid in southern Babylonia, and some Egyptian connections. *JEA* 8 (1922): 241-57.

964 ———. Egyptian antiquities. *British Museum Quart.* 1 (1926): 43.

965 ———. A pre-dynastic Egyptian double-axe. In *Essays in Aegean Archaeology Presented to Sir Arthur Evans.* (Oxford, 1927): 42.

966 ———. Some Egyptian axeheads in the British Museum. *LAAA* 16 (1929): 23-24.

967 ———. Antiquities from Badari (al-Mostagedda). *British Museum Quart.* 5 (1930): 76.

968 **Hamdan, G.** Evolution of irrigation agriculture in Egypt. *Arid Zone Research* 17 (1961): 119-42.

969 **Hamroush, Hamy A.** Preliminary report on the Quaternary geology and geoarchaeology of Hierakonpolis. In entry 1062, pp. 93-100.

970 **Hamy, Théodore Jules Ernest.** <132> L'Age de pierre en Egypte. *BSAP,* 2nd ser., 4 (1869): 685-88.

971 ———. L'Egypte quaternaire et l'ancienneté de l'homme. *BSAP,* 2nd ser., 4 (1869): 711-19.

972 ———. Sur l'Egypte préhistorique. *BSAP,* 2nd ser., 5 (1870): 15-18.

973 ———. Les Nègres de la vallée du Nil. *Revue d'Anthropologie* 4 (Paris, 1881): 22-35.

974 ———. Etudes sur les peintures ethniques d'un tombeau thébain de la XVIIIe dynastie. *Revue d'Ethnogr.* 3 (1884): 273-94. Also publ. separately, Paris, 1885.

975 ———. Aperçu sur les races humaines de la basse vallée du Nil. *BSAP,* 3rd ser., 9 (1886): 718-43. Also publ. separately, Paris, 1887.

———. See also entries 81 and 530.

976 **Hamy, Théodore J.E.** and **Françoise Lenormant.** Découvertes de restes de l'âge de pierre en Egypte. *CrASP* 69 (1869): 1090-91. Also publ. separately, Paris, 1869. [See also entry 75.]

977 ———. Sur quelques ateliers superficiels de silex taillés récemment découvertes en Egypte. *CrASP* 69 (1869): 1313-15.

978 ———. Silex taillés dans la Haute-Egypte. *Les Mondes,* 2nd ser., 21 (Paris, 1869): 574 and 795.

Harding-King, J. See entries 139 and 1219.

979 **Harlan, J. Fred.** *Excavations at Locality II, Hierakonpolis: 1978 and 1979.* Unpubl. M.A. Thesis, Washington Univ., St. Louis, 1980.

980 ———. Excavations at Locality IIC. In entry 1062, pp. 14-25.

981 **Hansen, C.L.** and **Karl W. Butzer.** Early Pleistocene deposits of the Nile Valley in Egyptian Nubia. *Quaternia* 8 (1966): 177-85.

Hansen, C.L. See entries 417-20.

982 **Harris, J.A.** A new fragment of the battlefield palette. *JEA* 46 (1960): 104-05.

Hassan, A. See entry 2387.

983 **Hassan, Fekri A.** *Demographic Archaeology of Hunters-Gatherers.* Unpubl. ms. N.d.

984 ———. *The Predynastic of Egypt: A Cultural Ecology.* Unpubl. ms. N.d.

985 ———. Notes on Sebilian sites from Dishna Plain. *CdE* 47 (1972): 11-16.

986 ———. Population dynamics and the beginning of domestication in the Nile Valley. [Paper presented at the 71st annual meeting of the Amer. Anthrop. Assoc.] (Toronto, 1975).

987 ———. On mechanisms of population growth during the Neolithic. *Current Anthropology* 14, 5 (1973): 535-40.

988 ———. *The Archaeology of the Dishna Plain, Egypt. Geological Survey of Egypt, paper* 59 (Cairo, 1974).

989 ———. Population growth and cultural evolution. *Anthropology* 2 (1974): 205-12.

990 ———. Determinants of size, density, and growth rate of hunting - gathering populations. In S. Polgar (ed.), *Population, Ecology and Social Evolution.* (The Hague, 1975): 27-52.

991 ———. Heavy minerals and the evolution of the modern Nile. *Quaternary Research* 6 (1976): 425-44.

992 ———. Prehistoric studies of the Siwa Oasis region: Preliminary report, 1975 season. *Nyame Akuma* 9 (1976): 18-34.

993 ———. Diet, nutrition and agricultural origins in the Near East. In Eric Higgs (ed.), *Origine de l'Elevage et de la Domestication.* (Paris, 1976): 227-47.

994 ———. Archaeological explorations of the Siwa Oasis, Egypt. *Current Anthropology* 19, 1 (1978): 146-48.

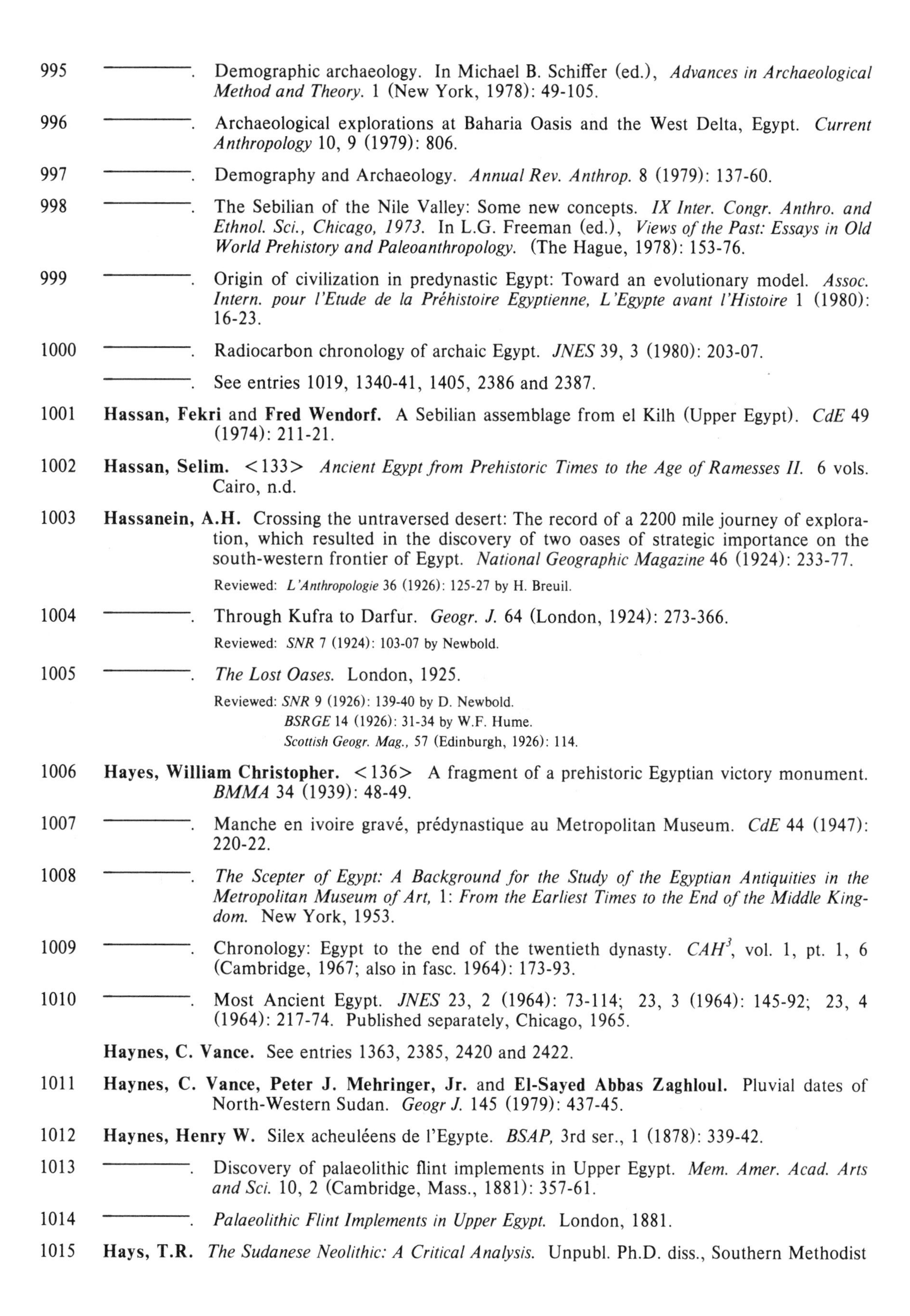

995 ———. Demographic archaeology. In Michael B. Schiffer (ed.), *Advances in Archaeological Method and Theory.* 1 (New York, 1978): 49-105.

996 ———. Archaeological explorations at Baharia Oasis and the West Delta, Egypt. *Current Anthropology* 10, 9 (1979): 806.

997 ———. Demography and Archaeology. *Annual Rev. Anthrop.* 8 (1979): 137-60.

998 ———. The Sebilian of the Nile Valley: Some new concepts. *IX Inter. Congr. Anthro. and Ethnol. Sci., Chicago, 1973.* In L.G. Freeman (ed.), *Views of the Past: Essays in Old World Prehistory and Paleoanthropology.* (The Hague, 1978): 153-76.

999 ———. Origin of civilization in predynastic Egypt: Toward an evolutionary model. *Assoc. Intern. pour l'Etude de la Préhistoire Egyptienne, L'Egypte avant l'Histoire* 1 (1980): 16-23.

1000 ———. Radiocarbon chronology of archaic Egypt. *JNES* 39, 3 (1980): 203-07.

———. See entries 1019, 1340-41, 1405, 2386 and 2387.

1001 **Hassan, Fekri** and **Fred Wendorf.** A Sebilian assemblage from el Kilh (Upper Egypt). *CdE* 49 (1974): 211-21.

1002 **Hassan, Selim.** <133> *Ancient Egypt from Prehistoric Times to the Age of Ramesses II.* 6 vols. Cairo, n.d.

1003 **Hassanein, A.H.** Crossing the untraversed desert: The record of a 2200 mile journey of exploration, which resulted in the discovery of two oases of strategic importance on the south-western frontier of Egypt. *National Geographic Magazine* 46 (1924): 233-77.

Reviewed: *L'Anthropologie* 36 (1926): 125-27 by H. Breuil.

1004 ———. Through Kufra to Darfur. *Geogr. J.* 64 (London, 1924): 273-366.

Reviewed: *SNR* 7 (1924): 103-07 by Newbold.

1005 ———. *The Lost Oases.* London, 1925.

Reviewed: *SNR* 9 (1926): 139-40 by D. Newbold.
BSRGE 14 (1926): 31-34 by W.F. Hume.
Scottish Geogr. Mag., 57 (Edinburgh, 1926): 114.

1006 **Hayes, William Christopher.** <136> A fragment of a prehistoric Egyptian victory monument. *BMMA* 34 (1939): 48-49.

1007 ———. Manche en ivoire gravé, prédynastique au Metropolitan Museum. *CdE* 44 (1947): 220-22.

1008 ———. *The Scepter of Egypt: A Background for the Study of the Egyptian Antiquities in the Metropolitan Museum of Art,* 1: *From the Earliest Times to the End of the Middle Kingdom.* New York, 1953.

1009 ———. Chronology: Egypt to the end of the twentieth dynasty. *CAH*[3], vol. 1, pt. 1, 6 (Cambridge, 1967; also in fasc. 1964): 173-93.

1010 ———. Most Ancient Egypt. *JNES* 23, 2 (1964): 73-114; 23, 3 (1964): 145-92; 23, 4 (1964): 217-74. Published separately, Chicago, 1965.

Haynes, C. Vance. See entries 1363, 2385, 2420 and 2422.

1011 **Haynes, C. Vance, Peter J. Mehringer, Jr.** and **El-Sayed Abbas Zaghloul.** Pluvial dates of North-Western Sudan. *Geogr J.* 145 (1979): 437-45.

1012 **Haynes, Henry W.** Silex acheuléens de l'Egypte. *BSAP,* 3rd ser., 1 (1878): 339-42.

1013 ———. Discovery of palaeolithic flint implements in Upper Egypt. *Mem. Amer. Acad. Arts and Sci.* 10, 2 (Cambridge, Mass., 1881): 357-61.

1014 ———. *Palaeolithic Flint Implements in Upper Egypt.* London, 1881.

1015 **Hays, T.R.** *The Sudanese Neolithic: A Critical Analysis.* Unpubl. Ph.D. diss., Southern Methodist

Univ., Dallas, Texas, 1971.

1016 ————. 'Wavy line' pottery: An element of Nilotic diffusion. *S. Afr. Archaeol. Bull.* 29 (1974): 27-32.

1017 ————. Neolithic settlement of the Sahara as it relates to the Nile Valley. In entry 2388, pp. 193-201.

1018 ————. Predynastic Egypt: Recent field research. *Current Anthropology* 17 (1976): 552-54.

1019 **Hays, T.R.** and **Fekri Hassan.** Mineralogical analysis of Sudanese Neolithic ceramics. *Archaeometry* 16, 1 (1974): 71-79.

1020 **de Heinzelin, J.** Geological history of the Nile Valley in Nubia. In entry 2375, pp. 19-35.

————. See entries 2191 and 2423.

1021 **de Heinzelin, J., P. Haesaerts** and **F. Van Noten.** Géologie récent et préhistoire au Jebel Uweinat. *Africa-Tervuren* 15 (1969): 120-25.

1022 **de Heinzelin, J.** and **R. Paepe.** The geological history of the Nile Valley in Sudanese Nubia: Preliminary remarks. In entry 2371, pp. 29-56.

1023 **Heizer, Robert F.** (ed.). *The Archaeologist at Work.* New York, 1959.

1024 **Helbaek, Hans.** Ancient Egyptian Wheats. *PPS* 21 (1955): 93-95.

1025 ————. *Queen Ichetis' Wheat: A Contribution to the Study of Early Dynastic Emmer of Egypt. Der Kongelige Daushe Videnshabernes Selskab. Biologishe Meddelelser* 21 (Munksgard, 1953).

1026 **Helck, Wolfgang.** Das Horusgeleit. *ArOr.* 18, 3 (1950): 120-43.

1027 ————. *Zur Vorstellung von des Grenze in der ägyptischen Frügeschichte. Vorträge der orientalistischen Tagung in Marburg.* (Hildesheim, 1951).

Reviewed: *Orientalia* 20 (1951): 382 by J. Pohl.

1028 ————. Die Herkunft des abydenischen Osirisrituals. *ArOr* 20, 1-2 (1952): 72-85.

1029 ————. Gab es einen König 'Menes'? *ZDMG* 103 (=n.f. 28) (1953): 354-59.

1030 ————. Herkunft und Deutung einiger Züge der frühagyptischen Königsbilder. *Anthropos* 49 (1954): 961-91.

1031 ————. *Untersuchungen du Manetho und den agyptischen Königslisten. Untersuch.* 19 (Berlin, 1956).

1032 ————. *Die Beziehungen Ägyptens zu Vorderasien im 3. und 2. Jahrtausend v. Chr. Agyptol. Abh.* 23 (Berlin, 1973).

1033 ————. Naqada. *LdÄ* 4 (1975-): 344-46.

1034 ————. Narmer. *LdÄ* 4 (1975-): 348-50.

1035 **Hellström, Pontus.** Incisioni rupestri ad Abka (Sudan). *Bollettino del Centro Comuno di Studi Preistorici* 2 (1966): 103-22.

1036 ————. *The Rock Drawings.* [In Collaboration with H. Longball.] Including: *The Results of the Gordon Memorial College Expedition, Abka. Scandinavian Joint Expedition to Sudanese Nubia* 1. 2 vols. Stockholm, 1970.

Reviewed: *Riv Studi Orienali* 46 (1971): 217-23 by S. Donadoni.
CdE 47 (1972): 163-66 by P. Huard.
JEA 62 (1966): 192-96 by B.J. Kemp.

1037 **Hennelberg, M., J. Piontek** and **J. Strzalko.** [Anthropological analysis of the early Neolithic human mandible from Jebel Nabta (Egypt, Western Desert).] *Przeglad Antropologiczny* 42 (1976): 307-12. [In Polish with English summary]

1038 **Henning, C.L.** Die neuster Forschungen über die Steinzeit und die Zeit der metalle in Ägypten.

Globus 72 (Braunschweig, 1897): 263-69.

1039 **Henry, D.O.** The utilization of the micro-burin technique in the Levant. *Paléorient* 2 (1974, publ. 1976): 389-98.

1040 **Henry, D.O.** and **P. Goldberg.** Ouadi T'mila: un atelier moustérien dans le nord du Sinai. *BSPF* 72 (1975): 223-24.

1041 **Herer, Johann Gottfried von.** *Reflections on the Philosophy of History.* [Abridged and with an introduction by Frank E. Manuel.] Chicago, 1968.

von Herder, J. G. See Supplement entry 2494.

1042 **Hertz, Amelia.** L'Egypte sous les quatre premières dynasties et l'Amérique centrale. Une contribution à la methode de l'histoire de la civilisation. *Revue et Synthèse historique* 35 (Paris, 1923-1924): 37-54; and 37 (1925-1926): 9-38.

1043 ———. Stammen die ägyptischen Gefässe mit Wellenenkeln aus Palästina? *WZKM* 35 (1928): 66-83.

1044 ———. Die Entwicklung der ältesten Kulturen im Agypten und ihre Beziehungen zu Vorderasien. *Rocznik Orientalistz* 9 (1934): 136-64.

Reviewed: *L'Anthropologie* 45 (1935): 418-19 by S.A. Huzayyin.

Hester, James J. See entry 1049.

1045 **Hester, James J.** and **Philip M. Hoebler.** *Prehistoric Settlement Patterns in the Libyan Desert. Univ. of Utah Papers in Anthro.* 92 (=Nubian series, 4). (Salt Lake City, 1969).

1046 **Hester, T.R.** Functional analysis of ancient Egyptian chipped stone tools: The potential for future research. *J. Field Archaeology* 3 (1976): 346-51.

Hey, R.W. See entry 1362.

el-Hinnawi, Mohammed. See entry 1117.

1047 **el-Hitta, Abdel Tawab.** Un nouvel éstablissement neolithic. *RC* 33 (1954): 3-4.

1048 **Heuzy, L.** Egypte ou Chaldée. *CRAIBL,* 4th ser., 27 (1899): 60-67.

Hodges, H. W. M. See entry 2264.

Hoebler, Philip M. See entry 1045.

1049 **Hoebler, Philip M.** and **James J. Hester.** Prehistory and environment in the Libyan Desert. *S. Afr. Archaeol. Bull.* 33 (1969): 120-30.

1050 **Hoffman, Inge.** *Die Kulturen des Nilstals von Aswan bis Sennar, vom Mesolithikum bis zum end der christlicher Epoche. Monographien zur Völkerkunde, hamburgischen Museum für Völkerkunde* 4 (Hamburg, 1967).

1051 ———. Deformierung. *LdÄ* I (1975-): 1004-6.

1052 ———. Hamiten. *LdÄ* II (1975-): 936-37.

1053 **Hoffman, Michael.** *Cultural History and Cultural Ecology at Hierakonpolis from Palaeoltihic Times to the Old Kingdom.* Unpubl. Ph.D. diss., Univ. of Wisconsin, Madison, 1970.

1054 ———. Occupational features at the Kom el Ahmar. *JARCE* 9 (1972): 35-47.

1055 ———. Excavations at locality 14. *JARCE* 9 (1972): 49-74.

1056 ———. The social context of trash disposal in the early dynastic Egyptian town. *American Antiquity* 39 (1974): 35-50.

1057 ———. City of the Hawk — Seat of Egypt's ancient civilization. *Expedition* 18 (1976): 32-41.

1058 ———. *Egypt before the Pharaohs: The Prehistoric Foundations of Egyptian Civilization.* New York, 1979.

Reviewed: *JAOS* (in press) by F. Hassan.
JARCE 17 (1980) by K. Weeks.

1059 ————. A rectangular Amration house from Hierakonpolis and its significance for predynastic research. *JNES* 39, 2 (1980): 119-37.

1060 ————. New excavations at Hierakonpolis: A multi-disciplinary approach to the origins of the Egyptian state. *Anthropology* 4 (1980): 51-70.

1061 ————. Ghosts in the sand. *Arts in Virginia Magazine* 21 (1980): 2-17.

1062 ————. *The Predynastic of Hierakonpolis — An Interim Report. Egyptian Studies Association,* Publ. 1 (Giza and Macomb, Illinois, 1982). [With sections by Barbara Adams, Michael Berger, M. Nabil el-Hadidi, J. Fred Harlan, Hamy A. Hamroush, Carter Lupton, John McArdle, William McHugh, Ralph O. Allen and Marianne S. Rogers.]

1063 **Hölscher, W.** *Libyer und Ägypter: Beitrage zur Ethnologie und Geschichte libyscher Völkerschaftern nach dem altägyptischen Quellen. ÄF* 4 (Glückstadt, 1937).

1064 **Hommel, Fritz.** <143> *Die vorsemitischen Kulturen in Agypten und Babylonien.* Leipzig, 1882.

1065 ————. *Der babylonischen Ursprung der ägyptischen Kultur.* Munich, 1892.

1066 ————. Identität der ältesten babylonischen und ägyptischen Gottergeneaologie und der babylonischen Ursprung der ägypischen Kultur. *Trans. Inter. Congr. Orientalists* (London, 1892): 218-44.

1067 ————. Zum babylonischen Ursprung der ägyptischer Kultur. *Memnon: Zeits. für die Kunst- und Kulturgeschichte der alten Orient* 1 (1907): 80-85.

1068 **Hornblower, George Davis.** <145> An humped bull of ivory. *JEA* 13 (1927): 222-25.

1069 ————. Some predynastic carvings. *JEA* 13 (1927): 240-46.

1070 ————. A spiral design in predynastic Egypt. *Ancient Egypt* (1928): 68-69.

1071 ————. Ancient reaping hooks. *Man* 29 (1929): 95.

1072 ————. Predynastic figures of women and their successors. *JEA* 15 (1929): 29-47.

1073 ————. Funerary designs on prehistoric jars. *JEA* 16 (1930): 10-18.

1074 ————. Prehistoric Egypt and North Africa. *Man* 30 (1930): 48-49.

1075 ————. Reed-floats in modern Egypt. *JEA* 17 (1931): 53-54.

1076 ————. The foundation of ancient Egyptian religion. *Islamic Culture* 6, 4 (Hyderabad, 1932) and 7, 14 (Hyderabad, 1933).

1077 ————. The 'Golden Horus' title. *JEA* 24 (1938): 129.

1078 **Hornell, James.** The palm leaves on boats' prows of Gerzean age. *Man* 45 (1945): 25-27.

1079 **Hornemann, Bodil.** *Types of Ancient Egyptian Sculpture.* 7 vols. Copenhagen, 1951-1959.

1080 **Houtart, Albert.** Les chiens dans l'ancienne Egypte. *CdE* (1934): 28-31.

1081 **Hours, F., L. Copeland** and **O. Aurenche.** Les industries paléolithiques du Proche-Orient: Essai de corrélation. *L'Anthropologie* 77 (1973): 229-80.

1082 **Hrdlička, Ales.** Note sur la variation morphologique des égyptiens depuis les temps préhistoriques ou prédynastiques. *BSAP,* 5th ser., 10 (1909): 143-44.

1083 **Huard, P.** Figurations sahariennes de boeufs porteurs, montés et attelés. *Rivista di Storia dell'Agriculture* 4 (1962): 3-23.

1084 ————. Etat des recherches sur les rapports entre cultures anciennes du Sahara Tchadien, de Nubie et du Soudan. *BiOr* 21 (1964).

1085 ————. Recherches sur les traits culturals des chasseurs anciens des Sahara centre-oriental et du Nil. *RdE* 17 (1965): 21-80.

1086 ————. Contribution saharienne à l'étude des questions intéressant l'Egypte ancienne. *BSFE* 45 (1966): 5-18.

1087 ————. Matériaux archéologiques pour la paléoclimatologie postglaciaire du Sahara oriental et tchadien. *Actes du Congr. Panafricain de Préhist., Dakar, 1967.* (Dakar, 1972): 207-17.

1088 ————. Nouvelles gravures et peintures rupèstres d'Uweinat (Libye orientale). *BSPF* 70 (1972): 197-99.

1089 ————. Datation de squelettes néolithiques, post-néolithiques et préislamiques du Nord-Tibesti. *BSPF* 70 (1973): 100-102.

1090 ————. Onze datations absolues pour la préhistoire et l'écologie ancienne du Nord-Tibesti et de la Libye méridionale. *BSPF* 70 (1973): 69-71.

1091 **Huard, P.** and **L. Allard.** Nouvelles gravures rupèstres d'In Habeter (Fezzan, S.W. Libye). *BSPF* 68 (1971): 618-28.

1092 **Huard, P., G. Bréaud** and **J.M. Massip.** Répertoire de sites paléolithiques du Sahara central, tchadien et oriental. *Bull. de l'Institut Fondamental d'Afrique Nord* 31 (1969): 853-74.

1093 **Huard, P.** and **J. Leclant.** *Problèmes Archéologiques entre le Nil et le Sahara. Etudes Scientifiques.* Cairo, 1972.

1094 ————. Figurations de pièges des chasseurs anciens du Nil et du Sahara. *RdE* 25 (1973): 136-77.

1095 **Hubbard, A.J.** *The Fate of Empires.* London, 1913.

Reviewed: *Ancient Egypt* (1914): 44.

1096 **Hugot, H.-J.** The origins of agriculture: Sahara. *Current Anthropology* 9 (1968): 483-88.

1097 ————. *Le Sahara avant le Désert.* Toulouse, 1977.

1098 ————. The prehistory of the Sahara. In J. Ki-Zerbo (ed.), *General History of Africa* 1: *Methodology and African Prehistory.* (London and Berkeley, 1981): 585-610.

————. See Supplement entry 2495.

1099 **Hummel, Christine.** Falle. *LdÄ* 2 (1975-): 99-101.

Humphreys, S.B. See entry 2389.

1100 **Hunt, E.E.** Anthropometry, genetics and racial history. *Amer. Anthrop.* 61 (1959): 64-87.

1101 **Huntingford, G.W.B.** On the connection between Egypt and the Masai-Nandi group of East Africa. *Ancient Egypt* (1926): 10-11.

1102 ————. The peopling of East Africa by its modern inhabitants. In R. Oliver and G. Mathew, *History of East Africa.* 1 (Oxford, 1963): 58-93.

1103 **Huntington, Ellsworth.** *Civilization and Climate.* New Haven, 1915; 2nd ed. 1922; 3rd ed. 1924.

1104 ————. Climate and the evolution of civilization. In Richard Swain (ed.), *The Evolution of the Earth.* (New Haven, 1918): 147-93.

Hurwitz, S.T.H. See entry 1373.

1105 **Hussein, Kamel.** A description of some bones examined. In entry 1974, pp. 257-58.

1106 **Huzayyin, S.A.** The place of the Sahara-Arabian area in the Palaeolithic culture sequence of the Old World: A synoptic review of recent data. *BIE* 20 (1938): 263-95.

1107 ————. Some new light on the beginnings of Egyptian civilization: A synopsis of culture complexes and contacts of Egypt in late prehistoric and protohistoric times. *BSRGE*

20 (1939): 203-73.

Reviewed: *L'Anthropologie* 51 (1947): 86-88 by R. Vaufrey along with entry 1106.

1108 ———. *The Place of Egypt in Prehistory: A Correlated Study of Climate and Cultures in the Old World. MIE* 43 (Cairo, 1941).

1109 ———. New light on the Upper Palaeolithic of Egypt. *Proc. Pan-Afr. Congr. on Prehistory, 1947.* (Oxford, 1952): 202-4.

1110 ———. Origins of Neolithic and settled life in Egypt. *BSRGE* 23 (1950): 175-81.

1111 ———. Recent studies on the technological evolution of the Upper Palaeolithic of Egypt. *Congr. Intern. des Sci. Prehist. et Protohist., Zurich, 1950* (Zurich, 1953): 174-76.

1112 ———. The flint industry. [Not Seen.]

———. See entries 44, 506 and 858.

I

1113 **Irwin, H., J.B. Wheat** and **L.F. Irwin.** *University of Colorado Investigations of Paleolithic and Epipaleolithic Sites in the Sudan, Africa. Univ. of Utah Papers in Anthrop.* 69 (Salt Lake City, 1968).

Irwin, L.F. See entry 1113.

Isaac, Glynn Ll. See Supplement entry 2496.

Ishige, N. See entry 1445.

1114 **Iskander, Zaki.** African archaeology and its techniques including dating techniques. In Ki-Zerbo, J. (ed.), *General History of Africa,* 1: *Methodology and African Prehistory.* (London and Berkeley, 1981):206-32.

1115 **Issawi, Bahay.** An introduction to the physiography of the Nile Valley. In entry 2407, pp. 3-25.

1116 ———. The geology. In entry 2416, pp. 11-17.

———. See entries 1363, 2401 and 2419.

1117 **Issawi, Bahay** and **Mohammed el-Hinnawi.** Contributions to the geology of the plain west of the Nile between Aswan and Kom Ombo. In entry 2416, pp. 311-30.

J

1118 **Jackson, W.** Résultats anthropologiques des fouilles. In entry 1447.

James, T.G.H. See entry 720.

1119 **Jarry, J.** Etude des graffite rupestres de Sebu'a. *BIFAO* 68 (1969): 53-62.

1120 **Jesi, Furio.** Bés initiateur. Eléments d'institutions préhistoriques dans le culte et le magie de l'ancienne Egypte. *Aegyptus* 38 (1958): 171-83.

1121 ———. *La Ceramica Egizia dalle Origine al Termine dell'età Tinita.* [With a chapter by P. Gilbert. Preface by B. de Rachewiltz.] Turin, 1958.

1122 ———. Elementi africani della civilità di Nagada. *Aegyptus* 37 (1957): 219-25.

1123 **Jéquier, Gustave.** <151> Les temples primitifs et la persistance des types archaiques dans l'architecture religieuse. *BIFAO* 6 (1908): 25-41.

1124 ———. Le sanctuaire primitif d'Amon. *BIFAO* 7 (1910): 87-88.

1125 ———. *Histoire de la Civilisation Egyptienne.* Paris, 1913. [See also entry 1741.]

Reviewed: *Ancient Egypt* (1914): 87-88 by W.M.F. Petrie.

1126 ———. *Manuel d'Archéologie Egyptienne,* 1: *Les Eléments de l'Architecture.* Paris, 1924.

Jones, F.W. See entry 2166.

1127 **Jukes-Browne, Alfred John.** On some flint implements from Egypt. *JRAI* 7 (1878): 396-411.

1128 **Junker, Hermann Josef Bartholomaeus.** <154> *Bericht über die Grabungen de kaiserliche Akademie der Wissenschaften in Wien auf dem Friedhof in Turah, Winter, 1909-1910. DAWW* 56 (Vienna, 1913).

1129 ———. *Bericht über die Grabungen auf den Friedhöfen von el-Kubanieh Süd. DAWW* 63 (1919).

1130 ———. *Bericht über die Grabungen auf den Friedhöfen von el-Kubanieh Nord. DAWW* 63, 3 (1920).

1131 ———. The first appearance of Negroes in history. *JEA* 7 (1921): 121-32.

1132 ———. Bericht über die von der Akademie der Wissenschaften in Wien nach dem Westdelta entsendete Expedition (20. Dezember 1927 bis 25. Februar 1926). *DAWW* 68, 3 (1928): 14-24.

1133 ———. Die Entwicklung der vorgeschichtlichen Kultur in Ägypten. *Festschrift P.W.*

Schmidt (Vienna, 1928): 865-96.

1134 ———. Vorläufiger Bericht über die Grabung der Akademie der Wissenschaften in Wien auf der neolitischen Siedlung von Merimde-Benisalame (Westdelta) vom 1 bis 30 März 1929. *AnzÖAW* 16-18 (1929): 156-250.

1135 ———. Bericht über die vom deutschen Institut für agyptische Altertumskunde nach dem Ost-delta-Rand unternommene Erkundungsfahrt. *MDAIK* 1 (1930): 1-37.

1136 ———. Vorläufiger Bericht über die Grabung der Akademie der Wissenschaften in Wien auf der neolitischen Siedlung von Merimde-Benisalame vom 7. Feb. bis 8. Apr. 1930. *AnzÖAW* 5-13 (1930): 21-83.

1137 ———. Die Grabungen der Akademie der Wissenschaften in Wien auf der vorgeschichtlichen Siedlung Merimde-Benisalame. *MDAIK* 3 (1932): 168-69.

1138 ———. Vorbericht der Dritten von der Akademie der Wissenschaften in Wien in Verbindung mit dem Egyptiska Museet in Stockholm unternommene Grabung auf der neolitischen Siedlung von Merimde-Benisalame. *AnzÖAW* 1-4 (1932): 36-97.

Reviewed: *L'Anthropologie* 43 (1933): 369 by A. Baschmakoff.
Antiquity 7 (1933): 501-2 by G. Brunton.

1139 ———. Vorläufiger Bericht über die von der Akademie der Wissenschaften in Wien in Verbindung mit dem Egyptiska Museet in Stockholm unternommene Grabung auf der neolitischen Siedlung von Merimde-Benisalame, vom 2. Jan. bis 20. Feb. 1933. *AnzÖAW* 16-27 (1933): 54-97.

Reviewed: *L'Anthropologie* 45 (1935): 143-44 by S. Huzayyin.

1140 ———. Vorläufiger Bericht über die von der Akademie der Wissenschaften in Wien in Verbindung mit dem Egyptiska Museet in Stockholm unternommene Grabung auf der neolitischen Siedlung von Merimde-Benisalame. *AnzÖAW* 10 (1934): 118-32.

1141 ———. Vorläufiger Bericht über die von der Akademie der Wissenschaften in Wien in Verbindung mit dem Egyptiska Museet in Stockholm unternommene Grabung auf der neolitischen Siedlung von Merimde-Benisalame. *AnzÖAW* 1-4 (1940): 55-56.

1142 ———. Geisthaltung der Agypter. *AnzÖAW* 1-4 (1940): 55-56.

1143 ———. Die Götterlehre von Memphis. *Abh. Berlin, 1939.* (Berlin, 1940): 23.

1144 ———. Zu der Frage der Rassen und Reiche in der Urzeit Ägyptens. *AnzÖAW* 86 (1950): 845-93.

Reviewed: *Orientalia* 20 (1951): 383 by A. Pohl.

1145 ———. Die Geistehaltung der Ägypter in der Frühzeit. *SAWW* 237, 1 (1961).

———. See entry 1421.

1146 **Junker, Hermann** and **Louis Delaporte.** *Die Völker des antiken Orients,* 1: *Die Ägypter.* Freiburg im Breisgau, 1933.

K

Kaczmarczyk, A. See entry 1671.

1147 **Kaiser, Werner.** *Studien zur Vorgeschichte Ägyptens.* Inaugural-Dissertation Erklarung der Doktorwürde der Philosophischen Fakultät der Ludwig-Maximillians Universität zu München, 1955.

1148 ———. Stand und Problem der ägyptischen Vorgeschichtsforschung. *ZÄS* 81 (1956): 87-109.

1149 ———. Zur inneren Chronologie der Naqadakultur. *Archaeologia Geographica* 6 (1957): 69-77.

1150 ———. Zur vorgeschichtlichen Bedeutung von Hierakonpolis. *MDAIK* 16 (1958): 183-92.

1151 ———. Bericht über eine archäologische-geologische Felduntersuchung in Ober- und Mittelägypten. *MDAIK* 17 (1961): 1-53.

1152 ———. Einige Bemerkungen zur ägyptischen Frühzeit, 1: Zu den *šmsw hr.* *ZÄS* 86 (1959): 119-32; and 85 (1960): 118-37.

1153 ———. Einige Bemerkungen zur ägyptischen Frühzeit, 2: Zur Frage einer über Menes hinausreichenden ägyptischen Geschichtsüberlieferung. *ZÄS* 86 (1961): 39-61.

1154 ———. Einige Bemerkungen zur ägyptischen Frühzeit, 3: Die Reichseinigung. *ZÄS* 91 (1963): 86-125.

1155 ———. El Badari. *LdÄ* 1 (1975-): 599-600.

1156 ———. Maadi. *LdÄ* 3 (1975-): 1110.

1157 ———. Zu den Königsgräber der I. Dynastie in Umm el-Qaab. *MDAIK* 37 (1981): 247-54. (=Festschr. Habachi).

1158 ———. *Studien zur Vorgeschichte Ägyptens,* 1: *Die Naqadakultur.* (In press).

1159 **Kantor, Helene J.** The early relations of Egypt with Asia. *JNES* 1 (1942): 174-213.

1160 ———. The final phase of predynastic culture, Gerzean or Semainean? *JNES* 3 (1944): 110-36.

1161 ———. A predynastic ostrich egg with incised decorations. *JNES* 7 (1948): 46-51.

1162 ———. Further evidence for early Mesopotamian relations with Egypt. *JNES* 11 (1952): 239-50.

1163 ———. The relative chronology of Egypt and its foreign correlations before the Late Bronze Age. In R. Ehrich (ed.), *Relative Chronologies in Old World Archaeology.* (Chicago, 1954): 1-27; and 2nd ed. (1965): 1-46.

1164 ———. Ägypten. In Matcheld J. Mellink and Jan Filip, *Frühe Stufen der Kunst. Propyläen Kunstgeschichte* 13 (Berlin, 1974), I: 227-55 and pls. 188-225.

1165 **Kaplan, Haya Ritter.** The problem of the dynastic position of Meryet-Nit. *JNES* 38, 1 (1979): 23-27.

1166 **Kaplan, J.** The connection of the Palestine Chalcolithic culture with prehistoric Egypt. *IEJ* 9 (1959): 134-36.

1167 **Kaplony, Peter.** Sechs Königsnamen der I. Dynastie in neuer Deutung. *Or. Suecana* 7 (1958): 54-59.

1168 ———. Zwei neue Götterfestung der ägyptischen Frühzeit. *ZDMG* 11 (=n.f. 36) (1961): 379-80.

1169 ———. Gottespalast und Götterfestungen in der ägyptischen Frühzeit. *ZÄS* 88 (1962): 5-16.

1170 ———. *Die Inschriften der ägyptischen Frühzeit.* 3vols. *AÄA* 8 (Wiesbaden, 1963-1964).

1171 ———. *Kleine Beiträge zu den Inschriften der ägyptischen Frühzeit. AÄA* 15 (1966).

1172 ———. *Steingefässe mit Inschriften der Frühzeit und des Alten Reiches. MonAeg.* 1 (1968).

1173 ———. Aha. *LdÄ* 1 (1975-): 94-96.

1174 ———. Djer. *LdÄ* 1 (1975-): 1109-11.

1175 ———. Heluan. *LdÄ* 2 (1975-): 115.

1176 ———. *Die Rollsiegel des Alten Reiches,* 1: *Allgemeine Teil mit Studien zum Königtum der Alten Reichs. MonAeg* 2 (1977).

1177 **Kees, Hermann Alexander Jakob.** <155> *Kulturgeschichte des Alten Orients, Ägypten. Handbuch der Altertumwiss.* Münich, 1923.

1178 ———. *Horus and Seth als Götterpaar. MVAG* 1 (1923) and 1 (1924).
Reviewed: *Ancient Egypt* (1924): 30-31 by L.B. Ellis.

1179 ———. Zum Ursprung der sog. Horusdiener. *NGWG* (1927): 196-207.

1180 ———. Memphis. *Pauly-Wissowa* 29, cols. 660-88 (Stuttgart, 1931).

1181 ———. Kulttopographische und mythologische Beiträge, 1: Die beiden Kinder des Horus im Kult von Hierakonpolis. *ZÄS* 64 (1929): 102-104.

1182 ———. Kulttopographische und mythologische Beiträge, 2: Der nördliche und südliche Horus. *ZÄS* 64 (1929): 102-4.

1183 ———. Kulttopographische und mythologische Beiträge, 3: Der älteste Horus (Hr śmsw̓). *ZÄS* 64 (1929): 104-107.

1184 ———. Kulttopographische und mythologische Beiträge, 4: Ein oberägyptischen Krokodilsgott als 'Horus'. *ZÄS* 64 (1929): 107-12.

1185 ———. *Kultlegende und Urgeschichte. NGWG* (1930).

1186 ———. Kulttopographische und mythologische Beiträge, 5: Hike, der älteste des heiligen Platzes des Urbeginns. *ZÄS* 65 (1930): 83-84.

1187 ———. Kulttopographische und mythologische Beiträge, 6: Anubis, Herr des weissen Landes. *ZÄS* 71 (1935): 150-55.

1188 ———. Die Opfertanzdarstellung auf einem Siegel des Königs Usaphis. *NGWG,* n.f., 3 (1938): 21-30.

1189 ———. *Der Götterglaube im Alten Ägypten.* *MVAG* 45 (Leipzig, 1941); 2nd ed. (Berlin, 1946). [Some chapters are translated in *CdE* 35 (1943): 93-102 by Mlle. M. van Bomberghen.]

Reviewed: *CdE* 35 (1943): 91-93 by J. Capart.
Aegyptus 23.2 (1943): 292-94 by Aristide Calderini.

1190 ———. Kulttopographische und mythologische Beiträge, 7: *'I3kś* und *Hpj,* zwei Königsinsignien als Gottheiten. *ZÄS* 77 (1942): 24-27.

1191 ———. Zur Problematik des archaischen Friedhofs bei Saqqara. *OLZ* 52 (1957): 12-20.

1192 ———. Neues vom archaischen Friedhofs von Saqqara. *OLZ* 54 (1959): 565-70.

1193 ———. *Das alte Ägypten: Eine kleine Landeskunde.* Berlin, 1955. Transl. as *Ancient Egypt: A Cultural Topography* by Ian F.D. Morrow, (London, 1961; repr. Chicago, 1977).

Reviewed: *CdE* 61 (1956): 283-84 by Paul Mertens.

1194 **Keimer, Ludwig.** <156> Bemerkungen zur Schiefertafel von Hierakonpolis. *Aegyptus* 7 (1926): 169-88.

Reviewed: *Ancient Egypt* (1927): 63 by M.A. Murray.

1195 ———. A propos d'une palette protohistorique en schist conservée au Musée du Caire. *BIFAO* 31 (1931): 121-34.

1196 ———. Sur deux vases prédynastiques de Khozâm. *ASAE* 35 (1935): 161-81.

1197 ———. Bemerkungen zu altägyptischen Bogen aus Antilopenhörnen. *ZÄS* 72 (1936): 121-28.

1198 ———. Remarques sur le porc et le sanglier dans l'Egypte ancienne. *BIE* 19 (1937): 147-56.

1199 ———. Sur deux representations égyptiennes de Gerenuk (Lithocranius Walleri). *ASAE* 42 (1942): 161-81.

1200 ———. Remarques sur le Tatouage dans l'Egypte ancienne. *MIE* 53 (Cairo, 1948).

1201 ———. Notes precis chez le Bišarin et les Nubiens d'Assouan. *BIE* 32 (1950): 47-101.

1202 **Keith, Arthur.** Were the ancient Egyptians a dual race? *Man* 6 (1906): 3-5.

1203 **Kelley, A.L.** Cylinder seals in predynastic Egypt. *JSSEA* 4, 2 (1973): 5-8.

1204 ———. Evidence for Mesopotamian influence in predynastic Egypt. *JSSEA* 4, 3 (1974): 2-11.

1205 **Kelly, Harper.** Collections africains du Département de Préhistoire exotique du Musée d'Ethnographie du Trocadéro, Comparaison avec l'Egypte. *J. Soc. des Africanistes* 4 (Paris, 1934): 135-43.

1206 **Kemal el-Din Hussein** [Prince]. L'Exploration du desert de Libye. *La Géographie* 50 (Paris, 1928): 171-84 and 320-36.

1207 **Kemal el-Din Hussein** [Prince] and **Henri Breuil.** Les gravures rupestres du Djebel Ouenat découvertes par le Prince Kemal el-Dine. *Revue Scient. Illust.* 66 (Paris, 1928): 105-17.

1208 **Kemp, Barry J.** Excavations at the Hierakonpolis Fort, 1905: A preliminary note. *JEA* 49 (1963): 24-28.

1209 ———. Abydos and the royal tombs of the First Dynasty. *JEA* 52 (1966): 13-22.

1210 ———. Merimda and the theory of house burial in prehistoric Egypt. *CdE* 43 (1968): 22-33.

1211 ———. Temple and town in Ancient Egypt. In entry 2265, pp. 657-80.

1212 ———. Photographs of the Painted Tomb at Hierakonpolis. *JEA* 59 (1973): 36-43.

1213 ———. Abydos. *LdÄ* 1 (1975-): 28-41.

1214 ———. The early development of towns in Egypt. *Antiquity* 51 (1977): 185-200.

1215 ———. Arkitektur der Frühzeit. In Claude Vandersleyen (ed.), *Das alte Ägypten. Propyläen Kunstgeschichte* 15 (Berlin, 1975): 99-112 and pls. 1-10.

1215a ———. Automatic analysis of predynastic cemeteries: A new method for an old problem. *JEA* 68 (1982): 5-15.

———. See Supplement entry 2514.

Kendall, E.A. See entry 651.

1216 **Kessler, Dieter.** Nekropolen. Frühzeit und AR. *LdÄ* 4 (1975-): 395-414.

1217 **el-Khouli, Ali.** *Egyptian Stone Vessels, Predynastic to Dynasty III: Typology and Analysis.* 3 vols. Mainz, 1978.

King, Leonard W. See Supplement entry 2497.

1218 **King, Leonard** and **H.R. Hall.** *Egypt and Western Asia in the Light of Recent Discoveries.* London, 1907.

1219 **King, W.J. Harding.** *Mysteries of the Libyan Desert: A Record of Three Years of Exploration in the Heart of that Vast and Waterless System.* London, 1925.

———. See entry 139.

1220 **Kink, Kh.** *[Artistic Handicrafts of Most Ancient Egypt and Adjacent Countries.]* Moscow, 1976. [In Russian]

1221 **Ki-Zerbo, J.** African prehistoric art. In J. Ki-Zerbo (ed.), *General History of Africa,* 1: *Methodology and African Prehistory.* (London and Berkeley, 1981): 656-86.

1222 ———. Editorial note: theories on the 'races' and history of Africa. *Ibid.,* pp. 261-70.

1223 **Klasens, A.** Van Neolithicum tot gnosis. Resultaten van tien jaren oudheidkundig bodemonderzoek in Egypt Museum. *Tijdschrift vour Filologie en Geschiedenis* 60 (1955): 129-42.

1224 ———. Een grafsteen uit de eerste dynastie. *OMRO* 37 (1956): 12-33 [With English summary 33-34.]

———. See also entries 720 and 726.

1225 **Kleindienst, Maxine R.** Brief observations on some stone age sites recorded by the Yale University Prehistoric Expedition to Nubia, 1964-1965. *C.r. Congr. intern. Panafricain de Préhistoire, Dakar* (1967): 111-12.

1226 **Knobel, E.B., W.W. Midgley, J.G. Milne, M.A. Murray** and **W.M.F. Petrie.** *Historical Studies,* vol. 2. *ERA* and *BSAE* 19 (London, 1911).

Kobusiewicz, H. See entries 2392 and 2422.

1227 **Kobusiewicz, Michal.** *[Prehistory of North-East Africa between 6 and 5 Millennia B.C.] Przeglad Archeologiczny* 24 (1976). [In Polish]

———. See entries 1987 and 2419.

1228 **Kobusiewicz, Michal** and **K. Morgan Banks.** Report on Site E-78-2. In entry 2416, pp. 55-76.

1229 **Kobusiewicz, Michal** and **William K. Singleton.** Report on Site E-78-9. In entry 2416, pp. 191-216.

1230 **Kozlowski, Janusz K.** (ed.). *Deir el-Bahari (Habitat Préhistorique).* Fasc. 1. *Travaux de la Mission Archéologique de l'Université Jagellonne en Egypte. Prace Archeologiczne* 24 (Krakow, 1976).

1231 ———. Recherches préhistoriques dans le cirque de Deir el-Bahari (Montaigne Thébaine) (Première saison, 1974). *Etudes et Travaux* 9 (1976): 47-66.

1232 ———. *Deir el-Bahari (Habitat Préhistorique).* Fasc. 2. *Travaux de la Mission Archéologique de l'Université Jagellonne en Egypte. Prace Archeologiczne* 25 (1977).

———. See entries 884 and 885.

1233 **Kozlowski, Janusz K.** and **Joachim Sliwa.** [Deir el-Bahari (Results of the Archaeology Mission of the Jaqiellonski University in 1974).] *Sprawozdania Archeologiczne* 28 (Krakow, 1976): 37-51. [In Polish]

1234 **Krader, Lawrence.** *Formation of the State.* [Foundations of Modern Anthropology series, M.D. Sahlins, (ed.).] Englewood Cliffs, N.J., 1968.

1235 **Kraeling, Carl** and **R. McC. Adams** (eds.). *City Invincible: An Oriental Institute Symposium.* Chicago, 1960.

1236 **Krebs, Walter.** Unterägypten und die Reichseingung. *ZÄS* 103 (1976): 76-78.

1237 ———. Die neolitischen Rinderhirten der Sahara und die Masai. *Ägypten und Kusch,* pp. 265-77.

1238 **Kreglinger, Richard.** *Etudes sur l'Origine et le Development de la Vie Religieux,* 1: *Les Primitifs, l'Egypte, l'Inde, et Perse.* Brussels, 1919.

Reviewed: *Ancient Egypt* (1920): 57-60.

1239 **Kroeber, Alfred Louis.** *A Roster of Civilization and Cultures.* Chicago, 1962.

1240 **Kromer, Karl.** Österreichische Felsbilderaufnahme in Sayala, Ägyptisch-Nubien. In E. Anati (ed.), *Symposium International d'Art Préhistorique, Valcomonica, 1968* (Brescia, 1970): 315-28.

1241 ———. Ausgrabungen im Aegypten. *Antike Welt* 4 (1973): 31-34.

1242 ———. Feuerstein. *LdÄ* 2 (1975-): 207-09.

1243 ———. Feuersteingeräte. *LdÄ* 2 (1975-): 209-15.

1244 **Krzyzaniak, Lech.** [The general developmental tendencies of societies living on the Nile in the period preceding plant and animal domestication.] *Fontes Archaeologici Posmamienses* 25 (Paznau, 1974): 196-204. [In Polish]

1245 ———. *Early Farming Cultures on the Lower Nile: The Predynastic Period in Egypt. Prace Zaktadu Archeologii Sród Ziemnomorskiej Polskiej Akademii Nauk* 21 (Warsaw, 1977).

Reviewed: *BiOr* 35 (1978): 73-74 by F. Hassan.

1246 ———. New archaeozoological studies on animal remains from the Neolithic Kadero. *Nyame Akuma* 11 (Calgary, 1977): 56.

1247 ———. New light on early food production in the Central Sudan. *J. African Hist.* 19 (1978): 159-72.

1248 ———. Some problems of current research on predynastic Egypt. *Assoc. Intern. pour l'Etude de la Préhistoire Egyptienne, L'Egypte Avant l'Histoire, Bull.* 1 (1980): 24-34.

1249 ———. Trends in the socio-economic developments of Egyptian predynastic societies. In entry 1898, pp. 402-12.

1250 **Kühn, H.** Die nordafridanischen und ägyptischen Felsbilder der Eiskeit. *Tagungsberichte der deutschen anthropologischen Gesellschaft, im Auftrage der kölner anthropologischen Gesellschaft.* (Leipzig, 1908): 68-79.

L

Labeyrie, J. See entry 649.

1251 **Lacovara, Peter.** Predynastic Egypt. *Bull. Field Museum of Natural History* 52 (1981): 7-12.

———. See Supplement entry 2498.

1252 **de Lacouperie, T.** The races of men in the Egyptian documents. *Babyl. and Orient. Record* 2 (1888): 133.

1253 **Lajard.** Deux stations de silex taillés dans le désert oriental. *BIE,* 3rd ser. (1894): 155-65.

1254 **Lajard** and **F. Regnault.** Stèles d'Egypte. *C.r. Assoc. Franç. pour l'Avancement des Sciences, 23e Session, Caen, 1894.* 1 (Paris, 1894): 190-91.

1255 **Landstrom, Bjorn.** *Ships of the Pharaohs: 4000 Years of Egyptian Shipbuilding.* London, 1970.

Lane, Mary Ellen. See entry 2426.

1256 **Langdon, S.** Early chronology of Sumer and Egypt. *Nature* 107 (1921): 315.

1257 ———. The early chronology of Sumer and Egypt and the similarities in their culture. *JEA* 7 (1921): 133-53.

1258 **Lange, Kurt** <163> and **Max Hirmer.** *Egypt. Architecture, Sculpture, Painting in Three Thousand Years.* Transl. by R.H. Boothroyd. 3rd ed. revised (London, 1961). Originally publ. in German (Munich, 1955); 2nd ed. (1956); French transl. (Paris, 1956).

Reviewed: *CdE* 63 (1957): 47-48 by A. Mekhitarian.
BiOr 13 (1956): 209-10 by Walter Wolf.
Erasmus 10 (1957): 747-51 by J. Leibovitch.
OLZ 53 (1958): 329-31 by Günther Roeder.
Universitas 2 (1956): 979-80 by H. Brunner.

1259 **Lansing, Ambrose.** <163> The Egyptian expedition: The Museum's excavations at Hierakonpolis. *BMMA* 30 (1935): 37-45.

1260 **Larrey,** [Baron] **Dominique Jean.** <164> Notice sur la conformation physique des égyptiens et des différentes races qui habitent l'Egypte, suivi de quelques réflexions sur l'embaumement des momies. *Descr. de l'Egypte* 18, 1 (1829): 59-70.

1261 **Larsen, Hjalmar.** Vorbericht über die schweidischen Grabungen in Abu Ghalib 1932-1934. *MDAIK* 6 (1935): 41-82.

1262 ———. A Second Dynasty grave at Wardan, Northern Egypt. *Or. Suecana* 5 (1957): 3-11.

1263 ———. On a detail of the Naqada plant. *ASAE* 54 (1957): 239-44.

1264 ———. Eine eigenartige Tongefass-Scherbe aus Merimde. *Or. Suecana* 6 (1958): 3-8.

1265 ———. Verzierte Tongefass-scherbe aus Merimde Benisalame in der ägyptischen Abteilung des Mittelmeermuseums in Stockholm. *Or. Suecana* 7 (1959): 3-53.

1266 ———. Knochengerate aus Merimde in der ägyptischen Abteilung der Mittelmeer-museums. *Or. Suecana* 9 (1960): 28-53.

1267 ———. Die Merimdekeramik im Mittelmeermuseums Stockholm. *Or. Suecana* 11 (1962): 3-88.

1268 **Lauer, Jean-Philippe.** Sur le dualisme de la monarchie égyptienne et son expression architectural sous les premières dynasties. *BIFAO* 55 (1955): 153-71.

1269 ———. Sur le 'fruit' des murs exterieurs dans les monuments de l'époque thinite et de l'Ancien Empire. *BIFAO* 59 (1960): 49-58.

1270 ———. Quelques remarques sur la Ire dynastie. *BIFAO* 64 (1966): 169-84.

1271 ———. *Saqqara: The Royal Cemetery of Memphis.* London, 1976.

1272 ———. La dévelopement des complexes funéraires royaux en Egypt depuis les temps prédynastiques jusqu'à la fin de l'ancien Empire. *BIFAO* 79 (1979): 355-94.

1273 ———. La signification et le rôle des fausses-portes de palais dans les tombeaux du type de Négadeh. *MDAIK* 37 (1981): 281-88.

Laurent-Täckholm, V. See Täckholm, V.L.

1274 **Lauth, Frans Joseph.** <164> *Aus Ägyptens Vorzeit: Eine übersichtliche Darstellung der ägyptischen Geschichte und Kultur, von den ersten Anfängen bis auf Augustus.* Berlin, 1851.

1275 ———. Age du fer en Egypte. *Les Mondes,* 2nd ser., 17 (Paris, 1868): 409.

1276 ———. Das Steinzeitalter in Ägypten. *Deutschen Gesellschaft für Anthropologie, Ethnologie und Urgeschichte. Korrespondenzblatt.* 3 (München, 1873): 36-38.

1277 **Lawson, A.C.** *The Valley of the Nile.* Berkeley, 1927.

Laycock, M.A. See entry 1860.

1278 **Leakey, Louis Seymour Bazett.** *Stone Age Africa: An Outline of Prehistory in Africa.* Oxford, 1936.

1279 **Leclant, Jean.** Afrika. *LdÄ* 1 (1975-): 84-94.

1280 ———. (ed), *Ägypten,* 1: *Das Alte und das Mittllere Reich. Von der Vorgeschichte bis zum Ende der Hyksoszeit (1560 v. Chr.). Universum der Kunst* 26 (Munich, 1979).

1281 ———. *Egypte pharaonique et Afrique. Séance Publique Annuelle des Cinq Académies.* Paris, 1980.

———. See entry 1093.

1282 **Leclerq, Elsa.** Les collections préhistoriques de Stambruges aux Musées Royaux d'Art et d'Histoire. *Bull. Musées R. d'Art et d'Hist.,* 3rd ser., 4 (Brussels, 1932): 13-16.

1283 ———. L'art préhistorique de l'Afrique du Nord: Quelques découvertes récentes. *CdE* 11 (1928): 324-28.

1284 ———. Dans le Delta, avant la 1re dynastie. *CdE* 16 (1933): 227-33.

1285 ———. Note de préhistoire africaine. *CdE* 17 (1934): 25-27. [See also entry 1334.]

1286 ———. Merimde-Benisalame, Méadi. *CdE* 19 (1935): 34-37.

———. See **Mounier-Leclerq** entries 1517-18.

1287 **Leclerq, Joannes.** *Atlas Antiquus, Sacer, Ecclesiasticus et Profanus, Collectus ex Tabulis*

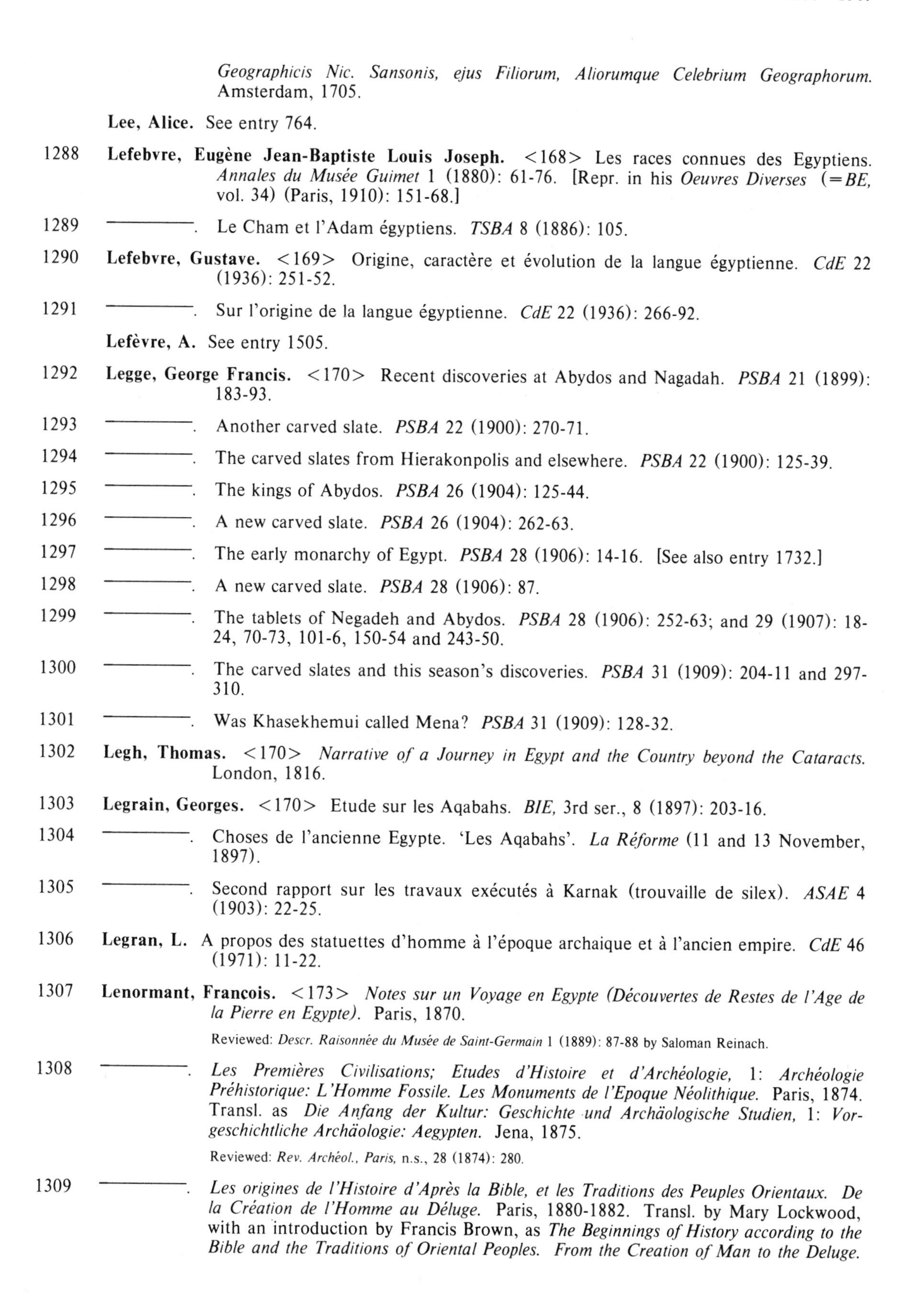

Geographicis Nic. Sansonis, ejus Filiorum, Aliorumque Celebrium Geographorum. Amsterdam, 1705.

Lee, Alice. See entry 764.

1288 **Lefebvre, Eugène Jean-Baptiste Louis Joseph.** <168> Les races connues des Egyptiens. *Annales du Musée Guimet* 1 (1880): 61-76. [Repr. in his *Oeuvres Diverses* (=*BE*, vol. 34) (Paris, 1910): 151-68.]

1289 ———. Le Cham et l'Adam égyptiens. *TSBA* 8 (1886): 105.

1290 **Lefebvre, Gustave.** <169> Origine, caractère et évolution de la langue égyptienne. *CdE* 22 (1936): 251-52.

1291 ———. Sur l'origine de la langue égyptienne. *CdE* 22 (1936): 266-92.

Lefèvre, A. See entry 1505.

1292 **Legge, George Francis.** <170> Recent discoveries at Abydos and Nagadah. *PSBA* 21 (1899): 183-93.

1293 ———. Another carved slate. *PSBA* 22 (1900): 270-71.

1294 ———. The carved slates from Hierakonpolis and elsewhere. *PSBA* 22 (1900): 125-39.

1295 ———. The kings of Abydos. *PSBA* 26 (1904): 125-44.

1296 ———. A new carved slate. *PSBA* 26 (1904): 262-63.

1297 ———. The early monarchy of Egypt. *PSBA* 28 (1906): 14-16. [See also entry 1732.]

1298 ———. A new carved slate. *PSBA* 28 (1906): 87.

1299 ———. The tablets of Negadeh and Abydos. *PSBA* 28 (1906): 252-63; and 29 (1907): 18-24, 70-73, 101-6, 150-54 and 243-50.

1300 ———. The carved slates and this season's discoveries. *PSBA* 31 (1909): 204-11 and 297-310.

1301 ———. Was Khasekhemui called Mena? *PSBA* 31 (1909): 128-32.

1302 **Legh, Thomas.** <170> *Narrative of a Journey in Egypt and the Country beyond the Cataracts.* London, 1816.

1303 **Legrain, Georges.** <170> Etude sur les Aqabahs. *BIE,* 3rd ser., 8 (1897): 203-16.

1304 ———. Choses de l'ancienne Egypte. 'Les Aqabahs'. *La Réforme* (11 and 13 November, 1897).

1305 ———. Second rapport sur les travaux exécutés à Karnak (trouvaille de silex). *ASAE* 4 (1903): 22-25.

1306 **Legran, L.** A propos des statuettes d'homme à l'époque archaique et à l'ancien empire. *CdE* 46 (1971): 11-22.

1307 **Lenormant, François.** <173> *Notes sur un Voyage en Egypte (Découvertes de Restes de l'Age de la Pierre en Egypte).* Paris, 1870.

Reviewed: *Descr. Raisonnée du Musée de Saint-Germain* 1 (1889): 87-88 by Saloman Reinach.

1308 ———. *Les Premières Civilisations; Etudes d'Histoire et d'Archéologie,* 1: *Archéologie Préhistorique: L'Homme Fossile. Les Monuments de l'Epoque Néolithique.* Paris, 1874. Transl. as *Die Anfang der Kultur: Geschichte und Archäologische Studien,* 1: *Vorgeschichtliche Archäologie: Aegypten.* Jena, 1875.

Reviewed: *Rev. Archéol., Paris,* n.s., 28 (1874): 280.

1309 ———. *Les origines de l'Histoire d'Après la Bible, et les Traditions des Peuples Orientaux. De la Création de l'Homme au Déluge.* Paris, 1880-1882. Transl. by Mary Lockwood, with an introduction by Francis Brown, as *The Beginnings of History according to the Bible and the Traditions of Oriental Peoples. From the Creation of Man to the Deluge.*

London, 1883., and New York, 1882, (Repr., 1883, 1886, 1891, 1893, 1899).

———. See entries 81 and 976-78.

1310 **Leonard, J.** Expédition scientifique belge dans le désert de Libye: Gebel Uweinat 1968-1969. *Africa-Tervuren* 15 (1969): 103-36.

1311 **Lepsius, Karl Richard.** <173> Ueber die Annahme einer sogenannten prähistorischen Steinalter in Aegypten. *ZÄS* 8 (1870): 89-97 and 113-21.

1312 **Letronne, Jean Antoine.** <176> Examen des passages relatifs à la population de l'ancienne Thèbes d'Egypte. *Nouvelles Annales des Voyages* 22 (1824).

1313 **Lhote, H.** *Le Peuplement de l'Afrique du Nord et du Sahara. Ethnologie Régionale,* 1: *Afrique-Océanie.* Paris, 1972.

1314 ———. Perioden der saharischen Vorgeschischte. In H. Schiffers, *Die Sahara und ihre Randgebiete. Darstellung eines Naturgrossraumes* 2 (Munich, 1972): 264-303.

1315 **Lieblein, Jens Daniel Carolus.** <178> Om Ziguenerne. In his *Aegyptologiska Studie.* (Christiania, 1870).

1316 **Lima, H. Pinto.** *A Ceramica Predinastica. Trabalhos da Sociedade Portuguesa de Antropologia e Etnologia* 6, 1 (1933).

1317 **de Lisle, Courtet.** Etudes sur les anciennes races de l'Egypte et de l'Ethiopie. *Annales des Voyages* 1 (1874): 326; and 2: 299.

1318 **Little, O.H.** Recent geological work in the Fayum and in the adjoining portion of the Nile Valley. *BIE* 18 (1936): 201-40.

1319 **Little, O.H., E.W. Gardner, K.S. Sandford** and **John Ball.** Further remarks on the Kharga Oasis. *Geogr. J.* 81 (1933): 526-32.

1320 **Lloyd, Alan B.** *Herodotus, Book II: Introduction.* In M.J. Vermaseren (ed.), *Etudes Preliminaries aux Religions Orientales dans l'Empire Romain* 43 (Leiden, 1975).

———. See Supplement entry 2514.

Loat, William Leward Stevenson. <181> See entries 121 and 1685.

1321 **Lockyer, Joseph Norman.** *The Dawn of Astronomy: A Study of the Temple-worship and Mythology of the Ancient Egyptians.* London, 1894.

1322 **Loret, Victor.** <183> Les enseignes militaires des tribus et les symboles hiéroglyphiques de divinités. *Rev. Eg.* 10 (1902): 94-101.

1323 ———. Horus le faucon. *BIFAO* 3 (1903): 1-24.

1324 ———. Quelques idées sur la forme primitive de certaines religions égyptiennes: à propos de l'identification de l'hiéroglyphe servant à écrire le mot dieu. *Rev. Eg.* 11 (1904): 69-100.

1325 ———. L'Egypte au temps du totémisme. Conférences du Musée Guimet. *BVMG* 19 (1906): 121-51.

1326 ———. Silex taillés dans les montagnes de Thèbes. *CrASP 35e session, Lyon, 1906* (Paris, 1906): 576-86.

1327 ———. A propos de la nécropole préhistorique de Khozam, en Haute Egypte. *BSAL* 27 (1908).

1328 ———. Station paléolithique désertique de Gebel-Souhan (Haute Egypte). *BSAL* 27 (1908): 87-92.

1329 ———. *La Vérité (Polémique).* Paris, 1908.

1330 **Lortet, Louis Charles.** <184> Crâne syphilitique et nécropoles préhistoriques de la Haute-Egypte. *BSAL* 27 (1907): 211-26. [See also entry 840.]

Reviewed: *L'Anthropologie* 19 (1908): 322-23 by Rivet.

1331 ————. *Résponse de M. le Docteur Lortet à M. Chantre sur l'Antiquité du Crâne Syphilitique Trouvé dans la Nécropole Préhistoirique de Roda (Haute Egypte).* Lyon, 1908.

1332 **Lortet, Louis Charles** and **Claude Gaillard.** *La Faune Momifée de l'Ancienne Egypte. Archives du Muséum d'Histoire Naturelle de Lyon,* vol. 8. (Lyon, 1907).

Reviewed: *L'Homme Préhistoirique* 6 (1908): 26-30 and 8 (1910): 56-58 by Edmond Hue.

1333 **[Louvre.]** *L'Egypte avant les Pyramides; 4e Millénaire.* [An exhibit at Le Grand Palais, 29 May-3 Sept. 1973.] Paris, 1973.

1334 **Lowe, C. van Reit.** Did the ancient Egyptians visit South Africa? *ILN* (29 April 1933). [See also entry 1285.]

1335 **Lubbock, John** [Baron] **Avebury.** Note on the discovery of stone implements in Egypt. *BIE,* 1st ser., 13 (1874): 57-58.

1336 ————. Note on the discovery of stone implements in Egypt. *JRAI* 4 (1874): 215-22.

1337 ————. Stone implements in Egypt. *Nature* 10 (1874): 138.

1338 ————. *The Origin of Civilization.* London, 1868; 2nd ed. 1870 (repr. 1871); 3rd ed. 1875; 4th ed. 1882 (repr. 1886); 5th ed. 1889 (repr. 1892, 1895, 1898); 6th ed. 1902. (New York, 1911); 7th ed. 1912. 2nd ed. trans. into French by Edward Barbier (Paris, 1873); 3rd ed. 1877 (repr. 1881). 4th ed. transl. into Spanish by Johé de Casa (Buenos Aires, 1943).

1339 **Lubell, David.** *The Fakhurian: A Late Palaeolithic Industry from Upper Egypt and its Place in Nilotic Prehistory.* Ph.D. diss., Columbia Univ., New York, 1971. *Geol. Survey of Egypt* Paper 58 (1974).

1340 **Lubell, D., J.L. Ballais, A. Gautier, F.A. Hassan, A.E. Close, C. Chippindale, J. Elmendorf** and **G. Aumassip.** The prehistoric cultural ecology of Capsian escargotières. *Libyca* 23 (1975): 43-121.

1341 **Lubell, David, Fekri A. Hassan, Achilles Gautier,** and **Jean-Louis Ballais.** The Capsian escargotières. *Science* 191 (1976): 910-20.

1342 **Lucas, Alfred.** <185> *Ancient Egyptian Materials and Industries.* London, 1924; 2nd ed. 1932; 3rd ed. 1948; 4th ed. revised and enlarged by J.R. Harris, 1962. Arabic transl. by Zaki Iskander and M. Zakariah Goneim, (Cairo).

1343 ————. Egyptian predynastic stone vessels. *JEA* 16 (1920): 200-12.

1344 ————. Black and black-topped pottery. *ASAE* 32 (1932): 93-96.

1345 **Lucas, J. Olumide.** *The Religion of the Yorubas.* Lagos, 1948. [Repr. in entry 575, pp. 29-35.]

1346 **Lugn, Pehr.** <186> *Svenska Gravninger i Egyptan Vintern 1931-1932, en Preliminar Redorgorelse. Arkeologiska Studier Tillagnade H.K.H. Kronprins Gustav Adolf.* Stockholm, 1932.

1347 **Lukas, J.** Bericht über die neolitische Station von Maadi bie Kairo. *Mitt. anthrop. Gessel. Wien* 56 (1931): 203-8.

1348 **Luppaciolu, M.** Considerazioni sul problema delle origini dell'economia pastorale nel Sahara. *Quaternia* 18 (1974): 439-72.

1349 **Lupton, C.** The other Egypt: In search of the lost pharaohs. *Lore* 31 (1981): 2-21.

————. See also entry 1062.

1350 **Luschan, Felix von.** Zur anthropologischen Stellung der alten Ägypter. *Globus Braunschweiger* 79 (1901): 197-200.

1351 ————. Ueber eine Beobachtung am Kieselmanufakten in Aegypten. *Zeitschrift für Ethnologie* 36 (Berlin, 1904): 317-21.

1352 ————. Über Petroglyphen bei Asswan und Demir-Kapu. *Zeitschrift für Ethnologie* 54 (1922): 177-92.

1353 **Lyons, Henry George.** <187> Introduction. In G.A. Reisner, *ASN Rep 1907-8,* 1 (1910): iii-iv.

1354 **Lythgoe, Albert Morton.** <187> The Egyptian expedition of the University of California: An early predynastic cemetery at Nag-ed-Dêr. *AJA* 9 (1905): 709.

1355 ————. The Predynastic Cemetery N7000. Naga-ed-Dêr IV. *UCPEA* 7 (Berkeley and Los Angeles, 1965). [Edited by Dows Dunham.]

M

McArdle, J. See entry 1062.

1356 **McBurney, Charles Brian Montague.** *The Stone Age of Northern Africa.* Hammondsworth, 1960.

1357 ————. *The Haua Fteah (Cyrenaica) and the Stone Age of the Southeast Mediterranean.* Cambridge, 1967.

1358 ————. Libyan role in prehistory. *LH 1968* (1970): 1-27.

1359 ————. Libya before the Greeks. *ARSLS* 2 (1970-1971): 19-25.

1360 ————. The archaeological context of the Hamitic languages in northern Africa. In J. and T. Bynon, (eds.), *Hamito-Semitica* (= *Janua linguarum,* ser. practica., 200), (The Hague, 1975): 495-506.

1361 ————. Current status of the Lower and Middle Paleolithic of the entire region from the Levant through North Africa. In entry 2388, pp. 411-23.

1362 **McBurney, Charles Brian Montagu** and **R.W. Hey.** *Prehistory and Pleistocene Geology in Cyrenaican Libya.* Cambridge, 1955.

1363 **McCauley, J.F., G.G. Schaber, C.S. Breed, M.J. Grolier, C.V. Haynes, B. Issawi, C. Elachi** and **R. Blom.** Subsurface valleys and geoarchaeology of the eastern Sahara revealed by shuttle radar. *Science* 218 (3 December 1982): 1004-19.

1364 **Mace, Arthur Cruttenden.** <189> *The Early Dynastic Cemeteries of Nag-ed-Dêr,* II. *UCPEA* 3 (Leipzig, 1909).

————. See entry 1861.

1365 **MacGaffey, Wyatt.** Concepts of race in the historiography of northeast Africa. *J. African History* 7 (1966): 1-17. [Reprinted in J.D. Fage and R.A. Oliver (eds.), *Papers in African Prehistory* (Cambridge, 1970): 99-116.]

1366 **McHugh, William P.** *Late Prehistoric Cultural Adaptation in the Southwestern Libyan Desert.* Unpubl. Ph.D. diss., Univ. of Wisconsin, Madison, 1971.

1367 ————. Cattle pastoralism in Africa. A model for interpreting archaeological evidence from the Eastern Sahara Desert. *Arctic Anthropology* 11 (1974): 236-44.

1368 ————. Late prehistoric cultural adaptation in southwest Egypt and the problem of the Nilotic origins of Saharan cattle pastoralism. *JARCE* 11 (1974): 2-29.

1369 ————. Some archaeological results of the Bagnold-Mond expedition to the Gilf Kebir and

Gebel Uweinat, southern Libyan Desert. *JNES* 34 (1975): 31-62.

———. See entry 1062.

Macintosh, N. M. G. See entry 705.

MacKay, Ernest John Henry. <190> See entry 1797.

1370 **MacKenzie, Donald A.** *Egyptian Myth and Legend: With Historical Narrative Notes on Race Problems, Comparative Beliefs, etc.* London, 1913.

1371 **MacLaurin, E.C.B.** Cultural diffusion in the Middle East during the Second Millennium B.C. In entry 705, pp. 175-96.

1372 **Macramallah, R.** *Un Cimetière Archaique de la Classe Moyenne du Peuple à Saqqara.* Cairo, 1940.

1373 **MacRitchie, D.** and **S.T.H. Hurwitz.** Les pygmées chez les anciens Egyptiens. *C.r. XIVe session du Congrès Inter. d'Anthrop., Genève 1912* (1912): 6.

Malay, Jean. See entry 520.

Málek, J. See entry 145.

1374 **Mallet, A.M.** *Description de l'Univers Contenant les Differents Systèmes du Monde.* 5 vols. Paris, 1683. [Esp. relevant are vol. 3, pls. 21 and 22, pp. 55 and 59.]

1375 **Manetho.** *The Aegyptiaca.* [An English translation by W.G. Waddell.] London and Cambridge, 1940.

1376 **Manouvrier, L.** and **L. Capitan.** Etude anthropologique et archéologique (d'après le récent livre de M. Chantre). *Rev. de l'Ecole d'Anthrop. de Paris* 15 (1905): 18-30.

1377 **Marchand, H.** and **A. Aymé.** Recherches stratigraphiques sur l'Atérian. *Bull. de la Soc. hist. naturelle d'Afrique du Nord* 26 (1935): 333-343.

1378 **de Marchesetti, Carlo.** La preistoria in Egitto. *Boll. della Soc. Adriatica di Sc. nat. in Trieste* 26 (1912): 89-120.

1379 **Mariette, François Auguste Ferdinand.** <194> De l'âge de pierre en Egypte. *RecTrav* 7 (1886): 132-40.

1380 ———. Communication de M. Mariette sur les fouilles qui s'exécutent en Egypte. *BIE,* 1st ser., (1870): 51-75.

1381 ———. Observations sur les antiquités, les silex taillés dans le désert Libyque et le Bahr Belà Mâ. *BIE,* 1st ser., (1873): 173-75.

1382 **Marks, Anthony J.** The Halfan industry. In entry 2375, pp. 393-460.

1383 ———. The Khormusan: An Upper Pleistocene industry in Sudanese Nubia. *Ibid.,* pp. 315-91.

1384 ———. The Mousterian industries of Nubia. *Ibid.,* pp. 193-314.

1385 ———. The Sebilian industry in the Second Cataract. *Ibid.,* pp. 461-531.

1386 ———. Survey and excavations in the Dongola Reach. *Current Anthropology* 9 (1968): 319-323.

1387 ———. The current status of Upper Paleolithic studies from the Maghreb to the Northern Levant. *Ibid.,* pp. 439-58.

———. See entries 2191, 2388 and 2423.

1388 **Marks, Anthony J., J.L. Shiner, F. Servello** and **F. Munday.** *Preceramic Sites. Scandinavian Joint Expedition to Sudanese Nubia* 2 (Helsinki, 1970).

1389 **Marples, E.A.** Ancient reaping hooks. *Man* 29 (1929): 54.

1390 **Marro, G.** L'Esplorazione della necropoli di Gebelan. Dai lavori della Missione Archeologica Italiana in Egitto. *Atti della Soc. Ital. per il Progresso delle Sc., Torino, 15-22*

Settembre 1928 (Rome, 1929): 592-636.

1391 ———. Scavi italiani in Egitto e loro scopo antropologico. *XVe Congr. Intern. d'Anthrop. et d'Archéol. Préhist., IVe Session de l'Institut International d'Anthropologie, Portugal, 21-30 Settembre 1930* (Paris, 1931).

1392 ———. Contributo alla paletnologia egiziana (dai lavori della Missione Archeologia Italiana in Egitto). *Atti della Soc. Ital. per il Progresso delle Sc., Milano, 12-18 Settembre 1931,* 2 (Milan, 1932): 452-55.

1393 **Martini, T.E.** Sull'origini del bronzo e sullo scettro di Pepi I, Re d'Egitto. *Bull. Sez. Fior. Soc. Afr. Ital.* 4 (Firenze, 1890): 279-80.

Mason, I.L. See entry 737.

1394 **Maspero, Gaston Camille Charles.** <197> Sur les dynasties divines de l'ancienne Egypte. *TSBA* 12 (1890): 419-32.

1395 ———. Chabas et les études sur l'antiquité historique d'après les sources égyptiennes et les monuments réputés préhistoriques. In his *Etudes de Mythologie et d'Archéologie Egyptiennes* (Paris, 1893-98): 917-1005. [See also entry 519.]

1396 ———. Notes sur différentes points de grammaire et d'histoire. *RecTrav* 17 (1895): 56-78.

1397 ———. *Histoire Ancienne des Peuples de l'Orient Classique. Les Origines: Egypte et Chaldée.* Paris, 1895. Transl. as *The Dawn of Civilization: Egypt and Chaldea* by M.L. McLure. New York, 1894; 2nd. ed. 1896; 3rd. ed. 1897.

1398 ———. Les fouilles de Kom el-Ahmar. In his *Etudes de Mythologie et d'Archéologie Egyptiennes. Bibl. Egyptol.* 40, 8 (Paris, 1916): 143-53.

1399 **Massey, Gerald.** *The Nature of Genesis; or, A Book of the Beginnings. Containing an Attempt to Recover and Reconstitute the Lost Origins of the Myths and Mysteries, Types and Symbols, Religion and Language, with Egypt for the Mouthpiece and Africa as the Birthplace.* 2 vols. London, 1881-83.

Reviewed: *J. of Sci.* (1883): 414-18 and 681f.
Athenaeum (1883): 864.
Notes and Queries (1884): 19.
Westminster Review (1884): 241.

Massip, J.M. See entry 1092.

1400 **Massoulard, Emile.** Lances fourchues et Peseshkhaf. A propos de deux acquistitions récentes du Musée du Louvre. *Rev. d'Egyptol.* 2 (1936): 135-63.

1401 ———. *Préhistoire et Protohistoire de l'Egypte. Travaux et Mémoires de l'Institut d'Ethnologie, Université de Paris* 53 (Paris, 1949).

1402 **Mauny, Raymond.** L'Afrique et les origines de la domestication. In W.W. Bishop and J.D. Clark (eds.), *Background to Evolution in Africa.* (Chicago, 1966): 583-99.

1403 **Mauny, Raymond** and **L. Balou.** Bibliographie préhistorique, Maghreb-Sahara-Soudan, ânnées 1953, 1954-1955. *Libyca* 2 (1954): 165-89; and 3 (1955): 185-217.

1404 **Mayassis, S.** *Mystères et initiations dans la préhistoire et protohistoire. De l'anté-diluvian à Sumer-Babylone. La Familiarité divine originelle. Bibliothèque d'Archéologie Orientale d'Athènes* 3 (Athens, 1961).

Meeks, N. See entry 165.

Mehringer, Peter J. See entry 1011.

1405 **Mehringer, Peter J., Kenneth L. Petersen,** and **Fekri A. Hassan.** A pollen record from Birket Qarun and the recent history of the Fayum, Egypt. *Quaternary Research* 11 (1979): 238-56.

Mellaart, J. See Supplement entry 2499.

1406 **Menghin, Oswald.** Die Grabung der Universität Kairo bei Maadi. *MDAIK* 2 (1932): 143-47.

1407 ———. Die Grabung der Universität Kairo bei Maadi: (Zweitesgrabungsjahr) *MDAIK* 3 (1932): 150-54.

1408 ———. Die Grabung der Universität Kairo bei Maadi: (Drittesgrabungsjahr). *MDAIK* 5 (1934): 111-18.

1409 ———. The excavations of the Egyptian University at Maadi (Egyptian University, Faculty of Arts). *Ancient Egypt* (1932): 108-9.

1410 ———. Paläolitische Funde in der Umgebung von Benisalame. *AnzAWW* 69 (1932): 889-97.

1411 ———. Die Primitivtypen des Neolithikums von Merimde-Benisalame. *Ibid.*, pp. 83-88.

1412 ———. The stone ages of North Africa with special reference to Egypt. *BSRGE* 18 (1932): 9-27.

1413 ———. Merimde-Benisalame und Maadi. *AnzAWW* 16 (1933): 82-97.

1414 ———. Die neolitisch Ansiedlung von Merimde-Benisalame und ihre Entwicklung des Neolithikums in Westeurope. *Proc. 1st Inter. Cong. Prehist. and Protohist. Sc.* (London, 1934): 177-80.

1415 ———. El origin del pueblo del antiguo Egipto. *Ampurias* 4 (1942): 25-41.

1416 ———. Zur Chronologie des Neolithikums in Ägypten. *Acta Praehistorica* 5-7 (Buenos Aires, 1961-1963): 128-47.

Reviewed: *L'Anthropologie* 72 (1968): 130-31 by Chr. Prost.

1417 **Menghin, Oswald** and **Mustafa Amer.** *The Excavations of the Egyptian University in the Neolithic Site at Maadi. First Preliminary Report (Season 1930-1931). Egy. Univ. Fac. of Arts., Publ. 19* (Cairo, 1932).

Reviewed: *Ancient Egypt* (1932): 79.
L'Anthropologie 43 (1933): 370-71 by R. Vaufrey.
JEA 19 (1933): 195-96 by G. Brunton.
LAAA 20 (1933): 202-4 by O.H. Meyers.

1418 ———. Stone age finds from the Kharga Oasis. *MDAIK* 3 (1932): 46-49.

1419 ———. *The Excavations of the Egyptian University in the Prehistoric Site at Maadi. Second Preliminary Report (Season 1932). Egy. Univ. Fac. of Arts., Publ. 20.* (Cairo, 1936).

Reviewed: *JEA* 24 (1938): 140-41 by G. Brunton.

1420 **Menghin, Oswald** and **Kurt Bittel.** Kasr el-Sagha. *MDAIK* 5 (1934): 1-10.

1421 **Menghin, Oswald** and **Hermann Junker.** Wissenschaftliche Unternehmungen in Aegypten und Nubien 1930/31. *MDAIK* 2 (1932): 141-49.

1422 **Mercer, Samuel A.B.** A study in Egyptian religious origins. *JASOR* 12 (1928): 83-96.

1423 ———. *Etudes sur les Origins de la Religion de l'Egypte.* [With a preface by A. Moret.] London, 1929.

1424 ———. Etudes sur les origines de la religion de l'Egypte. *JASOR* 13 (1929): 1-100.

1425 ———. Some religious elements in the civilization of predynastic Egypt. *Egy. Religion* 1 (1933): 121-26.

1426 ———. The civilization of the North and the South. *Egy. Religion* 1 (1933): 76-77.

1427 ———. The so-called first and second civilizations. *Egy. Religion* 1 (1933): 73-75.

1428 ———. Where in the Delta was Behdet? *Egy. Religion* 1 (1933): 35-37.

1429 ———. *Horus, Royal God of Egypt.* Grafton, Mass., 1942.

1430 **Merpert, I.Y.** and **O.G. Bollshakov.** [The Early Dynastic cemetery at Khor-Daud.] *Obshchaya Kharkteristika Drevnyaya Nubiya* (1964): 82-177. [In Russian]

1431 **du Mesnil du Buisson,** [Le Comte] **Robert.** Le décor asiatique du Couteau de Gebel-el-Arak. *BIFAO* 68 (1969): 63-83.

1432 **de Meulenaere, Hermann.** Elkab. *LdÄ* 1 (1975-): 1225-27.

1433 **Meyer, Eduard.** <201> *Geschichte des Altertums.* 5 vols. Stuttgart and Berlin, 1884-1902; 2nd. ed. 1901-3; 3rd. ed. 1907; 4th. ed. 1928; 5th. ed. 1931.

1434 **Meyerowitz, Eva L.R.** *The Divine Kingship in Ghana and Ancient Egypt.* London, 1960. [Pp. 228-29 and 232-35 are reprinted in entry 575, pp. 35-37.]

1435 **Michael, H.N.** and **E.V. Ralph.** Correction factors applied to Egyptian radiocarbon dates from the era before Christ. *Nobel Symposium* 12 (1970): 109-20.

Midgley, W. See entry 1226.

1436 **Millington, Thomas S.** *Signs and Wonders in the Land of Ham; A Description of the Ten Plagues of Egypt, etc., with Ancient and Modern Parallels and Illustrations.* London, 1873.

Milne, J.G. See entry 1226.

1437 **Milojčić, V.** *Chronologie der jüngeren Steinzeit Mittel und Südosteuropas.* Berlin, 1949.

1438 **Misonne, X.** and **F. Van Noten.** De rotsgraveringen en schilderingen van Uweinat. *Africa-Tervuren* 15 (1969): 126-30.

1439 **Mitra, Panchanan.** Prehistoric cultures and races in India. *Calcutta University Journal* (1920).
Reviewed: *Ancient Egypt* (1921): 18.

1440 **Mitwalli, M.** History of the relations between the Egyptian oases of the Libyan desert and the Nile Valley. *Bull. Inst. du Désert* 2 (1952): 114-31.

1441 **Möller, Georg Christian Julius.** <204> Ausgrabung der deutschen Orient-Gesellschaft auf dem vorgeschichtlichen Friedhofe bei Abusir el-Meleq im Sommer 1905. *MDOG* 30 (1906): 9.

1442 ————. Ausgrabung bei Abusir el-Meleq 1906. *MDOG* 34 (1907): 2-13.

1443 **Moir, J. Reid.** Some flint implements of rostro-carinate from Egypt. *Man* 18 (1918): 3-6.

1444 **Moll, H.** *Forty-two Maps of Asia, Africa, and America.* London, 1716.

1445 **Momono, S.** and **N. Ishige.** Palaeolithic tools from Fezzan province, Libya. *Kyoto Univ. African Studies* 8 (1973): 167-82.

1446 **Mond, Robert Ludwig** <205> and **W.B. Emery.** A preliminary report on the excavations at Armant. *LAAA* 16 (1929): 3-12.

1447 **Mond, Robert Ludwig** and **O.H. Myers.** *Cemeteries of Armant.* 2 vols. London, 1937.

1448 **Montelius, O.** Die Bronzezeit Aegyptens. *Korresp. d. Gesell. f. Anthrop. Münster* 18 (1888): 111-15. [See also entry 1807.]

1449 ————. Bronsaldern i Egypten. *Ymer* 8 (Stockholm, 1889): 3-49. [See also entry 1805.]

1450 ————. L'Age du bronze en Egypte. *L'Anthropologie* 1 (1890): 27-48. Transl. as The age of bronze in Egypt, in *Ann. Rep. Smithsonian Institution* (1890): 499-515.

1451 **Montet, Anita M.** Les industries levalloisiennes d'Héliopolis et d'Abou-Suweir (Egypte.) *BSPF* 54 (1957): 329-39.

1452 **Montet, Pierre.** <206> Tombeaux de la Ire et de la IVe dynasties à Abu Roach. *Kemi* 7 (1938): 11-69; and 8 (1946): 157-227.

1453 ————. *Isis, ou à la Recherche de l'Egypte Ensevelie.* Paris, 1956.

1454 ————. *Géographie de l'Egypte Ancienne.* 2 vols. Paris, 1957-61.

1455 ————. L'Egypte préhistorique. In André Varagnac, et al., *L'Homme avant l'Ecriture.* (Paris, 1959): 231-65.

1456 **Mook, Friedrich.** <207> Excavations in different parts of Egypt. *Nature* 18 (1878): 372.

1457 ———. *Aegyptens vormetallische Zeit.* Würzburg, 1880.

Moortgat, Anton. See entry 2036.

1458 **Morant, Geoffrey McKay.** A study of Egyptian craniology from prehistoric to Roman times; together with a series of measurements on crania of the First Dynasty from royal tombs at Abydos by G.H. Motley. *Biometrika* 17 (1925): 1-52.

1459 ———. A study of predynastic Egyptian skulls from Badari, based on measurements taken by Miss B.N. Stoessiger and Professor D.E. Derry. *Biometrika* 27 (1935): 293-309.

1460 ———. The predynastic skulls from Badari and their racial affinities. In entry 359: 63-66.

———. See entry 187.

1461 ———. Entry not used.

1462 **Moreau de Jounès, A.C.** *Ethnogenie Caucasienne.* Paris, 1861.

1463 **Morenz, Sigfried.** *Aegyptische Religion.* Stuttgart, 1960. Transl. as *Egyptian Religion* by Ann Keep. Ithaca, New York, 1973.

1464 **Moret, Alexandre.** <207> Le titre 'Horus d'Or' dans le protocole pharaonique. *RecTrav* 23 (1901): 23-32.

1465 ———. *Du Caractère Religieux de la Royauté Pharaonique.* Paris, 1902.

1466 ———. L'Egypte avant les pyramides. *Revue de Paris* (March 15, 1907): 389-419.

1467 ———. La Royauté dans l'Egypte Primitive: Totem et Pharaon. *BVMG,* fasc. 38 (Paris, 1912).

1468 ———. Fragments du mastaba de Shery, prêtre des rois Peribsen et Send. *MonPiot* 25 (1922-23): 273-98.

1469 ———. *Le Nil et la Civilisation Egyptienne.* Paris, 1926. Transl. as *The Nile and Egyptian Civilization* by M.R. Dobie. London, 1927.

Reviewed: *Ancient Egypt* (1926): 90.

1470 ———. *Histoire de la Nation Egyptienne,* 2: *L'Egypte Pharaonique.* Paris, 1932.

1471 ———. *Histoire Ancienne, Première Partie, Histoire de l'Orient,* 1: *Préhistoire.* Paris, 1936; 2nd. ed. 1941.

1472 **Moret, Alexandre** and **G. Davy.** *Des Clans aux Empire: l'Organisation Sociale chez les Primitifs et dans l'Orient Ancien.* Paris, 1923. Transl. as *From Tribe to Empire: Social Organization among Primitives and in the Ancient Near East.* by V. Gordon Childe. New York, 1926.

1473 **de Morgan, Henri.** Notes sur les stations quaternaires et sur l'âge du cuivre en Egypte. *Revue de l'Ecole d'Anthrop. de Paris* 18 (1908): 133-49.

Reviewed: *L'Anthropologie* 19 (1908): 629-31 by M. Boule.

1474 ———. Etude sur l'Egypte primitive. *Revue de l'Ecole d'Anthrop. de Paris* 19 (1909): 128-40, and 263-81.

Reviewed: *L'Anthropologie* 21 (1910): 201-3 by M. Boule.

1475 ———. Report on excavations made in Upper Egypt during the winter 1907-1908. *ASAE* 12 (1911): 25-50.

1476 **de Morgan, Jacques Jean Marie.** <82> *Recherches sur les Origines de l'Egypte.* 1: *L'Age de la Pierre et des Métaux.* 2: *Ethnographie Préhistorique et Tombeau Royal de Nagada.* [In collaboration with M.M. Weidmann, G. Jéquier and Dr. Fouquet.] 2 vols. Paris, 1896-97.

Reviewed: *Sphinx* 2 (1898): 104-7, by A. Eisenlohr.

BSAP 7 (1896) by G. Mortillet.
OLZ 1 (1898): 78-83 by Max Müller.

1477 ————. *Les Premières Civilisations.* Paris, 1900.

1478 ————. Observations sur les origines des arts céramiques dans le bassin méditerranéen. *Revue de l'Ecole d'Anthropologie* 17 (1907): 401-7.

1479 ————. *Les Premières Civilisations; Etudes sur la Préhistoire et l'Histoire jusqu'a la Fin de l'Empire Macédonien.* Paris, 1909.

Reviewed: *Rev. archéol.*, 4th ser., 15 (Paris, 1910): 303-4.
Rev. des Ethnogr. et Sociol. 2 (Paris, 1909): 378-79 by A. Van Gennep.
OLZ 13 (1910): 119-21 by E. Brandenburg.

1480 ————. La barque des morts chez les Egyptiens prédynastiques. *Rev. anthrop.* 30 (1920): 272-82.

1481 ————. *L'Humanité Préhistorique. Esquisse de Préhistoire Générale Bibliothèque de Synthèse Historique. L'Evolution de l'Humanité* 2 (Paris, 1921).

Reviewed: *Ancient Egypt* (1921): 116-18.
L'Anthrop., 5th ser., 4 (Paris, 1921): 420-421 by S. Reinach.

1482 ————. De l'influence asiatique sur l'Afrique à l'origine de la civilisation égyptienne. *L'Anthropologie* 31 (1921): 185-238 and 405-468.

1483 ————. Sur quelques formes curieuses des instruments de pierre en Egypte. *L'Anthropologie* 31 (1921): 52-65.

1484 ————. Le premiers temps de l'Egypte. *MonPiot* 25 (1921-22): 299-332.

1485 ————. L'Industrie néolithique et le proche-orient. *Syria* 4 (1923): 233-37.

1486 ————. L'Egypte et l'Asie aux temps antéhistoriques. *J. Asiat.* 203 (1923): 117-59.

1487 ————. Le monde oriental avant l'histoire: L'Asie antérieure et l'Egypte. *L'Anthropologie* 34 (1924): 17-56, 229-53.

1488 ————. *La Préhistoire Orientale.* 1: *Généralités.* 2: *L'Egypte et l'Afrique du Nord.* 3: *L'Asie Antérieure.* Paris, 1925.

Reviewed: *Ancient Egypt* (1928):55-58.
Historia 1 (1927): 120 by U. Antonielli.
OLZ 48 (1927): 1616-20 by A. Scharff.
BSPF (Paris, 1927): 386-87.
Jour. des Sav. (1926): 450-52 by L. Capitan.
Literarische Wochenschrift (1926): 1131 by G Röder.
Rev. des Questions hist. 54 (1926): 148-55 by A. Vincent.
J. Hell. Stud. (1926): 141-42.
Man 19 (1929): 15-26 by J.L. Myres.
L'Anthropologie 38 (1928): 139-42 by M. Boule.
La Géographie 45 (1926): 96 by E.D.
La Géographie 49 (1928): 516-17 by J.N.
Aegyptus 9 (1928): 161 and 10 (1929): 319 by A.C.
Rev. archéol., 4th ser., 22 (1925): 320 by S. Reinach.
CdE (1928-29): 106-12 by B. van de Walle.
Athenaeum 7 (1929): 85-113 by G. Latroni.

————. See also entry 876.

1489 **Mori, F.** Nuovi aspetti chronologici e culturali nel quadro della preistoria sahariana collegata all'arte rupestre. *Atti del congresso internazionale delle scienze preistoriche e protoistoriche* 6 (1962): 430-44.

1490 ————. Figure umane incise di tipo ittiomorfo scoperte nel Tadrart Acacus. *Origini* 1 (1967): 37-51.

1491 ————. Prehistoric Saharan art and cultures in the light of discoveries in the Acacus Massif (Libyan Sahara). *LH 1968* (1970): 31-39.

1492 ————. Proposition d'une chronologie absolue de l'art rupestre du Sahara d'après les fouilles du Tadrart Acacus (Sahara libyen). *Valcamonia Symposium, 1968: Actes du Symposium International sur les Religions de la Préhistoire.* 1 (1970): 345-56.

1493 ————. Proposta per una attribuzione alla fine del pleistocene delle incisioci della fase più antica dell'arte rupestre sahariana. *Origini* 5 (1971): 7-20.

1494 ————. Vorgeschichtliche Kunst und Kulturen der Sahara in Lichte der Entdeckungen im Massiv des Djebel Acacus (Libysche Sahara). *Almogaren* 2 (1971): 1-19.

1495 ————. A contribution to the study of magic co-religious thought based on some Saharan rock representations. *Bollettino del Centro Camuno di Studi Preistorici* 9 (1972): 161-62.

1496 ————. The earliest Saharan rock-engravings. *Antiquity* 48 (1974): 87-92.

1497 ————. Contributo allo studio del pensiero magico-religioso attraverso l'esame di alcune raffigurazioni rupestri preistoriche del Sahara. *Valcamonia Symposium, 1972: Actes du Symposium International sur les Religions de la Préhistoire.* (1975): 353-66.

1498 ————. The absolute chronology of Saharan prehistoric rock art. *Simposio internacional de arte rupestre.* E. Ripoll, (ed.), (Barcelona, 1968): 291-94.

————. See also entry 164.

1499 **Mori, F., P. Graziosi, T. del Gratta,** and **I. Fischietti.** *Arte Preistorica del Sahara.* Rome, 1959. [16mm film]

1500 **[Morbihan.]** La race celtique en Afrique, et ses luttes avec Egypte. *Bull. de la Soc. Polymathique du Morbihan* (Vannes, 1868): 103-108.

1501 **Morrison-Scott, T.C.S.** The mummified cats of ancient Egypt. *Proc. Zool. Soc. London* 121, 4 (1952): 861-67.

1502 **de Mortillet, A.** Discussion sur le fer en Egypte. *BSAP,* 3rd ser., 6 (1883): 808-19.

1503 ————. Le silex de l'Ile Riou. *L'Homme Préhistorique* 5 (Paris, 1907): 218-22.

1504 **Mortillet, Gabriel.** Nègres et civilisation égyptienne. *Matériaux pour l'Histoire Primitive et Naturelle de l'Homme,* 3rd ser., 1 (1884): 113-20.

1505 **Mortillet, Gabriel** and **André Lefèvre.** Egypte. In Ad. Bertillon, et al., *Dictionnaire des Sciences Anthropologiques* 1 (Paris, 1889): 414-32.

1506 **de Mortillet, Paul.** Les bracelets en pierre robenhaussiens. Bracelet en diorite, Rizakat (Egypte). *L'Homme Préhistorique* 9 (1911): 310-17.

1507 **Morton, Samuel George.** On the form of the head, and other ethnographic characters of the ancient Egyptians. *Proc. Amer. Phil. Soc.* 2 (1842): 239-41.

1508 ————. Summary of S.G. Morton's series of observations on Egyptian ethnography for spec. meeting, 5th session, 29th May, 10 a.m. *Proc. Amer. Phil. Soc.* 3 (1843): 115-18.

1509 ————. On the origin of the Nilotic or Egyptian population. *Edinburgh N. Phil. Jour.* 37 (1844): 308-11. [Summary in. *Frorief, Notijen* 32 (1844): 273.]

1510 ————. Observations on a second series of ancient Egyptian crania. *Proc. Acad. Nat. Sci. Philadelphia* 2 (1844): 122-26.

1511 ————. *Crania Aegyptica.* Philadelphia, 1844.

1512 ————. Observations on Egyptian ethnography, derived from anatomy, history, and the monuments. *Trans. Amer. Phil. Soc.* 9 (1846): 93-159.

1513 ————. Account of a craniological collection with remarks on the clarification of some families of the human race. *Trans. Amer. Ethnol. Soc.* 2 (1848): 215-22.

1514 ———. Remarks on embalmed heads of man, and the inferior animals from the Egyptian catacombs. *Proc. Acad. Nat. Sci. Philadelphia* 5 (1850): 122-23.

1515 **Mosso, Angelo.** *The Dawn of Mediterranean Civilization.* Transl. by Marian C. Harrison. London, 1910.

1516 **Mouillard, L.P.** Lettre de M.L.P. Mouillard à M. Gaillardot Bey sur les ateliers de silex en Egypte. *BIE,* 4th ser. (1901): 223-25.

1517 **Mounier-Leclerq, Elsa.** Deux palettes prédynastiques. *BMRAH,* 3th ser., 7 (1935): 134-38.

1518 ———. L'art préhistorique de l'Afrique du Nord. Quelques découvertes récentes. *CdE* 22 (1936): 324-28.

———. See also **Leclerq** entries 1282-86.

1519 **Moustafa, Yusef Shawki.** A contribution to the knowledge of animal life in predynastic Egypt. *Bull. Fac. Arts, Cairo Univ.* 15 (1953): 207-11.

1520 ———. Preliminary notice on gazelles from predynastic Wadi Digla. *Bull. Fac. Arts, Cairo Univ.* 15 (1953): 213.

1521 ———. 'Canis familiaris Aegyptica' from predynastic Maadi, Egypt. *BIE* 36 (1955): 105-9.

1522 **Müller, Friedrich Wilhelm Karl.** *Die anthropologischen Ergebnisse des vorgeschichtlichen Gräberfeldes von Abusir el-Meleq. WVDOG* 27 (Leipzig, 1915).

1523 **Müller, H.** *Die formale Entwicklung der Titular der ägyptischen Königs. ÄF* 7 (Glückstadt, 1938).

1524 **Müller, H.W.** Ein neues Fragment einer reliefgeschmückten Schminkpalette aus Abydos. *ZÄS* 84 (1957): 68-70.

1525 **Muller, Sophus.** Communautés stylistiques en Europe dans le récent âge de la pierre. *Mém. de la Soc. des Antiquaires du Nord,* n.s. (Copenhagen, 1920-24): 207-94. [Summary in *Ancient Egypt* (1926): 60.]

1526 **Müller, Valentin.** Die Petroglyphen von Demir-Kapu. *Zeitschrift für Ethnologie* 56 (1924): 176-79.

1527 **Muller, Wilhelm Max.** <209> An archaic cylinder from Egypt. *OLZ* 5 (1902): 90-92.

1528 ———. Hamites. *Encyclopaedia Britannica,* 11th ed., vol. 12 (Cambridge, 1910): 593-94.

Munday, F. See entry 1388.

1529 **Munro, Peter.** Bemalung. *LdÄ* 1 (1975-): 691-94.

1530 **Munro, Robert.** On prehistoric saws versus sickles. *Archaeol. Jour.* 49 (1892): 164-75.

1531 ———. Notes on flint saws and sickles. *BAAS, 63rd meeting, Nottingham, 1893* (1894): 899.

1532 **Murdock, George P.** *Africa: Its People and their Culture History.* New York, 1959. [Pp. 64-68 reprinted in entry 575, pp. 38-41.]

1533 **Murray, George William.** <210> Egypt, The Paleolithic age: A note on Dr. Seligman's paper. *Man* 22 (1923): 27-28.

1534 ———. *Sons of Ishmael: A Study of the Egyptian Bedouin.* London, 1935.

1535 ———. An archaic hut in Wadi Umm Sidrah. *JEA* 25 (1939): 38-39.

1536 ———. The Egyptian climate: An historical outline. *Geogr. J.* 117 (1951): 422-34.

1537 ———. Water from the desert: Some ancient Egyptian achievements. *Geogr. J.* 121 (1955): 171-87.

1538 **Murray, George William** and **D.E. Derry.** A predynastic burial on the Red Sea Coast of Egypt. *Man* 23 (1923): 129-31.

1539 **Murray, George William** and **O.H. Myers.** Some predynastic rock drawings. *JEA* 19 (1933): 129-32.

1540 **Murray, Margaret Alice.** <210> The first mace-head of Hierakonpolis. *Ancient Egypt* (1920): 15-17.

1541 ———. The costume of the early kings. *Ancient Egypt* (1926): 33-40.

1542 ———. An early Sed-festival. *Ancient Egypt* (1932): 70-72.

1543 ———. Rhymer and rain charms. *Ancient Egypt* (1933): 45-48.

1544 ———. Female fertility figures. *JRAI* 64 (1934): 93-100.

1545 ———. Dessication in Egypt. *BSRGE* 23 (1949): 19-34.

1546 ———. Burial customs and beliefs in the hereafter in predynastic Egypt. *JEA* 42 (1956): 86-96.

1547 ———. Egypt and Africa. *Man* 61 (1961): 25-26.
Reviewed: *Man* 61 (1961): 209-10 by G.A. Wainwright.

———. See entries 1226, 1770, 1786, 1794 and Supplement entry 2510.

Muzzolini, A. See Supplement entries 2500-06.

1548 **Myers, Charles S.** Note on the early dynastic period of Egypt. *Man* 2 (1902): 66-67.

1549 ———. Contributions to Egyptian anthropometry, 1: General introduction. *JRAI* 33 (1903): 82-89.

1550 ———. Contributions to Egyptian anthropometry, 2: The comparative anthropometry of the most ancient and modern inhabitants. *JRAI* 35 (1905): 80-91.

1551 ———. Contributions to Egyptian anthropometry, 3: The anthropometry of the modern Mohammedans. *JRAI* 36 (1906): 237-63.

1552 ———. Contributions to Egyptian anthropometry, 4: The comparison of the Mohammedans with the Copts and with the 'Mixed' Group. *JRAI* 36 (1906): 263-71.

1553 ———. Contributions to Egyptian anthropometry, 5: General conclusions. *JRAI* 38 (1908): 99-147.

1554 **Myers, Oliver Humphrys.** <211> Two prehistoric objects. *JEA* 19 (1933): 55.

1555 ———. The Sir Robert Mond Expedition of the Egypt Exploration Society. *Geogr. J.* 93 (1939): 287-91.

1556 ———. Drawings by the Sudanese artists of seven thousand years ago. Neolithic rock-drawings from the Pot-Holes of the Nile. *ILN* 213 (1948): 556-57.

1557 ———. Rock-drawings found by the Gordon College Expedition in the Second Cataract region of the Nile. *Actes du XXI Cong. Intern. des Orient.* (Paris, 1949): 375-76.

1558 ———. Abka re-excavated. *Kush* 6 (1958): 131-41.

1559 ———. Abka again. *Kush* 8 (1960): 174-81.

———. See entries 140, 1447 and 1539.

1560 **Myers, Oliver Humphrys** and **H.W. Fairman.** Excavations at Armant, 1929-1931. *JEA* 17 (1931): 223-32.

1561 **Myres, John L.** *The Dawn of History.* London, 1911.

N

1562 **de Nadaillac.** Silex taillés de l'Egypte. *BSAP,* 3rd ser., 5 (1882): 349.

1563 **Nagel, W.** Radio-carbon Datierung im orientalischen Neolithikum und die Zeitstellung der frühsumerischen Kultur. *Acta Praehistorica et Archaeologica* 4 (Berlin, 1973; publ. 1975) 33-74.

1564 **Naville, Henri Edouard.** <213> Figurines égyptiennes de l'époque archaique. *RecTrav* 21 (1899): 212-16 and 22 (1900): 65-71.

1565 ———. Les plus anciens monuments égyptiens. *RecTrav* 24 (1902): 109-20; and 25 (1903): 199-225.

1566 ———. Origine des anciens égyptiens: Rapport possibles avec Babylone. *Revue de l'Hist. des Religions* 52 (1905): 357-80.

1567 ———. The origin of Egyptian civilization. *JRAI* 36 (1907): 201-14. [Repr. in *Ann. Rep., Smithsonian Institution* (1907): 549-64.]

Reviewed: *Revue des Ethnogr. et de Sociol.* 3 (Paris, 1912): 393-94 by A.J. Reinach.

1568 ———. Origine des Anciens Egyptiens. In his *La Religion des Anciens Egyptiens.* (Paris, 1907). [See also entry 1567.]

1569 ———. The origin of Egyptian civilization. *BAAS, Report of the 77th Meeting, Leicester, 1904* (London, 1907): 650-52.

1570 ———. *The Old Egyptian Faith.* Transl. by Colin Campbell. London, 1909.

1571 ———. Deux rois de la période thinite. *ZÄS* 47 (1910): 65-67.

1572 ———. Les Anu. *RecTrav* 32 (1910): 52-61.

1573 ———. La population primitive de l'Egypte. *RecTrav* 33 (1911): 193-212. [Summary in *Le Globe* 50 (Geneva, 1911): 39-49.] [See also entries 1579 and 2243.]

1574 ———. Discours de clôture. *C.r. Congrès Internationale d'Anthropologie et de Archéologie Préhistoriques, Genève 1912* (Geneva, 1913): 1, 102-106. [See entry 1815 for summary.]

1575 ———. L'Origine africaine de la civilization égyptienne. *Revue Archéol.,* 4th ser., 22 (Paris, 1913): 47-65.

1576 ———. La poterie primitive en Egypte. *L'Anthropologie* 23 (1912): 313-20.

Reviewed: *BSAL* 32 (1913-17): 19-20 by E. Chantre.

1577 ————. Excavations at Abydos: The great pool and the tomb of Osiris. *JEA* 1 (1914): 159-67.

1578 ————. Le passage de la pierre au métal en Egypte. *Arch. Suisses d'Anthrop. Gén.* 1 (Geneva, 1914).

Reviewed: *BSAL* 32 (1913-17): 152-54.

1579 ————. Les dessins des vases préhistoriques égyptiens. *Arch. Suisses d'Anthrop. Gén.* 2 (Geneva, 1917): 77-82; and 4 (1921): 197-206. [See also entries 1573 and 2243.]

Reviewed: *Ancient Egypt* (1917): 95.
L'Anthropologie 29 (1919): 363-64 by M. Boule.

1580 ————. Les cimetières de Koubanieh. *Rev. Archéol.*, 5th ser., 14 (Paris, 1920): 158-65.

1581 ————. La Poterie nubienne. *Rev. Archéol.*, 5th ser., 16 (Paris, 1922): 44-45.

1582 ————. L'Age du cuivre en Egypte. *Rev. Archéol.*, 5th ser., 20 (Paris, 1924): 1-20.

Reviewed: *Isis* (1927): 545-46.

1583 **Naville, Edouard** and **T.E. Peet.** *The Cemeteries of Abydos. EEF* 33-35 (London, 1913-14).

1584 **Neck, James Hull.** *Egypt as a Field for British Enterprise, Trade, Commerce, Finance, and Agriculture. Requirements and Competition — General Information — Hints and Comments — Facts and Fallacies — Authoritative Opinions — Regeneration.* London, 1882.

1585 **Needham, John Turberville.** <215> *De Inscriptione Quadam Aegyptiaca Taurini Inventa et Characteribus Aegyptiis Olim et Sinis Communibus Exarata.* Rome, 1761.

1586 ————. *Résponses aux Deux Lettres de M. Bartholi sur l'Identité des Anciens Caractères Egyptiens et Chinois.* Turin, 1762.

1587 ————. *Letter sur le Génie de la Langue des Chinois et la Nature de leur Ecriture Symbolique Comparée celle des Egyptiens.* Brussels, 1773.

1588 **Needler, Winifred.** A flint knife of King Djer. *JEA* 42 (1956): 41-44.

1589 ————. Six predynastic human figures in the Royal Ontario Museum. *JARCE* 5 (1966): 11-17.

1590 ————. A rock-drawing on Gebel Sheikh Suliman (near Wadi Halfa) showing a scorpion and human figures. *JARCE* 6 (1967): 89-91.

1591 ————. Acquisitions by contribution: Latest finds from the Egyptian Exploration Society. *Rotunda, Bull. ROM* 2 (1969): 22-32.

1592 ————. Two important predynastic graves from H. de Morgan's excavations. *Assoc. Intern. pour l'Etude de la Préhistoire Eegyptienne, 'L'Egypte avant l'Histoire', Bulletin* 1 (1980): 1-15.

1593 ————. Federn's revision of Petrie's predynastic pottery classification. *JSSEA* 11 (1981): 69-74.

1594 **Neilson, J.** Flint implements from the Fayûm, Egypt. *Geol. Mag., London* 10 (1903): 192.

Neuffer, E. See entry 2053.

1595 **Neumann, .** *De Locis Aegypt. in Operib. Platonicis.* Vratislaviae, 1874.

1596 **de Neuville, René Victoire.** Affinités néolithiques du 'Chalossien' d'Egypte. *BSPF* 29 (1932): 469-71.

1597 **Newberry, Percy Edward.** <216> The Horus-title of the Kings of Egypt. *PSBA* 26 (1904): 295-99.

1598 ————. To what race did the founders of Sais belong? *PSBA* 28 (1906): 68-75.

1599 ————. The petty-kingdom of the harpoon and Egypt's earliest Mediterranean port. *LAAA* 1 (1908): 17-27.

1600 ————. Two cults of the Old Kingdom. *LAAA* 1 (1909): 24-29.

1601 ————. A bird cult of the Old Kingdom. *LAAA* 2 (1910): 49-51.

1602 ————. Two prehistoric slate palettes. *LAAA* 4 (1912): 140.

1603 ————. The wooden and ivory labels of the first dynasty. *PSBA* 34 (1912): 179-89.

1604 ————. List of vases with cult-signs. *LAAA* 5 (1913): 137-42.

1605 ————. Some cults of prehistoric Egypt. *LAAA* 5 (1913): 132-36.

1606 ————. Notes on some Egyptian nome ensigns and their historical significance. *Ancient Egypt* (1914): 5-8.

1607 ————. Ta Tahenu — 'Olive Land'. *Ancient Egypt* (1915): 97-100.

1608 ————. The Set rebellion in the IInd Dynasty. *Ancient Egypt* (1922): 40-46.

1609 ————. Egypt as field for anthropological research. *BAAS, 91st meeting* (1924): 175-96. [Reprinted in *Nature* 112 (1924): 422-23, 940-44; and in *Smithsonian Report* (1925): 436-59]. Transl. into German in *Das Alte Orient* 27, fasc. 1 (1927): 43, by G. Roeder. [See also entry 1133.]

Reviewed: *OLZ* 31 (1928): 191-96, by Scharff.
WZKM 36 (1929): 142-43 by W. Till.
Anthropos 25 (1930): 772-73 by Hischberg.

1610 ————. Miscellanea IV: A label of the First Dynasty. *JEA* 14 (1928): 110.

1611 ————. The pig and the cult-animal of Set. *JEA* 14 (1928): 211-25.

1612 ————. Menes: The founder of the Egyptian monarchy. In W. Brunton, et al., *Great Ones of Ancient Egypt.* (London, 1929): 35-53.

1613 ————. The shepherd's crown and the so-called 'flail' or 'scourge' of Osiris. *JEA* 15 (1929): 84-94.

1614 ————. Some African species of the genus Olea and the original home of the cultivated olive-tree. *Proc. Linnaean Society* 1 (1937-38): 3-16.

1615 **Newberry, Percy Edward** and **G.A. Wainwright.** King Udy-mu (Den) and the Palermo Stone. *Ancient Egypt* (1914): 148-55.

1616 **Newbold, Douglas.** A desert odyssey of a thousand miles. *SNR* 7 (1924): 43-83.

1617 ————. Explorations in the Libyan Desert. *Antiquity* 2 (1928): 206-7.

1618 ————. Rock pictures and archaeology in the Libyan Desert. *Antiquity* 2 (1928): 261-91.

1619 ————. Zerzura Oasis: Does it exist? *SNR* 11 (1928): 181-94.

1620 ————. The history and archaeology of the Libyan desert, being extracts from some letters of Douglas Newbold written between 1922 and 1923. *SNR* 26 (1945): 229-41.

————. See entry 139.

1621 **Newbold, Douglas** and **W.B.K. Shaw.** An exploration in the South Libyan Desert. *SNR* 11 (1928): 103-94.

1622 **Nicklin, T.** *Studies in Egyptian Chronology.* 1: *A Revised Text on Manetho's Dynasties.* 2: *The Sothic Cycle.* Blackbourne, 1928-29.

1623 **Nielson, O.V.** *Human Remains. Scandinavian Joint Expedition to Sudanese Nubia* 9 (Stockholm, 1970).

1624 **Noguera, Anthony.** *How African Was Egypt? A Comparative Study of Ancient Egypt and Black African Civilization.* New York, 1976.

1625 **Nordström, Hans-Ake.** A-group and C-group in Upper Nubia. *Kush* 14 (1966): 63-68.

1626 ————. *Neolithic and A-Group Sites. Scandinavian Joint Expedition to Sudanese Nubia* 3 (Stockholm, 1972).

1627 **Nott, J.C.** and **George R. Gliddon.** *Types of Mankind: Or, Ethnological Researches Based upon the Ancient Monuments, Paintings, Sculptures, and Crania of Races, and upon their Natural, Geographical, Philological, and Biblical History: Illustrated by Selections from the Inedited Papers of Samuel George Morton, M.D....* Philadelphia, 1855.

1628 **Nougier, L.-R.** Influence égyptienne dans le néolithique saharien. *Actes de la IIe Congrès de Préhistoire, Algiers, 1952* (Paris, 1955): 641-45.

1629 **Novak, Grga.** *Egipat Prehistoriia-faraoni Osvaja-kultura.* Zagreb, 1967.

Reviewed: *Telegram* 408 (Zagreb, 1968): 4 by Peter Selena.
Slobodua Dalmacya (Split, 1969): 5 by Peter Selena.

O

1630 **Oakley, Kenneth P.** The antiquity of the new Kom Ombo skull. *Man* 65 (1965): 104.

1631 **Obenga, Théophile.** *Méthode et Conception Historique de Cheikh Anta Diop.* Paris, 1970.

1632 ———. *L'Afrique dans l'Antiquite: Egypte Pharaonique — Afrique noire.* Paris, 1973.

1633 **Obermaier, Hugo.** Aegypten, A. Palaeolithikum. In M. Ebert (ed.), *Reallexikon der Vorgesch.* 1 (Berlin, 1924): 48-50.

1634 **O'Connor, David.** The geography of settlement in ancient Egypt. In entry 2265, pp. 681-98.

1635 ———. A regional population in Egypt to circa 600 B.C. In B. Spooner (ed.), *Population Growth: Anthropological Implications.* (Cambridge, Mass., 1972): 78-100.

1636 ———. Political systems and archaeological data in Egypt, 2600-1700 B.C. *World Archaeology* 6 (1974): 15-38.

———. See Supplement entry 2514.

1637 **Octobon, E.** Le micro-burin est-il sébilien? *BSPF* 32 (1935): 483.

1638 **Oetteking, Bruno.** Kraniologische Studien an Altägypten. *Archiv für Anthrop.*, n.f., 8 (1908): 1-90. Also publ. separarately, Braunschweig, 1908. [Briefly summarized by G. Elliot Smith, *ASN* 18-19.]

1639 **Offord, Joseph.** Egyptology in France. Figures upon prehistoric Egyptian and Dipylon early Hellenic pottery. *Ancient Egypt* (1916): 167-68.

1640 **Ogdon, Jorge R.** Observations on some priestly titles of the Old Kingdom. *JSSEA* 12 (1982): 87-90.

1640a **Ogden, Ricardo Edgard.** *Observaciones Sobres los Entes Llamados Tekenu.* Buenos Aires, 1977.

1641 **Ollivier-Beauregard, G.M.** L'antiquité du fer en Egypte. *BSAP,* 3rd ser., 7 (1884): 104-27.

1642 ———. Egypt in prehistoric times. *Nature* 40 (1889): 92. A transl. and summary of L'Antiquité de l'Egypte et les formules de la préhistoire. *BSAP,* 3rd ser., 11 (1888): 515-32.

1643 ———. *En Oriens: Etudes Ethnologiques et Linguistiques à Travers les Ages et les Peuples.* Paris, 1889.

1644 ———. L'Age du bronze en Egypte. *L'Anthropologie* 1 (1890): 383-84.

1645 **Ortelius, Abraham.** *Aegyptus Antique. . . Ex Conatibus Geographicus A. Ortelii.* Antwerp, 1595.

1646 ————. *Epitome of the Theatre of the World.* London, 1603.

1647 **Orton, W., Jr.** The Bible and Egyptology. *Biblical Review* 4 (1919): 203.

1648 **Osburn, William.** <219> *Ancient Egypt, Her Testimony to the Truth of the Bible. Being an Interpretation of the Inscriptions and Pictures which Remain upon her Tombs and Temples.* London, 1846.

1649 **Osten, Lawrence W.** An estimate of the climate along the Nile Valley between 18,000 and 14,000 BC based on pectoral fin spines of catfish. In entry 2388, pp. 331-34.

Otte, M. See entries 2291-94.

1650 **Otto, Eberhard.** *Beiträge zur Geschichte der Stierkulte in Aegypten.* *UGAÄ* 13 (Leipzig, 1938).

1651 ————. Ein Beitrag zur Deutung der ägyptischen Vor- und Frügeschichte. *Welt des Orient* 1 (1952): 431-53.

1652 ————. *Topographie des Thebanischen Gaues.* *UGAÄ* 16 (Berlin, 1952).

1653 ————. Der Gebrauch des Königstitels *bjtj.* *ZÄS* 85 (1960): 143-52.

1654 **Otto, Karl-Heinz.** Shaqadud: A new Khartoum Neolithic site outside the Nile Valley. *Kush* 11 (1963): 108-115.

1655 ————. Khartoum: Neolithikum am Jebel Shaqadud. In Paul Grimm (ed.), *Varia Archaeologica Wilhelm Unverzagt zum 70. Geburtstag dargebrecht. (=DAWB, Sektion für Vor- und Frühgesch.)* (Berlin, 1964): 9-13.

1656 **Owen, Richard.** Contributions to the ethnology of Egypt. *JRAI* 4 (1875): 223-54.

P

1657 **Pachundaki.** Observations sur le préhistoire en Egypte. *Revue Intern. d'Egypte* 2 (Alexandria, 1905): 15-24.

Paepe, Roland. See entries 1022 and 2191.

1658 **Paepe, Roland** and **J. Guichard.** Preliminary report on the prehistorical research around the temples of Abu Simbel. Columbia University Expedition in Nubia, Season October 1961 - February 1962. *AO: Fouilles en Nubie 1957-1961* (Cairo, 1963): 95-97.

1659 **Palmer, H.R.** The white races of North Africa. *SNR* 9 (1926): 69-74.

Palmieri, A. See entry 1854.

1660 **Papillault, G.** Crânes d'Abydos. *BSAP,* 5th ser., 6 (1905): 260-69.

Papworth, M.L. See entry 110.

1661 **de Paravey, Charles Hippolyte.** <221> *Essai sur l'Origine Unique et Hiéroglyphique des Chiffres et des Lettres de Tours le Peuples...* Paris, 1826.

1662 **Parker, O.F.** and **M.C. Burkitt.** Rock engravings from Onib, Wadi Allaki, Nubia. *Man* 27 (1932): 249-50.

1663 **Parker, Richard A.** *The Calenders of Egypt. SAOC* 26 (Chicago, 1950).

1664 ———. Sothic dates and calendar 'adjustment'. *Revue d'Egyptologie* 9 (1952): 101-8.

1665 **Parrat, H.J.F.** *Les 36,000 Ans de Manéthon, Suivis d'un Tableau des Concordances Synchroniques des Rois d'Egypte et des Hébreux.* Bern, 1855.

1666 **Passarge, S.** *Die Urlandschaft Ägyptens und die Lokalisierung der Wiege der altägyptischen Kultur. Neue Acta Leopoldina,* n.f., 9, 58 (Halle, 1940).

Reviewed: *AO* 14 (1941-1944): 359-61 by U. Hölscher.

1667 **Passemmard, E.** Une nouvelle industrie du paléolithique inférieur plus ancienne que le chelléen: Le chalossien. *Bull. Soc. Franç. Avancement des Sciences* (1925): 478-81.

1668 ———. Le chalossien en France, en Egypte et en Syrie. *Syria* 8 (1927): 342-51.

Paulissen, E. See entries 2290-94.

1669 **Paulme, D.** *Les Civilisations Africaines.* Paris, 1953.

1670 **Payne, Joan Crowfoot.** Tomb 100: The decorated tomb at Hierakonpolis. *JEA* 59 (1973): 31-35.

1671 **Payne, Joan Crowfoot., A. Kaczmarczyk** and **S.J. Fleming.** Forged decoration on predynastic pots. *JEA* 63 (1977): 5-12.

1672 **Peake, Harold J.E.** The beginning of civilisations. *JRAI* 57 (1927): 19-38.

1673 ———. *The Origins of Agriculture.* London, 1928.

1674 **Pearson, Karl.** Note on Dr. Keith's review of 'The Ancient Races of the Thebaid' by Prof. Arthur Thomson and D. Randall-MacIver. *Man* 5 (1905): 116-19. [See also entry 2238.]

1675 **Peck, William H.** A newly discovered example of decorated pre-dynastic pottery in the Detroit Institute of Arts. *Bull. Detroit Inst. Arts* 55 (1977): 216-18.

1676 **Peel, R.F.** Rock-paintings from the Libyan desert: An appendix to Dr. H.A. Winkler's 'Rock-drawings of Southern Upper Egypt, II'. *Antiquity* 13 (1939): 389-402. [See also entry 2461.]

1677 ———. Denudational landforms of the central Libyan Desert. *J. of Geomorphology* 4 (1941): 3-23.

———. See entry 140.

1678 **Peel, R.F.** and **R.A. Bagnold.** Archaeology: Additional notes. *Geographical J.* 93 (1939): 291-95.

1679 **Peet, Thomas Eric.** <223> *The Cemeteries of Abydos,* part 2, *1911-12. EES* 34 (London, 1914).

1680 ———. The art of the predynastic period. *JEA* 2 (1915): 88-94.

1681 ———. Primitive stone buildings in Sinai. *Man* 15 (1915): 151-58.

1682 ———. Egypt: The predynastic period. *CAH*[1], vol. 1 (Cambridge, 1924): 238-56. Also plate vol. (1927): 22-29.

1683 ———. Early Egyptian life and culture: The civilization of the Nile in predynastic times and its flowering under the Old Kingdom. In John Alexander Hammerton (ed.), *Universal History of the World.* 1 (London, 1927): 543-66.

1684 ———. The classification of Egyptian pottery. *JEA* 19 (1933): 62-64.

———. See entry 1583.

1685 **Peet, Thomas Eric** and **W.L.S. Loat.** *The Cemeteries of Abydos,* part 3, *1912-1913. EES* 35 (London, 1913).

1686 **Pelagaud, F.** Les débuts de l'histoire d'Egypte. *BSAL* 28 (1909): 42.

1687 **Penderel, H.W.G.J.** The Gilf Kebir. *Geogr. J.* 83 (London, 1934): 449-56.

1688 **Pendlebury, John David Stringfellow.** <224> *Aegyptiaca: A Catalogue of Egyptian Objects in the Aegean Area.* Cambridge, 1930.

1689 ———. Egypt and the Aegean in the Late Bronze Age. *JEA* 6 (1930): 75-92.

1690 **Penniman, T.K.** Origins of civilization in the Afrasian dry zone. *Antiquity* 19 (1945): 96-99.

1691 **Périer, Joanna André Napoleon.** Sur l'ethnogénie égyptienne. (A l'occasion d'un mémoire de Pruner-Bey). *MSAP,* 1st ser., 1 (1860-63): 435-504.

1692 ———. Paléogéographie de la Palestine et du Sinai. *Et. Théol. et Religieuses* (Paris, 1929): 242-60 and 345-60.

1693 **Perkins, Dexter, Jr.** Three faunal assemblages from Sudanese Nubia. *Kush* 13 (1965): 56-61.

1694 **Perry, William J.** *The Children of the Sun.* London, 1923.

1695 ———. Sumer and Egypt. *Man* 29 (1929): 76.

1696 ———. *The Growth of Civilization.* Harmondsworth, 1937.

1697 **Pervinquiere, L.** Archéologie préhistorique, l'âge du bronze. *Chronique Scientifique* (1912): 263-80.

1698 **Pesce, A.** Prehistoric rock carvings of the Jebel Bzema in Southern Cyrenaica. *La Arti* 5 (1968): 99-103.

1699 ————. Rock carvings in Wadi Bouzna, Wadi el Ajal Valley, Fezzan. *La Arti* 5 (1968): 109-12.

————. See entry 2356.

1700 **Peschel, Oscar.** *The Races of Man, and Their Geographical Distribution.* London, 1876; New York, 1906; transl. into German as *Völkerkund,* Leipzig, 1874; and 2nd ed. 1877.

Petersen, Kenneth L. See entry 1405.

1701 **Peterson, Bengt J.** Swedish travellers in Egypt during the period 1700-1850. *Opuscula Athenien-sia* 7 (Lund, 1967): 17-18.

1702 **Petrie,** Lady **Hilda Mary Isabel.** <227> *Egyptian Hieroglyphs of the First and Second Dynasties.* London, 1927.

————. See entries 1770 and 1786.

1703 **Petrie,** Sir **William Matthew Flinders.** <228> Pottery and implements collected at Gizeh and the neighbourhood, from December 1880 to June 1881. *PSBA* 4 (1882): 76.

1704 ————. Ethnographic casts from Egypt. *Babylonian and Oriental Record* 2 (1887-88): 134-37.

1705 ————. *Kahun, Gurob and Hawara.* London, 1890.

1706 ————. *Illahun, Kahun and Gurob.* London, 1891.

1707 ————. Prehistory of Egypt. *Nature* 45 (1891-92): 580.

1708 ————. *Medum.* London, 1892.

1709 ————. *Ten Years Digging in Egypt, 1881-1891.* London, 1892; New York, 1892; 2nd. ed. London, 1893; New York, 1893.

1710 ————. *Koptos.* London, 1896.

1711 ————. Excavations at Hierakonpolis: The earliest monuments of Egyptian history. *EEF, Archaeological Report for 1897-98* (London): 6-10.

1712 ————. Antiquities in Egypt: Prehistoric rock drawings. *The Graphic* (1st January, 1898).

1713 ————. On our present knowledge of early Egyptians. *JRAI* 28 (1898): 202-3.

1714 ————. Prehistoric Egypt. *Nature* 58 (1898): 31.

1715 ————. Excavations at Abadiyeh and Hû. *EEF, Archaeological Report for 1898-1899* (London, 1899): 1-3.

1716 ————. Flint implements from Egypt: An exhibition of flint implements shown by W.E. Hoyle to the Literary and Philosophical Society of Manchester. *Nature* 61 (1899-1900): 95.

1717 ————. *The Royal Tombs of the First Dynasty, 1900,* part 1. *EES, Mem.* 18 (London, 1900).

1718 ————. Sequences in prehistoric remains. *JRAI* 29 (1900): 295-301.

1719 ————. Sequences of prehistoric remains. *BAAS, Report of the 69th Meeting, Dover, 1899* (London, 1900): 876-77.

1720 ————. Tatouage des indigènes de l'Algérie. Représentations de navires égyptiens. *L'Anthropologie* 11 (1900): 485-86.

1721 ————. *Diospolis Parva. EEF, Special Extra Publication* 20 (London, 1901).

Reviewed: F.Ll. Griffith, See entry 942.
L'Anthropologie 13 (1902): 110-12 by M. Boule.
EEF, Archaeological Report for 1900-1901: 45.

1722 ———. The races of early Egypt. *JRAI* 31 (1901): 248.

1723 ———. *The Royal Tombs of the Earliest Dynasties, 1901,* part 2. *EEF* 21 and plate vol. (London, 1901).

1724 ———. Excavations at Abydos. *Man* 2 (1902): 88-90.

1725 ———. Prehistoric Egyptian carvings. *Man* 2 (1902): 161-62.

1726 ———. Prehistoric Egyptian figures. *Man* 2 (1902): 17.

1727 ———. Prehistoric Egyptian pottery. *Man* 2 (1902): 113.

1728 ———. Les plus anciens rois de l'Egypte. *RecTrav* 24 (1902): 214-16.

1729 ———. The races of early Egypt. *Man* 2 (1902): 248-55.
Reviewed: *L'Anthropologie* 14 (1903): 80-86.

1730 ———. *Abydos. EEF, Mem.* 22 and 24 (London, 1902-3).

1731 ———. The beginnings of the Egyptian kingdom. *BAAS, Report of the 73rd Meeting, Southport, 1903* (London, 1904).

1732 ———. The early monarchy of Egypt. *PSBA* 27 (1905): 279-85. [See also entry 1297.]

1733 ———. The Sinai expedition, 1904-1905. *Man* 5 (1905): 113-16.

1734 ———. Migrations. *JRAI* 36 (1906): 189-231.

1735 ———. *Gizeh and Rifeh. ERA* and *BSAE* 13 (London, 1907).

1736 ———. *Arts and Crafts of Ancient Egypt.* Chicago, 1910.

1737 ———. A cemetery of the earliest dynasties. *Man* 12 (1912): 73.

1738 ———. The earliest inscriptions. *Ancient Egypt* (1914): 61-77.

1739 ———. Egypt in Africa, 1: Funerary customs. *Ancient Egypt* (1914): 115-27.

1740 ———. Egypt in Africa, 2: Royalty, religious beliefs. *Ancient Egypt* (1915): 159-70.

1741 ———. For reconsideration (Onkh-em-ma'ot): Paintings of prehistoric towns. *Ancient Egypt* (1914): 33-34. [See also entry 1125.]

1742 ———. On the palaeolithic age and its climate in Egypt. *Proc. Geol. Soc.* (London, 1914): 19-20.

1743 ———. *Tarkhan II. BSAE* 26 (London, 1914).

1744 ———. The Egyptian Museum, University College. *Ancient Egypt* (1915): 168-80.

1745 ———. Egyptian wrought flints. *Nature* 95 (1915): 238.

1746 ———. The metals in Egypt. *Ancient Egypt* (1915): 12-23.

1747 ———. More of the earliest inscriptions. *Ancient Egypt* (1915): 78-83.

1748 ———. Palaeolithic age and climate in Egypt. *Geol. Mag.*, n.s., 2 (1915): 90-91.

1749 ———. Palaeolithic age and its climate in Egypt. *Nature* 94 (1914): 497.

1750 ———. The stone age in Egypt. *Ancient Egypt* (1915): 59-76 and 122-35.

1751 ———. The stone age in Egypt. *Nature* 95 (1915): 490.

1752 ———. New portions of the annals. *Ancient Egypt* (1916): 114-20.

1753 ———. Egypt and Mesopotamia. *Ancient Egypt* (1917): 26-36. [See also entry 226.]

1754 ———. *Prehistoric Egypt. Illustrated by over 1000 Objects in University College. ERA* and *BSAE* 31 (London, 1917).

1755 ———. Racial types at Abu Simbel. *Ancient Egypt* (1917): 57-61.

1756 ———. *Tools and Weapons. ERA* and *BSAE* 31. (London, 1917).

1757 ———. Entry not used.

1758 ———. Proceedings of the Session, 1918-1919 [on prehistoric Egypt.] *JMEOS* (1918-1919): 10.

1759 ———. The sphinxes of Tanis. *Ancient Egypt* (1920): 105.

1760 ———. *Corpus of Prehistoric Pottery and Palettes. ERA* and *BSAE* 32. (London, 1921). Repr., Warminster, n.d.

1761 ———. Egyptian palaeoliths. *Man* 21 (1921): 129-30.

1762 ———. [A comment on Northcote W. Thomas' 'Dualism in African Religions'.] *Ancient Egypt* (1922): 108-10.

1763 ———. The antiquity of Egyptian civilisation. *JEA* 9 (1923): 153-56.

1764 ———. Current fallacies about history. *Ancient Egypt* (1923): 78-84.

1765 ———. The British School in Egypt. *Ancient Egypt* (1924): 33-38.

1766 ———. The British School in Egypt: Excavations at Qau. *Ancient Egypt* (1924): 16-17.

1767 ———. The Caucasian Atlantis and Egypt. *Ancient Egypt* (1924): 123-24.

1768 ———. Prehistoric ivory figurine from Egypt. *Nature* 114 (1924): 587.

1769 ———. Early man in Egypt. *Man* 25 (1925): 129-30.

1770 ———. *Tombs of the Courtiers and Oxyrhynchus.* London, 1925. [With chapters by Alan Gardiner, Hilda Petrie and M.A. Murray.]

1771 ———. The Badarian civilisation. *Man* 26 (1926): 63.

1772 ———. Early Egypt and the Caucasus. *Nature* 118 (1926): 514-15.

1773 ———. Early Egypt and the Fayum. *Nature* 118 (1926): 696.

1774 ———. Early man in Egypt. *Oriens: The Oriental Review* 1 (1926): 19.

1775 ———. Observations on 'The recent geology and neolithic industry of the northern Fayum' by Miss E.W. Gardner and G. Caton-Thompson. *JRAI* 56 (1926): 325-26. [See also entry 855.]

1776 ———. The origins of the Book of the Dead. *Ancient Egypt* (1926): 41-45.

1777 ———. Small objects from Nagadeh. *Ancient Egypt* (1927): 14-15.

1778 ———. Osiris in the tree and pillar. *Ancient Egypt* (1928): 40-44.

1779 ———. The age of Egypt. *Ancient Egypt* (1929): 33-42.

1780 ———. The Egyptian lily. *Ancient Egypt* (1929): 65-73.

1781 ———. The linking of Egypt and Palestine. *Antiquity* 4 (1930): 279-84.

1782 ———. The peoples of Egypt. *Ancient Egypt* (1931): 77-85.

1783 ———. A revision of history. *Ancient Egypt* (1931): 1-20.

1784 ———. *Seventy Years in Archaeology.* London, 1931.

1785 ———. Egyptian shipping. *Ancient Egypt* (1933): 1-14.

1786 ———. *Ceremonial Slate Palettes. BSAE* 66a (London, 1935). [With preface and intro. by Hilda F. Petrie; additional notes to text by M.A. Murray.] Repr., 1953.

Reviewed: *CdE* 57 (1954): 62-63 by P. Gilbert.

1787 ———. The dynastic invasion of Egypt. *Syro-Egypt* 2 (London, 1937): 6-8.

1788 ———. The junction of geology and Egyptology. *Syro-Egypt* 2 (London, 1937): 9-10.

1789 ———. The prehistoric constitution of Egypt. *Syro-Egypt* 2 (London, 1937): 6-9.

1790 ———. The meaning of the Fayum. *Syro-Egypt* 3 (London, 1938): 12-15.

1791 ———. The Upper Palaeolithic in the light of recent discoveries. *Syro-Egypt* 4 (London, 1938): 8-9.

1792 ———. *The Making of Egypt.* London, 1939.

1793 ———. *Corpus of Proto-Dynastic Pottery: 30 Plates of Drawings. BSAE* 66b (London, 1953).

———. See entries 363, 1226 and 1852.

1794 **Petrie, William Matthew Flinders, Guy Brunton** and **M.A. Murray.** *Lahun II. ERA* and *BSAE* 23 (London, 1923).

1795 **Petrie, William Matthew Flinders** and **J.E. Quibell.** *Naqada and Ballas. ERA* and *BSAE* 1. (London, 1896).

1796 **Petrie, William Matthew Flinders, G.A. Wainwright** and **A.H. Gardiner.** *Memphis V and Tarkhan I. ERA* and *BSAE* (London, 1913).

Reviewed: *JEA* 1 (1914): 77-78 by J.G. Milne.

1797 **Petrie, William Matthew Flinders, G.A. Wainwright** and **E. Mackay.** *The Labyrinth, Gerzeh and Mazghuneh. ERA* and *BSAE* 21 (London, 1912).

1798 **Phillips, G.B.** The composition of some ancient bronzes. *Amer. Anthrop.* 24 (1922): 129-43.

1799 **Phillips, J.L.** *Two Final Palaeolithic Sites in the Nile Valley and their External Relations. Geological Survey of Egypt,* paper 57 (Cairo, 1973).

———. See entries 178 and 557.

1800 **Phillips, J.L.** and **O. Bar-Yosef.** Notes and news: Jebel Maghara (Northern Sinai). *IEJ* 23 (1973): 106-7.

1801 ———. Gebel Maghara, Northern Sinai. *Paléorient* 2 (1974, publ. 1976): 83-84.

1802 **Phillips, J.L.** and **K.W. Butzer.** A Silsilian occupation site (65-2B-II) of the Kom Ombo Plain, Upper Egypt: Geology, archaeology and palaeo-ecology. *Quaternaria* 17 (1973): 343-86.

1803 **Phillips, W.** Recent discoveries in the Egyptian Fayum and Sinai. *Science* 107 (1948): 666-70.

1804 **Pickering, Charles.** *The Races of Man.* London, 1840. Revised ed. 1854.

1805 **Piehl, Karl Fredrik.** <232> Bronsalder i Egypten. *Ymer* 8 (Stockholm, 1889): 94-102. [See also entry 1449.]

1806 ———. Sur le sens du groupe . *PSBA* 11 (1889): 139-42.

1807 ———. Varia: 63: A propos d'un prétendu âge du bronze en Egypte. Examen de la thèse de M. Montelius. *ZÄS* 28 (1890): 17-19. [See also entry 1448.]

Piontek, J. See entry 1037.

1808 **Piotrovski, Boris.** Miscellanea. *Publ. de la soc. égyptol. de l'Univ. de l'Etat de Leningrad* 2 (1929): 33.

1809 ———. Deux enseignes sur les barques égyptiens prédynastiques. *Publ. de la Soc. égyptol. de l'Univ. de l'Etat de Leningrad* 5 (1930): 17.

Reviewed: *Ancient Egypt* (1930): 124.

1810 ———. *The Early Dynastic Settlement of Khar-Daoud.* Cairo, 1967.

1811 **Piotrovski, Boris** and **I. Snegizeff.** Ägyptische vordynastische Altertümer aus den Kollektionen der staatlichen Ermitage. *Publ. de la Soc. Eegyptol. de liv. de l'Etat de Leningrad* 5 (1930): 18-24.

1812 **Pirenne, Jacques.** *Histoire des Institutions et du Droit Privé de l'Ancienne Egypte.* 1: *Des Origines à la Fin de la IVe Dynastie.* Brussels, 1932.

1813 ———. Les origines et la genèse de la monarchie en Egypte. *Annales du Centre d'Etude des Religion* 1 (Brussels, 1962): 49-59.

1814 **Piroutet, Maurice.** Questions relatives à l'âge du bronze. Apparition du bronze en Orient. *L'Anthropologie* 28 (1917): 55-91.

1815 **Pittard, E.** *Les races et l'Histoire. Introduction Ethnologique à l'Histoire. L'Evolution de l'Humanité* 5 (Paris, 1924). Transl. by V.C.C. Collum as *Race and History: An Ethnographical Introduction to History.* London, 1926.

1816 **Pitt-Rivers, Augustus Henry Lane Fox.** On the discovery of chert implements in stratified gravel, in the Nile Valley, near Thebes. *JRAI* 11 (1882): 382-400.

1817 **Pollard, W.B.** Black topped predynastic pottery. *Cairo Science J.* 6 (1912): 72-75.

1818 **Polotsky, Hans J.** Egyptians at the dawn of civilization. In *The World History of the Jewish People,* series 1 (1964).

1819 **Pond, Alonzo William et al.** *Prehistoric Habitation Sites in the Sahara and North Africa. Beloit: Beloit College, Logan Museum Bulletin* 5 (n.d.).

1820 **Pons, A.** *Les Origines de l'Embaumement et l'Egypte Prédynastique.* Montpellier, 1910.

1821 **Poole, Reginald Stuart.** <236> *Horae Aegyptiacae: Or, the Chronology of Ancient Egypt, Discovered from Astronomical and Hieroglyphical Records upon its Monuments.* London, 1851.

1822 ———. The ethnology of Egypt. *Trans. Ethnol. Soc.* 2 (1863): 260-64.

1823 ———. On the ethnic relations of the Egyptian race. *Rep. Brit. Assoc.* 34 (1864): 146-47.

1824 ———. On the Egyptian classification of the races of man. *JRAI* 16 (1887): 370-77.

1825 **Poplin, F.** Deux cas particuliers de débitage par Usure. *Premier Colloque Intern. sur l'Industrie de l'Os dans la Préhistoire, Univ. de Provence* (1977): 85-92.

1826 **Porteres, R.** and **J. Barrau.** Origin, development and expansion of agricultural techniques. In J. Ki-Zerbo (ed.), *General History of Africa,* 1: *Methodology and African Prehistory.* (London and Berkeley, 1981): 687-705.

1827 **Posnansky, Merrick.** Kingship, archaeology and historical myth. *The Uganda Journal* 1 (1966): 1-12. [Repr. in entry 575, pp. 45-55.]

1828 **Postovskaya, N.M.** [Study of the formation of the ancient Egyptian state.] *BECTHNK* 1 (1947): 233-49. [In Russian]

1829 ———. [Abydos et Memphis. Pour déterminer les monuments de la première dynastie.] *BECTHNK* 3 (1959): 103-29. [In Russian]

1830 **Prausnitz, M.W.** Abydos and combed ware. *PEQ* 86 (1954): 91-96.

1831 **Priault, Osmond de Beauvoir.** *Quaestiones Mosaicae; or, the First Part of the Book of Genesis Compared with the Remains of Ancient Religions.* London, 1854.

1832 **Price, Frederick George Hilton.** <237> Notes upon ancient Egyptian implements. *JRAI* 16 (1885): 56-64.

1833 ———. Notes upon some predynastic and early dynastic antiquities from Egypt in the writer's collection. *Archaeologia* 56 (1889): 337-50.

1834 ———. Two objects from prehistoric tombs. *ZÄS* 37 (1899): 47.

1835 ————. On some remarkable flint lance-heads from Luxor. *Proc. Soc. Antiquaries,* 2nd ser., 16 (1900): 277.

1836 ————. Some ivories from Abydos. *PSBA* 22 (1900): 160-61.

Pritchard, D.H. See entry 422.

1837 **Pritchard, James Cowles.** <237> *Natural History of Man.* London, 1855.

1838 ————. *Researches into the Physical History of Man.* [Ed. and with an introduction by George W. Stocking, Jr.] Chicago, 1973.

1839 **de Prorok, Byron K.** Découvertes néolithiques dans le désert de Libye. *L'Illustration* 86 (Paris, 1928) 172-77.

1840 **Protsch, R.** and **R. Berger.** Earliest radiocarbon dates for domesticated animals. *Science* 179 (1973): 235-39.

1841 **Pruner, Franz.** <239> *Die Ueberbleibsel der aegyptischen Menschenrace. Eine Abhandlung gelesen am 24 Aug. 1846* (Munich, 1846).

1842 ————. Recherches sur l'origine de l'ancienne race égyptienne. *MSAP* 1 (1860-63): 399-433.

1843 ————. Sur l'âge de pierre en Egypte. *BSAP,* 2nd ser., 4 (1869): 705-10.

Q

1844 **Quetelet, L.A.J.** Des proportions du corps humain chez les Grecs, chez les Egyptiens, les Romains . . . *Bull. Acad. Sci.* 15, 1 (Bruxelles, 1848): 580-93; 15, 2 (1848): 16-27; 16, 2 (1849): 17-27; 17, 2 (1850): 38-48 and 95-108.

1845 **Quibell, James Edward.** <240> On the date of the period in Egypt called Neolithic, Libyan and New Race. *ZÄS* 35 (1897): 134-40.

1846 ———. Slate palette from Hierakonpolis. *ZÄS* 36 (1898): 81-84.

1847 ———. *El-Kab. ERA* and *BSAE* 3 (London, 1898).

1848 ———. Flint dagger from Gebelein. *ASAE* 2 (1901): 131-32.

1849 ———. *Catalogue générale des antiquités égyptiennes du Musée du Cairo, nos. 11001-12000 et 14001-14754: Archaic Objects.* Vols. 23 and 24. Cairo, 1904-5.

1850 ———. *Excavations at Saqqara (1912-1914): Archaic Mastabas.* Cairo, 1923.

———. See entry 1795.

1851 **Quibell, J.E.** and **F.W. Green.** *Hierakonpolis II. ERA* and *BSAE* 5 (London, 1902).

1852 **Quibell, J.E.** and **W.M.F. Petrie.** *Hierakonpolis I. ERA* and *BSAE* 4 (London, 1900).

Reviewed: *L'Anthropologie* 11 (1900): 759 by M. Boule.

R

Race, G.J. See entry 2389.

1853 **Raglan** [Lord]. Mr. Frankfort and the Hamites. *Man* 49 (1949): 48. [See also entry 811.]

1854 **Raikes, R.L.** and **A. Palmieri.** Environmental conditions in the Nile Valley over the past 10,000 years. *J. Human Evol.* 1 (1973): 147-54. [Repr. in entry 332.]

Ralph, E.V. See entry 1435.

1855 **Randall-MacIver, David.** <190> Prehistoric cemeteries. *EES Archaeological Report for 1899-1900* (1900): 1-2.

1856 ———. On recent anthropometrical work in Egypt. *BAAS, Report of the 69th Meeting, Dover, 1899* (London, 1900): 875.

1857 ———. Recent anthropometrical work in Egypt. *JRAI* 30 (1900): 95-103.

1858 ———. *The Earliest Inhabitants of Abydos: A Craniological Study.* Oxford, 1901.

1859 ———. Libyan notes. *Man* 1 (1901): 75-77.

1860 **Randall-MacIver, David** and **M.A. Laycock.** A prehistoric cemetery at El-Amrah in Egypt: Preliminary report of excavations. *Man* 1 (1901): 49-54.

1861 **Randall-MacIver, David** and **A.C. Mace.** *El-Amrah and Abydos, 1899-1901. EEF Special Extra Publication* 23 (London, 1902). [With a chapter by F. Ll. Griffith.]

Reviewed: *Man* 3 (1903): 126-27.

1862 **Ranke, Hermann.** <242> *Alter und Herkunft der ägyptischen 'Löwenjagd-Palette'. SHAW* 5 (Heidelberg, 1925).

1863 ———. Eine Bemerkung zur 'Narmer Palette'. *Studia Orientalia Edidit Societas Orientalis Fennica I Commentationes in Honorem Knut Tallqvist, Helsingforisise* 4 (1925): 167-75.

1864 ———. The origin of the Egyptian tomb statue. *Harvard Theological Review* 28, 1 (1935): 45-53.

1865 ———. The beginnings of civilization in Egypt. *JAOS* 59, suppl. (1939): 3-16.

1866 **Raphael, Max.** *Prehistoric Pottery and Civilization in Egypt. Bollingen Series,* no. 8. (Princeton, N.J., 1947). Transl. from German by Norbert Guterman.

1867 **Ravenstein, Ernest G.** *Illustrations of the Principal Varieties of the Human Race, Arranged According to the System of Dr. Latham.* London, 1856.

1868 **Rawlinson, George.** <242> *Egypt and Babylon, from Scripture and Profane Sources.* London, 1885.

1869 **Ray, Sudhansu Kumar.** *Prehistoric India and Ancient Egypt.* New Delhi, 1956.

Reviewed: *Artibus Asiae* 20 (1957): 229 by J.D. Cooney.

1870 **Read, F.W.** Boats or fortified villages? *BIFAO* 13 (1917): 145-51.

1871 **Rebuffat, R.** Protohistoire et histoire en Libye intérieure au IIIe siècle de notre ère. L'Age du fer en méditerranée. *Ajaccio Pâques* (1947): 49-68.

1872 **Reder, D.G.** Ancient Egypt, a Centre of Agriculture. *J. World History* 4 (1958): 801-17. [This Journal is also publ. in Engl., Fr., & Span.]

1873 ————. [The economic development of Lower Egypt (the Delta) in the Archaic Period (5th-4th millennia before present).] *Drevenu Egupet* (1960): 172-79. [With French summary 179-80.]

1874 **Reed, Charles A.** A natural history of Kurkur Oasis, Libyan Desert, Egypt, part 1: Introduction. *Postilla* (Peabody Museum, Yale Univ., 1964).

1875 ————. Animal domestication in the prehistoric Near East. *Science* 130 (1959): 1629-39. [Reprinted in J.R. Caldwell (ed.), *New Roads to Yesteryear: Essays in Archaeology, Articles from Science.* (London, 1966): 178-209.]

1876 ————. A human frontal bone from the late Pleistocene of the Kom-Ombo plain. *Man* 95 (1965): 101-4.

1877 ————. The Yale University Prehistoric Expedition to Nubia, 1962-1965. *Discovery: The Magazine of the Peabody Museum of Natural History, Yale University* 1, 2 (1966): 16-23.

1878 ————. *Preliminary Report on the Archaeological Research of the Yale University Prehistoric Expedition to Nubia 1962-1963.* Cairo, 1967.

1879 ————. Origins of agriculture: Discussion and some conclusions. In his *Origins of Agriculture.* (The Hague, 1977): 879-953.

————. See entry 2424.

1880 **Reed, Charles A., Martin A. Baumhoff, Karl W. Butzer, Heinz Walter** and **David S. Boloyan.** Preliminary report on the archaeological aspects of the research of the Yale University Prehistoric Expedition to Nubia, 1962-1963. *Fouilles en Nubie (1961-63).* (Cairo, 1967): 145-56.

1881 **Reil,** Dr. **Wilhelm.** <244> Bearbeitete Feuersteine von Helwân (Aegypten). *Verh. Berlin Gesells. für Anthrop.* (1876): 156.

1882 **Reilly, Frank E.** *Guidebook to the Geology and Archaeology of Egypt.* [Petroleum Exploration Society of Libya, 6th Annual Field Conference.] Tripoli, 1964.

1883 **Reinach, Adolphe-J.** L'Egypte préhistorique. *Revue des Idées* 8 (1908): 154-92. Also publ. separately, Paris, 1908.

Reviewed: *L'Anthropologie* 19 (1908): 631.
Revue des Et. ethnol. et sociol. 1 (1908): 533 by C. Boreux.
Anthropos 3 (Vienna, 1908): 839.
OLZ (1908): 508-9 by Max Muller.
RSO 2 (1908-1909): 254-55.

1884 **Reinach, Salomon.** Description raisonnée du Musée de Saint-Germain.

1885 ————. Note sur un passage de Strabon (Dolmens en Egypt). L'Anthropologie 7 (1891): 202-3.

1886 ————. L'Age du bronze en Egypte. *L'Anthropologie* 2 (1896): 104-8.

1887 ————. Le préhistoire en Egypte, d'après de récentes publications. *L'Anthropologie* 8

(1897): 327-43.

1888 ———. Nouvelles découvertes égéenes. *L'Anthropologie* 10 (1899): 513-21.

1889 ———. A propos de bateaux égyptiens. *L'Anthropologie* 11 (1900): 347.

1890 ———. Le Musée Ashmoléen d'Oxford en 1901. *Revue Archéol.*, 3rd ser., 40 (1902): 407-9.

1891 ———. Les Thraces en Egypte. *Revue Archéol.*, 4th ser., 2 (1903): 347.

1892 ———. Le fer en Egypte. *L'Anthropologie* 15 (1904): 116-17.

1893 ———. Les tombes 'prédynastiques' en Egypte. *Revue Archéol.*, 4th ser., 18 (1911): 185.

1894 ———. Silex aurignaciens en Egypte. *Revue Archéol.*, 5th ser., 16 (1922): 341-42.

1895 ———. La civilization badarienne. *Revue Archéol.*, 5th ser., 22 (1925): 292.

1896 ———. L'homme préhistoirique en Egypte. *Revue Archéol.*, 5th ser., 24 (1926): 269.

1897 ———. Gravures rupestres du désert Libyque. *Revue Archéol.*, 5th ser., 27 (1928): 346.

1898 **Reineke, Walter F.** (ed.). *Acts of the 1st Inter. Congress of Egyptology, Cairo, Oct. 2-10, 1976. (=Akad. der Wiss. der DDR Zentralinstitut für alte Geschichte und Archäologie; Schriften zur Geschichte und Kultur des alten Orients* 14). Berlin, 1979.

1899 **Reisner, George Andrew.** <244> Amélineau's excavations. *AJA* 2 (1898): 101.

1900 ———. Work of the University of California at El-Ahaiwah and Naga-ed-Dêr. *EES Archaeological Report for 1900-1901* (London, 1901): 23-25.

1901 ———. Work of the University of California at Naga-ed-Dêr. *ASAE* 4 (1904): 105-9.

1902 ———. *The Early Dynastic Cemeteries of Naga-ed-Dêr,* part 1. *UCPEA* 2 (Leipzig, 1928).
Reviewed: *Revue des Et. ethnol. et sociol.* 1 (1908): 371-73 by A.J. Reinach.

1903 ———. The significance of the predynastic period in Egypt. *Cairo Science J.* 2, 17 (1908): 47-50.

1904 ———. *The Archaeological Survey of Nubia: Report for 1907-1908. First Archaeological Report.* Cairo, 1910.

1905 ———. A scribe's tablet found by the Hearst Expedition at Giza. *ZÄS* 48 (1910): 113-14.

1906 ———. Outline of the ancient history of the Sudan. *SNR* 1 (1918): 3-15.

1907 ———. *Excavations at Kerma. Harvard African Studies,* vols. 5-6 (Cambridge, 1923).
Reviewed: *SNR* 7 (1924): 117 by J. Crowfoot.

1908 ———. The position of early grave stelae. In entry 941, pp. 324-31.

1909 ———. *The Development of the Egyptian Tomb Down to the Accession of Cheops.* Cambridge, 1936.

1910 ———. *A History of the Giza Necropolis,* 1. Cambridge, 1942.

1911 ———. *Excavations at Kerma: The Eastern Cemetery. Harvard African Studies,* vol 5, part 3 (Cambridge, 1923): 68-72, 77, 280. [Reprinted as 'Suttee Burial at Kerma' in entry 1023, pp. 105-12.]

1912 ———. Black-topped pottery. *JARCE* 5 (1966) 7-10. [Ed. with intro. by E.L.B. Terrace.]

1913 **Reisner, George Andrew, Grafton Elliot Smith** and **Douglas E. Derry.** *The Archaeological Survey of Nubia,* bulletin 11. Cairo, 1909.

1914 **Reiss, W.** Funde aus der Steinzeit Aegyptens. *Verh. Berlin Gesells. für Anthrop.* (1890): 700-12.

1915 ———. Neue Feuersteingeräte aus Aegypten und Hrn. Flinders Petrie's neueste Forschungen. *Verh. Berlin Gesells. für Anthrop.* (1891): 474-78.

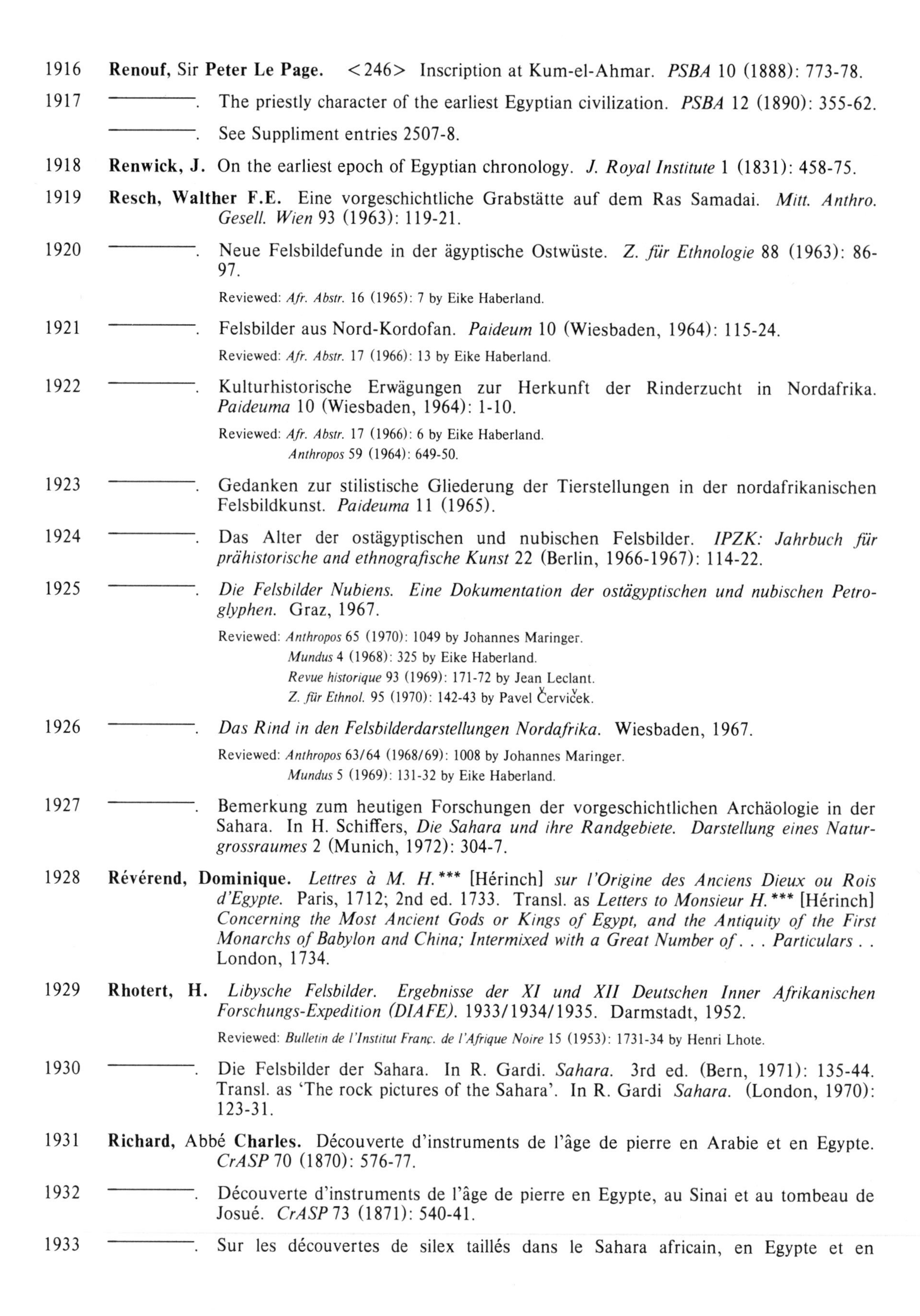

1916 **Renouf,** Sir **Peter Le Page.** <246> Inscription at Kum-el-Ahmar. *PSBA* 10 (1888): 773-78.

1917 ———. The priestly character of the earliest Egyptian civilization. *PSBA* 12 (1890): 355-62.

———. See Suppliment entries 2507-8.

1918 **Renwick, J.** On the earliest epoch of Egyptian chronology. *J. Royal Institute* 1 (1831): 458-75.

1919 **Resch, Walther F.E.** Eine vorgeschichtliche Grabstätte auf dem Ras Samadai. *Mitt. Anthro. Gesell. Wien* 93 (1963): 119-21.

1920 ———. Neue Felsbildefunde in der ägyptische Ostwüste. *Z. für Ethnologie* 88 (1963): 86-97.

Reviewed: *Afr. Abstr.* 16 (1965): 7 by Eike Haberland.

1921 ———. Felsbilder aus Nord-Kordofan. *Paideum* 10 (Wiesbaden, 1964): 115-24.

Reviewed: *Afr. Abstr.* 17 (1966): 13 by Eike Haberland.

1922 ———. Kulturhistorische Erwägungen zur Herkunft der Rinderzucht in Nordafrika. *Paideuma* 10 (Wiesbaden, 1964): 1-10.

Reviewed: *Afr. Abstr.* 17 (1966): 6 by Eike Haberland.
Anthropos 59 (1964): 649-50.

1923 ———. Gedanken zur stilistische Gliederung der Tierstellungen in der nordafrikanischen Felsbildkunst. *Paideuma* 11 (1965).

1924 ———. Das Alter der ostägyptischen und nubischen Felsbilder. *IPZK: Jahrbuch für prähistorische and ethnografische Kunst* 22 (Berlin, 1966-1967): 114-22.

1925 ———. *Die Felsbilder Nubiens. Eine Dokumentation der ostägyptischen und nubischen Petroglyphen.* Graz, 1967.

Reviewed: *Anthropos* 65 (1970): 1049 by Johannes Maringer.
Mundus 4 (1968): 325 by Eike Haberland.
Revue historique 93 (1969): 171-72 by Jean Leclant.
Z. für Ethnol. 95 (1970): 142-43 by Pavel Červiček.

1926 ———. *Das Rind in den Felsbilderdarstellungen Nordafrika.* Wiesbaden, 1967.

Reviewed: *Anthropos* 63/64 (1968/69): 1008 by Johannes Maringer.
Mundus 5 (1969): 131-32 by Eike Haberland.

1927 ———. Bemerkung zum heutigen Forschungen der vorgeschichtlichen Archäologie in der Sahara. In H. Schiffers, *Die Sahara und ihre Randgebiete. Darstellung eines Naturgrossraumes* 2 (Munich, 1972): 304-7.

1928 **Révérend, Dominique.** *Lettres à M. H.**** [Hérinch] *sur l'Origine des Anciens Dieux ou Rois d'Egypte.* Paris, 1712; 2nd ed. 1733. Transl. as *Letters to Monsieur H.**** [Hérinch] *Concerning the Most Ancient Gods or Kings of Egypt, and the Antiquity of the First Monarchs of Babylon and China; Intermixed with a Great Number of. . . Particulars . .* London, 1734.

1929 **Rhotert, H.** *Libysche Felsbilder. Ergebnisse der XI und XII Deutschen Inner Afrikanischen Forschungs-Expedition (DIAFE).* 1933/1934/1935. Darmstadt, 1952.

Reviewed: *Bulletin de l'Institut Franç. de l'Afrique Noire* 15 (1953): 1731-34 by Henri Lhote.

1930 ———. Die Felsbilder der Sahara. In R. Gardi. *Sahara.* 3rd ed. (Bern, 1971): 135-44. Transl. as 'The rock pictures of the Sahara'. In R. Gardi *Sahara.* (London, 1970): 123-31.

1931 **Richard,** Abbé **Charles.** Découverte d'instruments de l'âge de pierre en Arabie et en Egypte. *CrASP* 70 (1870): 576-77.

1932 ———. Découverte d'instruments de l'âge de pierre en Egypte, au Sinai et au tombeau de Josué. *CrASP* 73 (1871): 540-41.

1933 ———. Sur les découvertes de silex taillés dans le Sahara africain, en Egypte et en

Palestine. *C.r. Congr. Intern. Sc. Anthrop.* (Paris, 1878): 278-82.

1934 **Ricke, Herbert.** Der hohe Sand in Heliopolis. *ZÄS* 71 (1935): 107-11.

1935 ————. *Bemerkungen zur ägyptischen Baukunst des Alten Reichs. Beiträge Bf.* 4, 5. 2 vol. Zürich and Cairo, 1944-1950.

1936 **Ridley, R.T.** *The Unification of Egypt, as Seen through a Study of the Major Knife-Handles, Palettes and Mace Heads.* Deception Bay, Australia, 1973.

1937 **Ries, Julien.** La religion de la préhistoire égyptienne: Les étapes de la recherches. In Emmanuel Anati (ed.), *Valcomonica Symposium, 1972: Actes du Symposium International sur les Religions de la Préhistoire* (Brescia, Italy, 1975): 293-312.

1938 **Ritchie, Patrick Dunbar.** An examination of some predynastic pottery pigments. *Technical Studies in the Field of the Fine Arts* 4 (Lancester, Pa., 1936): 234-36.

1939 **Rizkana, Ibrahim.** Centres of settlement in prehistoric Egypt in the area between Helwan and Heliopolis. *Bull. de l'Inst. Fouad Ier du Désert* 2 (1952): 117-30.

1940 ————. Two new Egyptian cultures. *30 Pan-Afr. Congr. on Prehist., Livingstone 1955* (London, 1957): 391-93.

————. See entries 48-49.

1941 **Robertson, J.H.** and **R.J. Bradley.** On the presence of the Negro in the Nile Valley. *Current Anthropology* 19 (1978): 177-78.

1942 **Robertson, J.M.** and **H. Carpenter.** The metallography of some ancient Egyptian implements. *Nature* (1930): 859-62.

1943 **Robinson, Arthur E.** Egypt: Rock drawings. *Man* 34 (1934): 32.

1944 ————. Rock pictures. *J. African Society* 33 (1934): 353-60.

1945 ————. Nubian rock pictures. *Man* 35 (1935): 160.

1946 **Robinson, Ronald, John Gallagher** with **Alice Denny.** *Africa and the Victorians: The Official Mind of Imperialism.* New York, 1961; repr. Garden City, N.J., 1968. 2nd ed. 1981.

1947 **Roeder, Günther.** <251> Die vorgeschichtliche Plastik (Ägyptens in ihrer Bedeutung für die Bildung des ägyptischen Stils). *Jahrbuch für prähist. und ethnogr. Kunst* (1926): 64-84.

Reviewed: *L'Anthropologie* 37 (1927): 545.

Rogers, M.S. See entries 15 and 1062.

1948 **Rognon, P.** Essai d'interprétation des variations climatique au Sahara depuis 40,000 ans. *Revue de Géographie Physique et Géologie Dynamique* 18 (1976): 251-82.

1949 **Rognon, P.** and **M.A.J. Williams.** Late Quaternary climatic changes in Australia and North Africa. *Palaeogeography, Palaeoclimatology and Palaeoecology* 21 (1977): 285-327.

1950 **Rosen, Eric Gustav Bloomfield von.** Har den fornegyptiska kulturen spirat hos ett träskfold. *Ymer* 49 (Stockholm, 1929): 237-52. Also publ. separately as *Did Prehistoric Egyptian Culture Spring from a Marshdwelling People? Riksmuseets etnografiska advelning, Smarre Meddelanden,* nr. 8. (Stockholm, 1929).

Reviewed: L'Anthropologie 40 (1931): 488 by M. Boule.

1951 **Rösing, F.W.** Prädynastiche Menschenreste von der Nilinsel Elephantine von Aswan (Ägypten). *Homo* 21 (1970): 210-20.

1952 **Rössler-Köhler, Ursula.** Kannibalismus. *LdÄ* 3 (1975-): 314-15.

1953 **Rostovzev, M.** L'Age du cuivre dans le Caucase septentrional et les civilisations de Soumer et de l'Egypte protodynastique. *Revue Archéol.*, 5th ser., 12 (1920): 1-37.

1954 **Roubert, C.** Evolution de l'outillage lithique du néolithique de tradition capsienne. *Actes du premier Colloque International d'Archéologie Africaine, Fort-Lamy, Chad, 11-16 Decembre, 1966. Etudes et Documents Tchadiens, Mémoires* 1 (Fort-Lamy, Chad, 1969): 338-57.

1955 **de Rougé, Olivier Charles Camille Emmanuel.** <84> *Recherches sur les Monuments qu'on Peut Attribuer aux Six Premiers Dynasties de Manéthon. MAIBL* 25 (Paris, 1866).

1956 ———. Origine de la race égyptienne. *Mém de la Soc. Nationale des Antiquaires de France,* 6th ser., 4 (1894): 264-87.

1957 **Roulin, Dom E.** Ivoires de la Haute-Egypte. *Revue Archéol.,* 4th ser., 3 (1904): 97-110.

1958 **Rowe, Alan.** Studies in the archaeology of the Near East I: The derivations of the nomenclatures of the cultures of the Egyptian Palaeolithic and Predynastic periods. *Bull. John Rylands Library* 43 (Manchester, 1960-61): 480-91.

1959 **Rubensohn, O.** and **F. Knatz.** Bericht über die Ausgrabungen bei Abusir el-Mäläq in Jahre 1903. *ZÄS* 41 (1904): 1-21.

1960 **Rudbeck, Claus.** *Ichthyologiae Biblecae* . . . Upsalae, 1705.

1961 **Ruffer,** Sir **Marc Armand.** <256> On the physical effects of consanguineous marriage in the royal families of ancient Egypt. *Proc. Royal Soc. Med.* 7 (1919): 145-90. [Repr. in Moody, R.L. (ed.), *Studies in the Palaeopathology of Egypt.* (Chicago, 1921): 322-57.]

Reviewed: *Ancient Egypt* (1922): 126.

1962 **R[ugiu], G.** La spedizione Almasy-Penderel nel deserto Libico. *Boll. della Soc. R. Geogr. Ital.,* 6th ser., 11 (Roma, 1934): 578-80.

1963 **Rühle von Lilienstern.** *Geographische Darstellungen zur ältesten Geschichte und Geographie von Aethiopien und Aegypten.* Berlin, 1827.

1964 **Rusch, Adolf.** Die Entwicklung der Grabsteinformen im Alten Reich. *ZÄS* 58 (1923): 101-24.

1965 **de Rustafjaell, Robert.** <256> *Palaeolithic Vessels of Egypt; or, the Earliest Handiwork of Man.* London, 1907.

Reviewed: *Revue des Et. ethnogr. et sociol.* 1 (Paris, 1908): 302 by A.J. Reinach.
Nature 80 (1910): 247.

1966 ———. *The Light of Egypt from Recently Discovered Predynastic and Early Christian Records.* London, 1909.

Reviewed: *Nature* 83 (1910): 247.

1967 ———. *Antiquités d'Egypte Prédynastiques, Romaines et Chrétiennes, Provenant de l'Ancienne Collection de . . .* Paris, 1914.

1968 ———. Résumé sommaire de l'âge de pierre en Egypte. Civilisation et arts depuis les temps les plus reculés jusqu'à la fin de la Royauté moyenne. Traduit part Oscar Schmidt. *Congrès Préhistorique de France, C.r. de la 5e session, Beauvais, 1909* (Paris, 1910): 297-322.

1969 ———. *The Stone Age of Egypt. A Record of Recently Discovered Implements and Products of Handicraft of the Archaic Nilotic Races Inhabiting the Thebaid.* New York, 1914.

1970 ———. *Catalogue of the Collection of Egyptian Antiquities, Formed in Egypt by R. de Rustafjaell. Esq., Queen's Gate, S.W., Which Will Be Sold by Auction, by Messrs. Sotheby, Wilkinson and Hodge...* London, 1906.

1971 **Rutot, A.** Note préliminaire sur les silex paléolithiques de la vallée du Nil. *BSAB* 21 (1902-1903).

1972 ———. La géologie de la vallée du Nil et les nouvelles découvertes éolithiques et paléolithiques qui y ont été faites. *Bull. Soc. Belge de Géol., de Paléontol. et d'Hydrol.* 19 (Bruxelles, 1905): 260-62.

S

1973 **Saad, Zaki Youssef.** *Royal Excavations at Saqqara and Helwan (1941-1945). Suppl. ASAE,* Cahier 3 (Cairo, 1947).

1974 ————. *The Royal Excavations at Helwan.* Cairo, 1945-1947.

1975 ————. Recent excavations which throw new light on the Egyptian architecture of five thousand years ago: Aspects of art and life revealed in the First Dynasty Necropolis of Helwan. *ILN* 212 (1948): 644-45.

1976 ————. Fouilles royales —VIe campagne: 1942-1948. *CdE* 24 (1949): 48.

1977 ————. The royal excavations at Helwan. *Bull. Inst. Fouad Ier du Désert* 1 (1951): 151-56.

1978 ————. Nouvelles découvertes dans les fouilles de Hélouan. *La Revue du Caire* 33 (1954): 5-11.

1979 ————. *Ceiling Stelae in Second Dynasty Tombs from the Excavations at Helwan. Suppl. ASAE,* Cahier 21 (Cairo, 1957).

1980 ————. *The Excavations at Helwan: Art and Civilization in the First and Second Egyptian Dynasties.* [Ed. and with a foreward by J. Frank Autry.] Norman, Oklahoma, 1969.

Reviewed: *BiOr* 28 (1971): 42-49 by P. Kaplony.
CdE 45 (1970): 95-98 by Winifried Barta.
JARCE 8 (1969-1970): 95 by H. Goedicke.
Man 5 (1970): 137 by J.S.N. Wright.

————. See also entries 707 and 711.

1981 **Saffirio, Luigi.** L'alimentzione umana nell'Egitto preistorico (dalla raccolta alla produzione del Cibo). *Aegyptus* 45 (1965): 20-35.

1982 ————. L'Alimentazione umana nell'Egitto preistorico, part 3. *Aegyptus* 46 (1966): 26-59.

1983 ————. Food and dietary habits in ancient Egypt. *J. Human Evol.* 1 (1972): 297-305. [Repr. in entry 332, pp. 297-305.]

1983a ————. Le origini dell'agricoltura: l'ipotesti nilotica. *Archivo per l'Antropologia e la Etnologia* 104 (Florence, 1974): 245-60.

1984 **Said, Rushdi.** *The Geology of Egypt.* Amsterdam and New York, 1975.

1985 ————. Pleistocene geology of the Dungul region, Southern Libyan Desert, Egypt. In entry 1045, pp. 7-18.

1986 ———. The geological evolution of the River Nile. In entry 2388, pp. 7-44.

———. See entries 2390-96 and 2420-22.

1987 **Said, Rushdi, C.C. Albritton, F. Wendorf, R. Schild,** and **M. Kobusiewicz.** Remarks on the Holocene geology and archaeology of northern Fayum Desert. *Archaeologia Polona* 13 (1972): 7-22.

1988 **Said, Rushdi** and **H. Faure.** Chronological framework: African pluvial and glacial epochs. In J. Ki-Zerbo (ed.), *General History of Africa* 1: *Methodology and African Prehistory.* (London and Berkeley, 1981): 359-99.

1989 **Said, Rushdi, F. Wendorf** and **R. Schild.** The geology and prehistory of the Nile Valley in Upper Egypt. *Archaeologia Polona* 12 (1970): 43-60.

1990 **Said, Rushdi** and **F. Yousri.** Origin and Pleistocene history of River Nile near Cairo, Egypt. *BIE* 45 (1968): 1-30.

1991 **Saint-Hilaire, J. Berthelemy.** *Egypt and the Great Suez Canal: A Narrative of Travels.* London, 1857.

1992 **St. John, Bayle.** <257> *Village Life in Egypt.* 2 vols. London, 1852.

1993 **Sandford, Kenneth Stuart.** Preliminary remarks on early man in relation to river gravels and other deposits of Upper Egypt. *BAAS, Report of the 96th Meeting, Oxford, 1926* (London, 1927): 358.

1994 ———. The Pliocene and Pleistocene deposits of Wadi Qena and of the Nile Valley between Luxor and Assiut (Qau). *Quart. J. Geol. Soc.* 85 (London, 1929): 493-548.

1995 ———. Palaeolithic man in Nubia and Upper Egypt. In entry 945, pp. 454-56.

1996 ———. Recent developments in the study of Palaeolithic man in Egypt. *AJSL* 48 (1932): 170-83. [Based upon an earlier paper summarized in *Actes du XVIIIe Congr. Intern des Orientalistes, Leyden* (1931): 80-81.]

1997 ———. Past climate and early man in the southern Libyan Desert. *Geogr. J.* 82 (1933): 219-22.

Reviewed: *L'Anthropologie* 44 (1934): 612-13 by R. Vaufrey.

1998 ———. *Palaeolithic Man and the Nile Valley in Upper and Middle Egypt: A Study of the Region during Pliocene and Pleistocene Times. OIP* 18 (Chicago, 1934).

Reviewed: *L'Anthropologie* 46 (1936): 142-43 by S. Huzayyin.

———. See entry 1319.

1999 **Sandford, Kenneth Stuart** and **William J. Arkell.** *First Report of the Prehistoric Survey Expedition. OIC* 3 (Chicago, 1928).

Reviewed: *Antiquity* 4 (1930): 270 by John Ball.

2000 ———. The relation of Nile and Faiyum in Pliocene and Pleistocene times. *Nature* 121 (1928): 670-71

2001 ———. On the relation of palaeolithic man to the history and geology of the Nile Valley. *Man* 29 (1929): 65-69 and 215-16.

2002 ———. The origin of the Faiyum depression: The Faiyum and Uganda. *Geogr. J.* 74 (1929): 578-84.

2003 ———. *Palaeolithic Man and the Nile-Faiyum Divide: A Study of the Region during Pliocene and Pleistocene Times. OIP* 10 (Chicago, 1929).

Reviewed: *Man* 30 (1930): 144-46.
OLZ 33 (1930): 985-86.

2004 ———. *Palaeolithic Man and the Nile Valley in Nubia and Upper Egypt: A Study of the Region during Pliocene and Pleistocene Times. OIP* 17 (Chicago, 1933).

2005 ———. *Palaeolithic Man and the Nile Valley in Lower Egypt; With Some Notes upon a Part of the Red Sea Littoral: A Study of the Region during Pliocene and Pleistocene Times. OIP* 46 (Chicago, 1939).

2006 **Sarasin, P.B.** Die ägyptische Prähistorie und das drei Periodsystem. *Verh. Natur. Gesellsch., Basel* 21 (1910): 245-65.

2007 **Sauneron, Serge** and **Jean Yoyotte.** La naissance du Monde selon l'Egypte ancienne. In A.-M. Esnoul, et al., (eds.), *Sources Orientales,* 1: *La Naissance du Monde.* (Paris, 1959): 17-91.

Sauter, Marc. R. See Supplement entry 2509.

2008 **Säve-Söderbergh, Torgny.** *Ägypten und Nubien: Ein Beitrag zur Geschichte altägyptischen Aussenpolitik.* Lund, 1941.

2009 ———. Der Frühkulturen Ägyptens und Mesopotamiens. *AO* 41 (1941).

2010 ———. Preliminary report of the Scandinavian Joint Expedition: Archaeological survey between Faras and Gamai. *Kush* 10 (1961): 84-85.

2011 ———. Preliminary report of the Scandinavian Joint Expedition: Archaeological investigations between Faras and Gemai, November 1962 - March 1963. *Kush* 12 (1964): 1969.

2012 ———. (ed.). *The Scandinavian Joint Expedition to Sudanese Nubia.* 10 vols. (Helsinki, 1970-).

2013 **Sayce, Archibald Henry.** <261> *The Races of the Old Testament.* London, 1891. 2nd ed. 1925.

2014 ———. The beginnings of the Egyptian monarchy. *PSBA* 20 (1898): 96-101.

2015 ———. Objects from the tomb of a pre-dynastic Egyptian King, 2: Some early Egyptian seal-cylinders. *PSBA* 22 (1900): 278-80.

2016 **Sayce, A.H.** and **Somers Clarke.** Report on certain excavations made at El-Kab during the years 1901, 1902, 1903, 1904. *ASAE* 6 (1905): 239-72.

2017 **Sayed, Abdel Monem Abdel Halim.** An attempt at the identification of the transmitters of the Mesopotamian cultural influences to Upper Egypt in Proto-Dynastic times. *Cairo University Faculty of Archaeology, the 50th Anniversary of Archaeological Studies, the Magazine of the Faculty of Archaeology* 1 (1976): 5-18.

Schaber, G.G. See entry 1363.

2018 **Schäffer, Heinrich.** Neue Altertümer der 'New Race' aus Negadeh. *ZÄS* 34 (1896): 158-61.

2019 **Scharff, Alexander.** <262> *Catalogue des Monuments Préhistoriques du Musée du Caire.* Cairo, n.d.

2020 ———. *Die Archäologischen Ergebnisse des Vorgeschichtlichen Gräberfeldes von Abusir el-Meleq nach den Aufzeichnungen Georg Möllers bearbeitet von. WVDOG* 41 (Leipzig, 1926).

2021 ———. *Grundzüge den ägyptischen Vorgeschichte. Morgenland* 12 (Leipzig, 1926). [See also entry 535.]

Reviewed: *Ypek* (1927): 105-7 by G. Roeder.
JEA 13 (1927): 281-82 by S.R.K. Glanville.
OLZ 28 (1927): 2547 by O. Menghin.
Revue archéol. 26 (1927): 304 by S. Reinach.
Anthropos 22 (1927): 669-70 by P. Schebesta.
Petermann's Mitt. (Gotha, 1931): 319-20 by B. Blanckenhorn.

2022 ———. *Aegypten in seinen ältesten Beziehungen zum Westen und Osten.* Leipzig, 1927.

2023 ———. Der heutige Stand der ägyptischen Vorgeschichtsforschung. *ZDMG* 81 (1927): 38.

2024 ———. Neues aus dem vor- und frühgeschichtlichen Saal der ägyptischen Abteilung.

Berliner Museen, Bericht aus den preussischen Kunstsammlungen 48 (1927): 56-61.

2025 ———. Vorgeschichtliches zur Libyerfrage. *ZÄS* 61 (1926): 16-30.
Reviewed: *Ancient Egypt* (1927): 29.

2026 ———. Some prehistoric vases in the British Museum and remarks on Egyptian prehistory. *JEA* 14 (1928): 261-76.

2027 ———. *Die Ältertümer der Vor- und Frühzeit Ägyptens.* 1: *Werkzeuge, Waffen, Gefässe.* 2: *Bestattung, Kunst, Amulette und Schmuck, Geräte zur Körperpflege, Spiel- und Schreibgeräte, Schnitzereien aus Holz und Elfenbein, Verschiedenes. Staatliche Museen zu Berlin, Mitteilungen aus der ägyptischen Sammlung,* vols. 4-5. (Berlin, 1929-1931).

2028 ———. Das Schiff in vorgeschichtlichen Aegypten. *Der Erdball* 5 (1931): 412-18.

2029 ———. Eine archaische Grabplatte des Berliner Museums und die Entwicklung der Grabplatten im frühen Alten Reich. In entry 945, pp. 346-57.

2030 ———. Neues zur Frage der ältesten ägyptisch-babylonischen Kulturbeziehungen. *ZÄS* 71 (1935): 89-106.

2031 ———. Der reliefgeschmückte Muschelangänger der Frühzeit in der Berliner ägyptischen Sammlung. *MDAIK* 6 (1935): 103-7.

2032 ———. *Archäologische Beiträge zur Frage der Entstehung der Hieroglyphenschrift. SBAW* 3 (1942).

2033 ———. Wesenunterschiede ägyptischer und vorasiatischer Kunst. *Der Alte Orient* 42 (Leipzig, 1943).

2034 ———. *Das Grab als Wohnhaus in der ägyptischen Frühzeit. SBAW* 6 (Munich, 1947).

2035 ———. *Die Ausbereit des Osiriskultes in der Frühzeits und während des Alten Reiches. SBAW* 4 (Munich, 1947).

2036 **Scharff, Alexander** and **A. Moortgat.** *Ägypten und Vorderasien in Altertum (Weltgeschichte in Einzeldarstellung).* Munich, 1950.

2037 **Schenkel, Wolfgang.** Horus. *LdÄ* 3 (1975-): 14-25.

2038 ———. *Die Bewässerungsrevolution im alten Ägypten.* Mainz, 1978.

2039 **Schiaparelli, Ernesto.** <263> La missione italiana a Gebelein. *ASAE* 21 (1921): 126-28.

2040 **Schild, Romuald.** [A new variety of the Levallois method of flaking from the Late Palaeolithic of Upper Egypt.] *Archeol. Polski* 16 (1971): 75-84. [In Polish with French and English summaries]

———. See 1987, 1989, 2384-85 and 2391-2422.

2041 **Schild, Romuald, M. Chmielewski** and **H. Wieckowska.** The Arkinian and Shamarkian industries. In entry 2375, pp. 651-767.

2042 **Schlüter, Hans.** *Index Libycus,* 1: *Titles.* Boston, 1979.

2043 **Schmidt, Emil.** Uber alt- und neuägyptische Schädel: Beiträge zu unseren Anschauungen über die Veränderlichkeit und Constanz der Schädelformen. *Archiv für Anthropologie* 17 (1888): 189-227.

2044 ———. Die Rasse der ältesten Bewohner Ägyptens. *ZÄS* 36 (1898): 114-21.

2045 **Schmidt, E.** Vorgeschichtliche Handelswege in Agyptens und Frühgeschichte als historische Wissenschaft. In *Ur- und Frühgeschichte als historische Wissenschaft. Festschrift zum 60. Geburtstag von E. Wahle.* (Heidelberg, 1950): 139-48.

2046 **Schmidt, F. Albrecht.** Prähistoriche Kulturen in Ägypten. *Vorzeit-Forschung* 1 (Aachen, 1954): 2-13.

2047 ———. Die Anfänge des alten Ägypten, 1: *Grundlagen der geschichtlichen ägyptischen Kultur.*

Vorzeit-Forschung 2 (1954): 1-4; and 3 (1954): 1-7.

2048 ———. Die Anfänge des alten Ägypten, 2: *Die Denkmäler des Könige von Hierakonpolis. Vorzeit-Forschung* 3 (1954): 8-12; 4 (1955): 1-3; 5 (1955): 1-6; and 6/7 (1955): 2-3.

2049 **Schott, Sigfried.** *Hieroglyphen Untersuchen zum Ursprung der Schrift. AAWLM* 24 (Wiesbaden, 1950).

2050 ———. Die Vertreibung der Libyer und der Ursprung der ägyptischen Kultur. In A.E. Jensen (ed.), *Mythe, Mensch und Umwelt.* (Bamburg, 1950): 139-48.

2051 ———. Vorgeschichtliche Handelswege in Ägypten. In *Ur- und Frühgeschichte als historische Wissenschaft. Festschrift zum 60. Geburtstag von Ernst Wahle.* (Heidelberg, 1950).

2052 ———. Kulturprobleme der Früzeit Ägyptens. *MDOG* 84 (1952): 1-37.

Reviewed: *Sefarad* 13 (Madrid, 1953): 188 by J.M. Peñuela.

2053 **Schott, S., E. Neuffer** and **K. Bittel.** Bericht über die zweite vom Deutschen Institut für aegyptische Altertumskunde nach dem Ostdelta-Rand und in das Wâdi Tumilât unternommene Erdundungsfahrt. *MDAIK* 2 (1931): 39-54.

2054 **Schrader, Friedrich.** Les origines planétaires de l 'Egypte. *Revue de l'Ecole d'Anthrop.* 19 (Paris, 1909): 15-27.

2055 **Schulz-Weidner, W.** *Vorgeschichte Afrikas südlich der Sahara. Abriss der Vorgeschichte.* Munich, 1957.

2056 **Schuster, Carl.** V-Shaped chert-markings re-considered: A Palaeolithic figurine as explanation of their wide modern distribution. *Anthropos* 63/64 (1968/69): 428-40.

2057 **Schweinfurth, Georg August.** <264> Notizen zur Kenntnis der Oase El-Chargeh. *Petermann's Mitt.* 21 (Gotha, 1875): 384-93.

2058 ———. Les ateliers d'outils en silex dans le désert oriental de l'Egypte. *BIE* 6 (1885): 229-38.

2059 ———. Kieselartefacte aus der arabischen Wüste und von Helouan. *Verh. Berl. Gesellsch. für Anthrop.* (1885): 406-7.

2060 ———. Kiesel-Nuclei aus der arabischen Wüste. *Verh. Berl. Gesellsch für Anthrop.* (1885): 128-31.

2061 ———. Steingeräte von Helouan und aus der arabischen Wüste. *Verh. Berl. Gesellsch. für Anthrop.* (1885): 302-6.

2062 ———. Kieselmanufacte vom Isthmus von Sues und von Qasre-es-Sàga (Moeris See). *Verh. Berl. Gesellsch. für Anthrop.* (1886): 646-48.

2063 ———. Reise in das Depressiongebiet im Umkreise der Fayum. *Zeits. der Gesell. für Erdkunde* 21 (Berlin, 1886).

2064 ———. Kieselartefacte aus neuen ägyptischen Fundstätten. *Verh. Berlin Gesellsch. für Anthrop.* (1887): 719.

2065 ———. Ornamentik der ältesten Kultur-Epoche Aegypteus. *Verh. der Berliner Anthropologischen Gesellschaft* (1897): 391-401.

2066 ———. De l'origine des égyptiens et sur quelques-uns de leurs usages remontant à l'âge de la pierre. *BSGE,* 4th ser., 12 (1897): 785-805.

2067 ———. Steingeräte der Abade. *Verh. Berl. Gesellsch. für Anthrop.* (1897): 95.

2068 ———. [Sur l'origine des Egyptiens.] *Zeits. für Ethnol.* (Berlin, 1897). [Also in *L'Anthropologie* 8 (1897): 719.]

2069 ———. Ueber den Ursprung der Aegypter. *Zeits. Berl. Gesell. für Anthrop.* (1897): 263-86.

Reviewed: *L'Anthropologie* 9 (1898): 444-46.

2070 ———. Die neusten Gräberfunde im Oberägypten und die Stellung der noch lebenden Wüstenstämme zu der altägyptischen Bevölkerung. *Verh. Berl. Gesellsch. für Anthrop.* (1898): 180-86.

2071 ———. Modelle von Steinwaffen in neolithischen Gräbern, vom Kom el-Ahmar (Hierakonpolis). *Verh. Berl. Gesellsch. für Anthrop.* (1898): 260-62.

Reviewed: *L'Anthropologie* 12 (1901): 699 by L. Laloy.

2072 ———. Aegyptischer Ring aus Kieselmasse. *Verh. Berl. Gesellsch. für Anthrop.* (1899): 496-97.

Reviewed: *L'Anthropologie* 11 (1900): 281-82 by L. Laloy.

2073 ———. Kieselartefacte in der diluvialen Schotter-Terrasse und auf den Plateau-Höfen von Theben. *Verh. Berl. Gesellsch. für Anthrop.* (1902): 293-308 and tables 10-12.

2074 ———. Mitteilung an Prof. R. Virchow (Ring von Brocatelle). *Verh. Berl. Gesellsch. für Anthrop.* (1902): 98-100.

2075 ———. Über palaeolithische Kieselartefacte von Theben mit zweifacher Bearbeitung. *Verh. Berl. Gesellsch. für Anthrop.* (1902): 261-62.

2076 ———. Aegyptische Tierbilder als Kieselartefacte. *Die Umschau* 6, 41 (Frankfurt, 1903): 804-6.

2077 ———. Brief an Prof. v. Luschan (aus Luksor). *Zeits. für Ethnol.* 2 (1903): 504-7.

2078 ———. Figures d'animaux fabriquées en silex provenant d'Egypte. *Revue de l'Ecole d'Anthrop.* (Paris, 1903): 395-96. [Repr. in *Egyptian Gazette* (1903), no. 305.]

2079 ———. Steinzeitliche Forschungen in Ober-Aegypten. *Zeits. für Ethnol.* 35 (1903): 798-822, tables 13-14; and 36 (1904): 766-825, table 6.

Reviewed: *L'Anthropologie* 15 (1904): 380-81.

2080 ———. Die umgegend von Schaghab und el-Kab. *Zeits. der Gesellsch. für Erdkunde* 8 (Berlin, 1904): 574-93.

2081 ———. Recherches sur l'âge de la pierre dans la Haute-Egypte. *ASAE* 6 (1905): 9-59.

2082 ———. Über die steinzeitlichen Forschungen in Oberägypten. *Zeits. für Ethnol.* 37 (1905): 622-24.

2083 ———. Über unerklärte Kiesel-Manufakte von Theben. *Zeits. für Ethnol.* 37 (1905): 622-24.

2084 ———. Brief aus Tunis über den Knochenfund von Metlaui. *Zeits. für Ethnol.* 38 (1906): 733-36.

2085 ———. Brief aus Biskra an Geh.-R. Prof. Lissauer, über das Problem eines libyschen Ammonskults. *Zeits für Ethnol.* 40 (1908): 88-95.

2086 ———. Brief aus Biskra. *ASAE* 9 (1908): 162-71.

2087 ———. Über altpaläolithische Manufakte aus dem Sandsteingebiet von Oberägypten. *Zeits. für Ethnol.* 41 (1909): 735-44.

Reviewed: *L'Anthropologie* 21 (1910): 199-201 by L. Laloy.

2088 ———. Über alte Tierbilder und Felsinschriften bei Assuan. *Zeits. für Ethnol.* 44 (1912): 627-58.

Reviewed: *L'Anthropologie* 24 (1913): by H. Obermaier.

2089 **Schweitzer, Ursula.** Reisebericht über die ägyptischen Altertumer. *Orientalia* 19 (1950): 242.

2090 **Schweitzer, V.** Archäologische Bericht aus Ägypten-Helwan. *Orientalia* 17 (1948): 119-22.

2091 **Sears, E.H.** Races of North Africa. *Christian Examiner* 41 (n.d.): 33.

2092 **Sebelein, John.** Early copper and its alloys. *Ancient Egypt* (1924): 6-15.

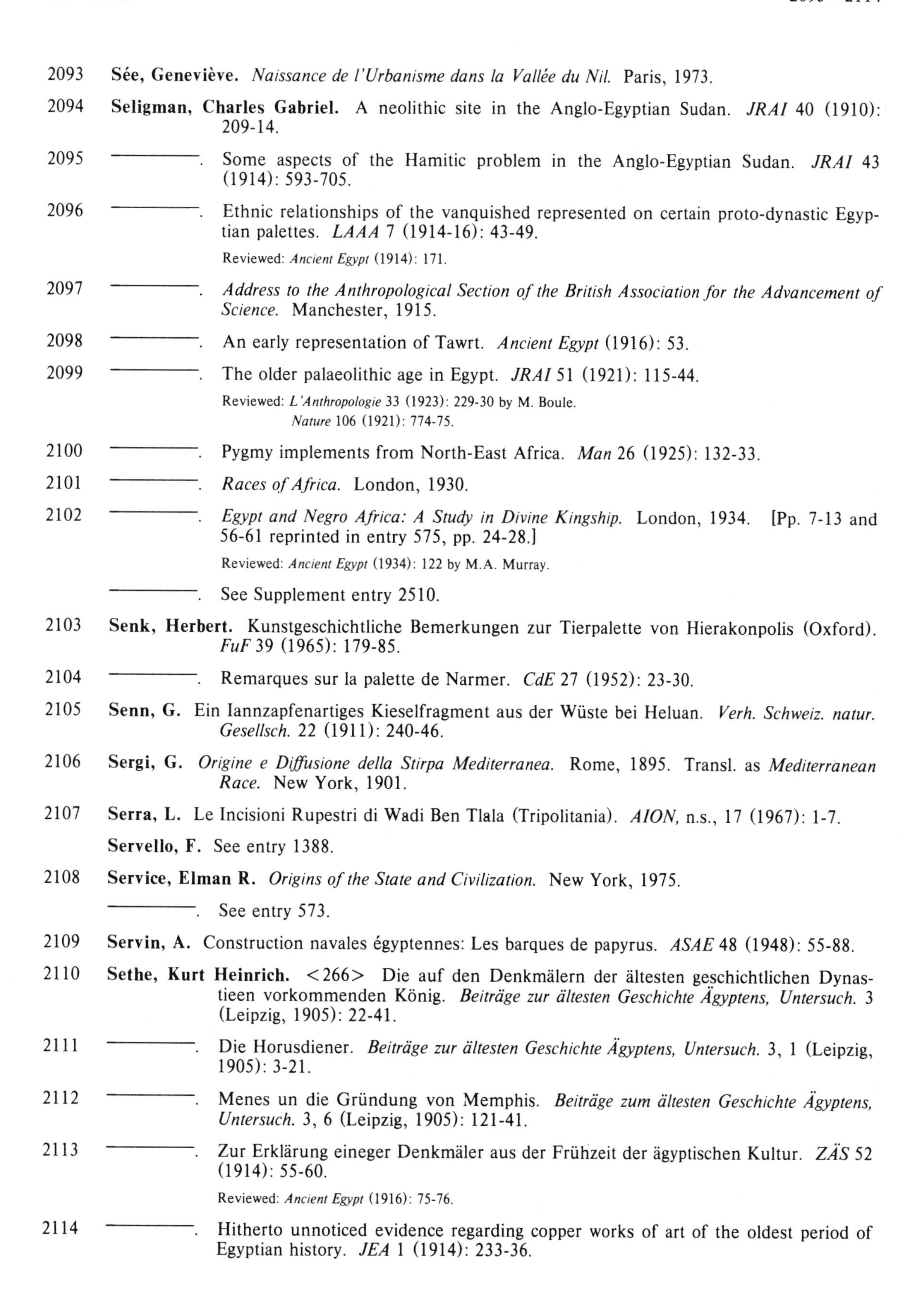

2093 **Sée, Geneviève.** *Naissance de l'Urbanisme dans la Vallée du Nil.* Paris, 1973.

2094 **Seligman, Charles Gabriel.** A neolithic site in the Anglo-Egyptian Sudan. *JRAI* 40 (1910): 209-14.

2095 ———. Some aspects of the Hamitic problem in the Anglo-Egyptian Sudan. *JRAI* 43 (1914): 593-705.

2096 ———. Ethnic relationships of the vanquished represented on certain proto-dynastic Egyptian palettes. *LAAA* 7 (1914-16): 43-49.

Reviewed: *Ancient Egypt* (1914): 171.

2097 ———. *Address to the Anthropological Section of the British Association for the Advancement of Science.* Manchester, 1915.

2098 ———. An early representation of Tawrt. *Ancient Egypt* (1916): 53.

2099 ———. The older palaeolithic age in Egypt. *JRAI* 51 (1921): 115-44.

Reviewed: *L'Anthropologie* 33 (1923): 229-30 by M. Boule.
Nature 106 (1921): 774-75.

2100 ———. Pygmy implements from North-East Africa. *Man* 26 (1925): 132-33.

2101 ———. *Races of Africa.* London, 1930.

2102 ———. *Egypt and Negro Africa: A Study in Divine Kingship.* London, 1934. [Pp. 7-13 and 56-61 reprinted in entry 575, pp. 24-28.]

Reviewed: *Ancient Egypt* (1934): 122 by M.A. Murray.

———. See Supplement entry 2510.

2103 **Senk, Herbert.** Kunstgeschichtliche Bemerkungen zur Tierpalette von Hierakonpolis (Oxford). *FuF* 39 (1965): 179-85.

2104 ———. Remarques sur la palette de Narmer. *CdE* 27 (1952): 23-30.

2105 **Senn, G.** Ein Iannzapfenartiges Kieselfragment aus der Wüste bei Heluan. *Verh. Schweiz. natur. Gesellsch.* 22 (1911): 240-46.

2106 **Sergi, G.** *Origine e Diffusione della Stirpa Mediterranea.* Rome, 1895. Transl. as *Mediterranean Race.* New York, 1901.

2107 **Serra, L.** Le Incisioni Rupestri di Wadi Ben Tlala (Tripolitania). *AION,* n.s., 17 (1967): 1-7.

Servello, F. See entry 1388.

2108 **Service, Elman R.** *Origins of the State and Civilization.* New York, 1975.

———. See entry 573.

2109 **Servin, A.** Construction navales égyptennes: Les barques de papyrus. *ASAE* 48 (1948): 55-88.

2110 **Sethe, Kurt Heinrich.** <266> Die auf den Denkmälern der ältesten geschichtlichen Dynastieen vorkommenden König. *Beiträge zur ältesten Geschichte Ägyptens, Untersuch.* 3 (Leipzig, 1905): 22-41.

2111 ———. Die Horusdiener. *Beiträge zur ältesten Geschichte Ägyptens, Untersuch.* 3, 1 (Leipzig, 1905): 3-21.

2112 ———. Menes un die Gründung von Memphis. *Beiträge zum ältesten Geschichte Ägyptens, Untersuch.* 3, 6 (Leipzig, 1905): 121-41.

2113 ———. Zur Erklärung eineger Denkmäler aus der Frühzeit der ägyptischen Kultur. *ZÄS* 52 (1914): 55-60.

Reviewed: *Ancient Egypt* (1916): 75-76.

2114 ———. Hitherto unnoticed evidence regarding copper works of art of the oldest period of Egyptian history. *JEA* 1 (1914): 233-36.

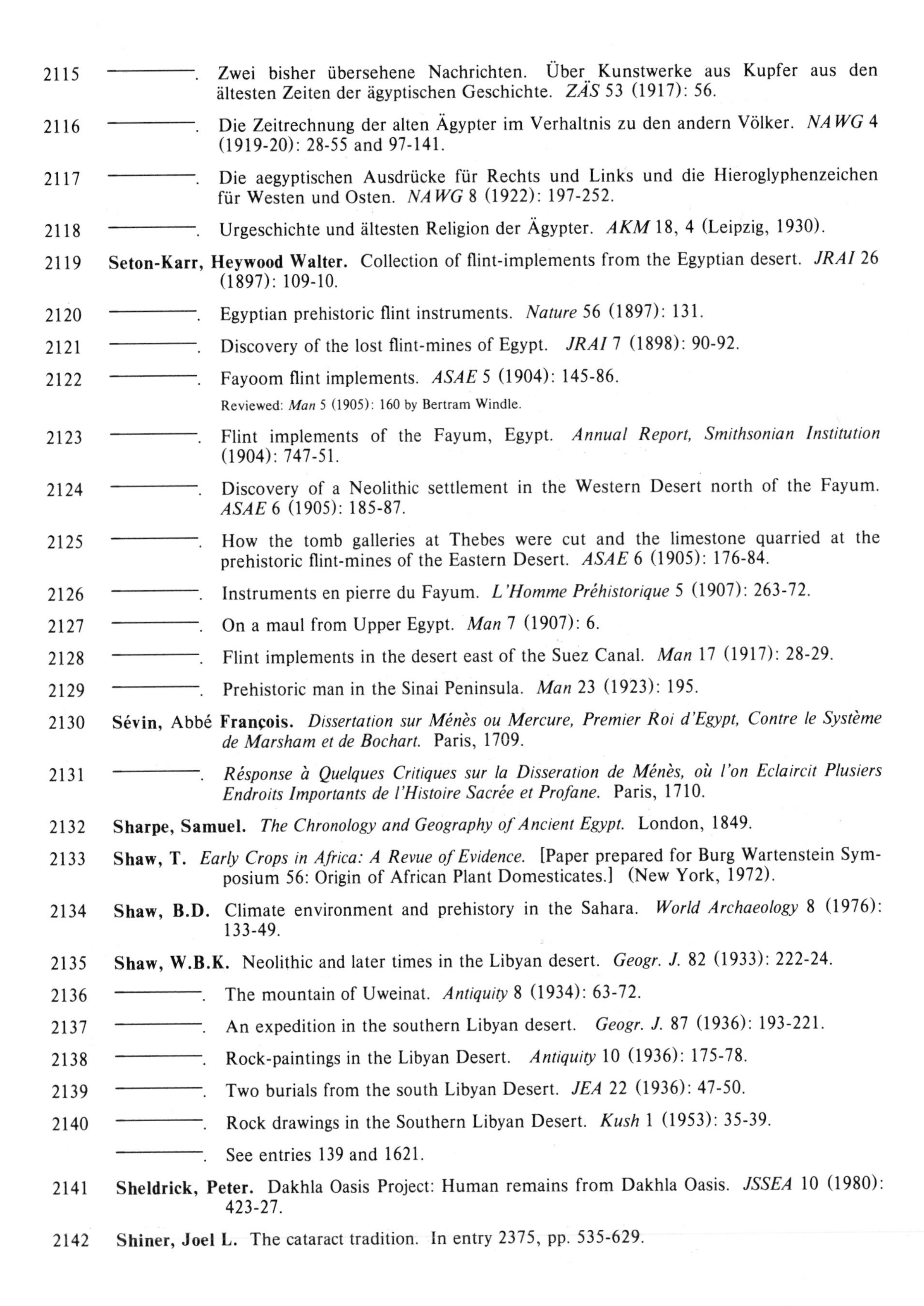

2115 ————. Zwei bisher übersehene Nachrichten. Über Kunstwerke aus Kupfer aus den ältesten Zeiten der ägyptischen Geschichte. *ZÄS* 53 (1917): 56.

2116 ————. Die Zeitrechnung der alten Ägypter im Verhaltnis zu den andern Völker. *NAWG* 4 (1919-20): 28-55 and 97-141.

2117 ————. Die aegyptischen Ausdrücke für Rechts und Links und die Hieroglyphenzeichen für Westen und Osten. *NAWG* 8 (1922): 197-252.

2118 ————. Urgeschichte und ältesten Religion der Ägypter. *AKM* 18, 4 (Leipzig, 1930).

2119 **Seton-Karr, Heywood Walter.** Collection of flint-implements from the Egyptian desert. *JRAI* 26 (1897): 109-10.

2120 ————. Egyptian prehistoric flint instruments. *Nature* 56 (1897): 131.

2121 ————. Discovery of the lost flint-mines of Egypt. *JRAI* 7 (1898): 90-92.

2122 ————. Fayoom flint implements. *ASAE* 5 (1904): 145-86.

Reviewed: *Man* 5 (1905): 160 by Bertram Windle.

2123 ————. Flint implements of the Fayum, Egypt. *Annual Report, Smithsonian Institution* (1904): 747-51.

2124 ————. Discovery of a Neolithic settlement in the Western Desert north of the Fayum. *ASAE* 6 (1905): 185-87.

2125 ————. How the tomb galleries at Thebes were cut and the limestone quarried at the prehistoric flint-mines of the Eastern Desert. *ASAE* 6 (1905): 176-84.

2126 ————. Instruments en pierre du Fayum. *L'Homme Préhistorique* 5 (1907): 263-72.

2127 ————. On a maul from Upper Egypt. *Man* 7 (1907): 6.

2128 ————. Flint implements in the desert east of the Suez Canal. *Man* 17 (1917): 28-29.

2129 ————. Prehistoric man in the Sinai Peninsula. *Man* 23 (1923): 195.

2130 **Sévin,** Abbé **François.** *Dissertation sur Ménès ou Mercure, Premier Roi d'Egypt, Contre le Système de Marsham et de Bochart.* Paris, 1709.

2131 ————. *Résponse à Quelques Critiques sur la Disseration de Ménès, où l'on Eclaircit Plusiers Endroits Importants de l'Histoire Sacrée et Profane.* Paris, 1710.

2132 **Sharpe, Samuel.** *The Chronology and Geography of Ancient Egypt.* London, 1849.

2133 **Shaw, T.** *Early Crops in Africa: A Revue of Evidence.* [Paper prepared for Burg Wartenstein Symposium 56: Origin of African Plant Domesticates.] (New York, 1972).

2134 **Shaw, B.D.** Climate environment and prehistory in the Sahara. *World Archaeology* 8 (1976): 133-49.

2135 **Shaw, W.B.K.** Neolithic and later times in the Libyan desert. *Geogr. J.* 82 (1933): 222-24.

2136 ————. The mountain of Uweinat. *Antiquity* 8 (1934): 63-72.

2137 ————. An expedition in the southern Libyan desert. *Geogr. J.* 87 (1936): 193-221.

2138 ————. Rock-paintings in the Libyan Desert. *Antiquity* 10 (1936): 175-78.

2139 ————. Two burials from the south Libyan Desert. *JEA* 22 (1936): 47-50.

2140 ————. Rock drawings in the Southern Libyan Desert. *Kush* 1 (1953): 35-39.

————. See entries 139 and 1621.

2141 **Sheldrick, Peter.** Dakhla Oasis Project: Human remains from Dakhla Oasis. *JSSEA* 10 (1980): 423-27.

2142 **Shiner, Joel L.** The cataract tradition. In entry 2375, pp. 535-629.

2143 ———. The Khartoum variant industry. *Ibid.*, pp. 768-90.

2144 ———. Miscellaneous sites. *Ibid.*, pp. 630-50.

———. See entries 1388 and 2423.

2145 **Shoukry, Mohammed Anwar.** The so-called stelae of Abydos. *MDAIK* 16 (1958): 292-97.

Siepel, W. See Supplement entry 2511.

Sigstad, J.S. See entry 457.

2146 **Siirianen, Ari.** The Wadi Halfa Region (Northern Sudan) in the Old Stone Age. *Studia Orientalia* 30 (1965): 3-34.

2147 **Simpson, William Kelly.** A statue of King Nyneter. *JEA* 42 (1956): 45-49.

2148 ———. Kenotaph. *LdÄ* 3 (1975-): 387-91.

———. See also entry 2187.

Singleton, William K. See entry 1229.

Sliwa, Joachim. See entries 885 and 1233.

2149 **Slow, Dorothy.** An ivory fragment from Hierakonpolis, Upper Egypt. *Liverpool Bull.* 12 (1963-64): 13-18.

2150 **Smith,** Sir **Grafton Elliot.** <273> On the presence of an additional incisor tooth in a prehistoric Egyptian. *Anatomy and Physiol.* 36. [Not seen.]

2151 ———. Prehistoric graves and remains at Girga to be investigated. *Nature* 65 (1901-1902): 571.

2152 ———. The people of Egypt. *Cairo Science J.* 3 (1909): 51-63.

2153 ———. Entry not used.

2154 ———. The people of Egypt. *BAAS, Report of the 80th Meeting, Sheffield, 1910* (London, 1911): 727-28.

2155 ———. The origin and meaning of the dolmen. *JMEOS* (1912-13): 76.

2156 ———. Physical characters of the ancient Egyptians. *BAAS, Report of the 82nd Meeting* (London, 1913): 268-70.

2157 ———. The evolution of the dolmen. *BAAS, Report of the 83rd Meeting, Birmingham, 1913* (London, 1914): 646-47.

2158 ———. The ancient inhabitants of Egypt and the Sudan. *BAAS, Report of the 84th Meeting, Australia, 1914* (London, 1915): 534.

2159 ———. *The Influence of Ancient Egyptian Civilisation in the East and in America.* Manchester, 1915. [Reprinted in V.F. Calverton (ed.), *The Making of Man* (New York, 1931): 393-420.] [See also entry 875.]

Reviewed: *Ancient Egypt* (1916): 141-42.

2160 ———. Influence of racial admixture in Egypt. *Eugenics Review* 7 (1915): 163-83.

2161 ———. *The Migrations of Early Culture. University of Manchester Publication* 102 (Manchester, 1915).

2162 ———. Physical characters of the ancient Egyptians. *BAAS, Report of the 84th Meeting, Australia, 1914* (London, 1915): 212-28.

2163 ———. Professor Guiffrida-Ruggeri's views on the affinities of the Egyptians. *Man* 15 (1915): 71-72. [See also entry 886.]

2164 ———. Anthropology. *Encyclopaedia Britannica,* 12th ed. Vol. 30 (London, 1922): 1454.

2165 ———. *The Ancient Egyptians and the Origin of Civilisation.* London and New York, 1923.

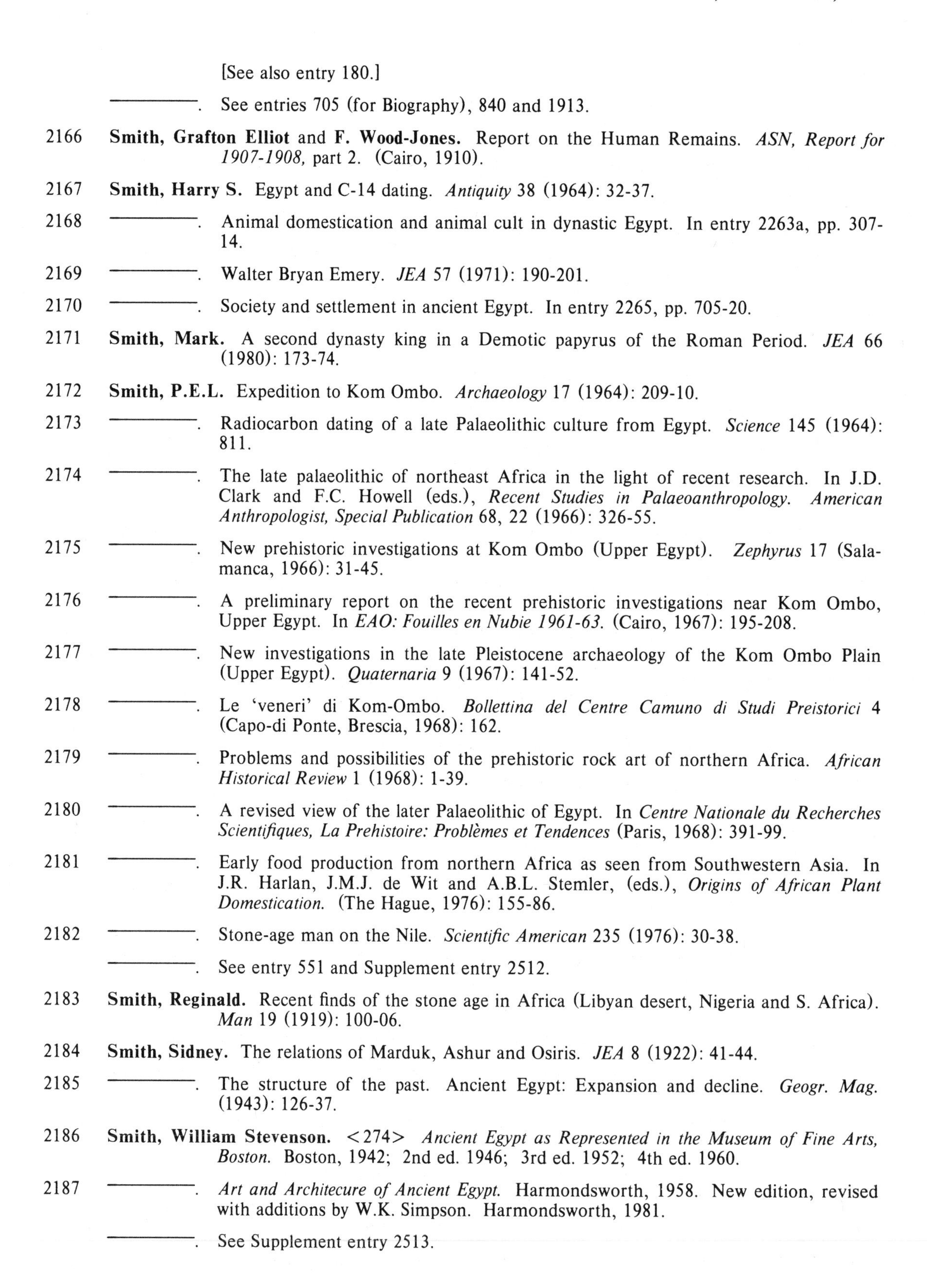

[See also entry 180.]

———. See entries 705 (for Biography), 840 and 1913.

2166 **Smith, Grafton Elliot** and **F. Wood-Jones.** Report on the Human Remains. *ASN, Report for 1907-1908,* part 2. (Cairo, 1910).

2167 **Smith, Harry S.** Egypt and C-14 dating. *Antiquity* 38 (1964): 32-37.

2168 ———. Animal domestication and animal cult in dynastic Egypt. In entry 2263a, pp. 307-14.

2169 ———. Walter Bryan Emery. *JEA* 57 (1971): 190-201.

2170 ———. Society and settlement in ancient Egypt. In entry 2265, pp. 705-20.

2171 **Smith, Mark.** A second dynasty king in a Demotic papyrus of the Roman Period. *JEA* 66 (1980): 173-74.

2172 **Smith, P.E.L.** Expedition to Kom Ombo. *Archaeology* 17 (1964): 209-10.

2173 ———. Radiocarbon dating of a late Palaeolithic culture from Egypt. *Science* 145 (1964): 811.

2174 ———. The late palaeolithic of northeast Africa in the light of recent research. In J.D. Clark and F.C. Howell (eds.), *Recent Studies in Palaeoanthropology. American Anthropologist, Special Publication* 68, 22 (1966): 326-55.

2175 ———. New prehistoric investigations at Kom Ombo (Upper Egypt). *Zephyrus* 17 (Salamanca, 1966): 31-45.

2176 ———. A preliminary report on the recent prehistoric investigations near Kom Ombo, Upper Egypt. In *EAO: Fouilles en Nubie 1961-63.* (Cairo, 1967): 195-208.

2177 ———. New investigations in the late Pleistocene archaeology of the Kom Ombo Plain (Upper Egypt). *Quaternaria* 9 (1967): 141-52.

2178 ———. Le 'veneri' di Kom-Ombo. *Bollettina del Centre Camuno di Studi Preistorici* 4 (Capo-di Ponte, Brescia, 1968): 162.

2179 ———. Problems and possibilities of the prehistoric rock art of northern Africa. *African Historical Review* 1 (1968): 1-39.

2180 ———. A revised view of the later Palaeolithic of Egypt. In *Centre Nationale du Recherches Scientifiques, La Prehistoire: Problèmes et Tendences* (Paris, 1968): 391-99.

2181 ———. Early food production from northern Africa as seen from Southwestern Asia. In J.R. Harlan, J.M.J. de Wit and A.B.L. Stemler, (eds.), *Origins of African Plant Domestication.* (The Hague, 1976): 155-86.

2182 ———. Stone-age man on the Nile. *Scientific American* 235 (1976): 30-38.

———. See entry 551 and Supplement entry 2512.

2183 **Smith, Reginald.** Recent finds of the stone age in Africa (Libyan desert, Nigeria and S. Africa). *Man* 19 (1919): 100-06.

2184 **Smith, Sidney.** The relations of Marduk, Ashur and Osiris. *JEA* 8 (1922): 41-44.

2185 ———. The structure of the past. Ancient Egypt: Expansion and decline. *Geogr. Mag.* (1943): 126-37.

2186 **Smith, William Stevenson.** <274> *Ancient Egypt as Represented in the Museum of Fine Arts, Boston.* Boston, 1942; 2nd ed. 1946; 3rd ed. 1952; 4th ed. 1960.

2187 ———. *Art and Architecure of Ancient Egypt.* Harmondsworth, 1958. New edition, revised with additions by W.K. Simpson. Harmondsworth, 1981.

———. See Supplement entry 2513.

Snegizeff, J. See entry 1811.

2188 **Sneguireff, I.** Sur le problème du culte de la grande déesse dans l'Egypte archaique. *PSEL* 2 (1929): 6-14.

2189 **Soldi Colbert de Beaulieu, Emile.** <276> Sur les migrations en Egypte. *BSAP,* 3rd ser., 3 (1880): 19-31.

2190 ———. Discussion sur le fer en Egypte. *BSAP,* 3rd ser., 7 (1884): 63-69.

2191 **Solecki, Ralph S., Jean de Heinzelin, Robert L. Stigler, Anthony J. Marks, Roland Paepe** and **Jean Guichard.** Preliminary statement of the prehistoric investigations of the Columbia University Nubian Expedition in Sudan, 1961-62. *Kush* 11 (1963): 70-92.

2192 **Sonnini de Manoncour, Charles Nicolas Sigisbert.** <276> *Travels in Upper and Lower Egypt, Undertaken by Order of the Old Government of France . . .* London, 1800. Repr., London, 1972.

2193 **Souville, G.** L'Industrie préhistorique recueilli à Bu Njem (1967-1968). *La Arte* 6-7 (1969-70): 169-73.

2194 **Spamaus, G.** *Historische-Kritisches zum Hamiten Problem.* [Memoriam Karl Weule.] Leipzig, 1929.

2195 ———. Zum Hamiten Problem in Afrika. *FuF* 7 (Berlin, 1931).

2196 **Spencer, A.J.** *Brick Architecture in Ancient Egypt.* Warminster, 1979.

2197 ———. *Catalogue of Egyptian Antiquities in the British Museum,* 5: *Early Dynastic Objects.* London, 1980.

2198 **Spiegel, Joachim.** Ätiologie. Ätiologische Mythen. *LdÄ* 1 (1975-): 80-83.

2199 **Spiegelberg, Wilhelm.** <278> Ein neuer Denkmal aus der Frühzeit der ägyptischen Kunst. *ZÄS* 35 (1897): 7-11.

2200 ———. Zu dem Stein von Hierakonpolis. *OLZ* 1 (1898): 232-38.

2201 **Spurrell, Flaxman Charles Joseph.** <280> Notes on early sickles. *Archaeol. J.* 49 (1892): 53-68.

2202 ———. Some flints from Egypt of the IVth dynasty. *Archaeol. J.* 49 (1892): 48-52.

2203 ———. On some flint implements from Egypt and Denmark. *Archaeol. J.* 53 (1896): 46-55.

2204 **Stahr, Hermann.** *Die Rassenfrage im antiken Aegypten: Kraniologische Untersuchungen an Mumienköpfen aus Theben.* Berlin, 1907.

Stanley, P.S. See entry 557.

2205 **Stemmler, Anne B.L.** and **Richard H. Falk.** A scanning electron microscope study of cereal grains from Wadi Kubbaniya. In entry 2416, pp. 299-306.

2206 **Steindorff, Georg.** <281> Eine neue Art ägyptischer Kunst. *Aegyptiaca: Festschr. für G. Ebers.* (Berlin, 1897): 122-24.

2207 ———. Steinzeitliche Forschungen in Ober Aegypten. *Zeits. für Ethnol.* 44 (1912): 627-58.

2208 **Sterns, F.H.** The palaeolithic of the Eastern Desert. *Harvard African Studies* 1 (1917): 48-83.
Reviewed: *Ancient Egypt* (1921): 53.
Rev. archéol., 5th ser., 7 (1918): 195 by S. Reinach.

2209 **Steward, Julian.** *Theory of Culture Change: The Methodology of Multilinear Evolution.* Urbana, Illinois, 1955.

2210 **Stewart, H.M.** *Egyptian Stelae, Reliefs and Paintings from the Petrie Collection,* part 2: *Archaic to Second Intermediate Period.* London, 1979.

Stigler, Robert L. See entry 2191.

2211 **Störk, Lothar.** Fauna. *LdÄ* 2 (1975-): 128-38.

2212 **Stock, Hans.** <282> Das Ostdelta Ägyptens in seiner entscheidenden Rolle für die politische und religiöse Entwicklung des Alten Reiches. *Die Welt des Orients* 3 (1948): 135-45.

Stocking, G.W. See entry 1838.

2213 **Stoessiger, Brenda N.** A study of the Badarian crania recently excavated by the British School of Archaeology in Egypt. *Biometrika* 19 (1927): 110-50.

Reviewed: *Ancient Egypt* (1927): 106.

2214 **Stopes, H.** On a Palaeolithic stone-implement from Egypt. *BAAS, Report of the 50th Meeting, Swansea, 1880* (London, 1881): 624.

2215 **Stracmans, M.** Les pygmées dans l'ancienne Egypte. *Mélanges Georges Smuts.* (Brussels, 1952): 621-31.

2216 ————. Une statuette pygmoide du Musée de Berlin. *BSAB* 63 (1952): 23-29.

2217 **Stromer von Reichenbach, E.** Ueber die Steinzeit Aegyptens. *Korresp. Anthrop. Gesellsch.* 33 (Munich, 1903): 34-36.

2218 **Strouhal, Eugen.** Contribution à la question du caractère de la population préhistorique de la Haute-Egypte. *Anthropologie* 6 (Bruno, 1968): 19-22.

2219 ————. Evidence of the early penetration of Negroes into prehistoric Egypt. *J. African History* 12 (1971): 1-9.

Strzalko, J. See entry 1037.

2220 **Stuart, Henry Windsor Villiers.** <283> Exhibition of flint instruments from Egypt. *PSBA* 5 (1883): 97-98.

2221 **Suret-Canale, J.** *L'Afrique Noire, Occidentale et Centrale.* Paris, 1958.

2222 **Sutton, J.E.G.** The prehistory of East Africa. In J. Ki-Zerbo, *General History of Africa,* 1: *Methodology and African Prehistory.* (London and Berkeley, 1981): 451-86.

T

2223 **Täckholm, V. Laurent.** The plant of Nagada. *ASAE* 51 (1951): 299-311.

2224 ————. Flora. *LdÄ* 2 (1975-): 267-75.

2225 **Taylor, Griffith.** *Environment and Race: A Study of the Evolution, Migration, Settlement and Status of the Races of Man.* Oxford, 1927.

2226 **Tcherezov, E.V.** [Les annales de la pierre de Palerme et les documents de l'ancien empire.] *[Drevenu Egupet]* (1960): 261-72. [In Russian with French summary]

2227 **Terrien de Lacouperie, Albert Etienne Jean Baptiste.** The races of man in the Egyptian documents: A bibliographical notice. *Babylonian and Oriental Record* 2 (1887-88): 133-34.

2228 **Te Velde, Herman.** Horus and Seth. *LdÄ* 3 (1975): 25-27.

2229 **Thausing, Gertrude.** Der Tiercult im alten Ägypten. *Antaios* 5 (Stuttgart, 1963): 309-24.

2230 **Thomas, Ernest S.** The branch on prehistoric ships. *Ancient Egypt* (1923): 97.

2231 ————. A comparison of drawings from ancient Egypt, Libya and the south Spanish caves. *JRAI* 56 (1926): 385-94.

2232 ————. Note on a decorated gourd. *Ancient Egypt* (1931): 28-29.

2233 ————. An ivory in the Petrie Collection. *Ancient Egypt* (1933): 89-92.

2234 ————. Note on early Egyptian slate-palettes. *Man* 34 (1934): 126-28.

Thommeret, J. See entry 430.

2235 **Thomson, Arthur.** Composite photographs of early Egyptian skulls. *Man* 5 (1905): 65-67.

2236 ————. A note on Dr. Keith's review of 'The Ancient Races of the Thebaid'. *Man* 5 (1905): 101-102. [See also entry 2238.]

2237 ————. Egyptian craniology. *Man* 6 (1906): 55.

2238 **Thomson, Arthur** and **David Randall MacIver.** *The Ancient Races of the Thebaid; Being an Anthropological Study of the Inhabitants of Upper Egypt from the Earliest Prehistoric Times to the Mohammedan Conquest, Based on the Examination of over 1,500 Crania.* Oxford, 1905. [See also entries 1674 and 2236.]

Reviewed: *Man* 5 (1905): 91-96 by A. Keith.

2239 **Titicomb,** Bishop. On ethnic testimonies to the Pentateuch. *Trans. Victoria Inst.* 6 (1873): part 23.

2240 **Tixier, J.** Les témoignages des vestiges Cithiques. In *Méthode pour l'Etude des Outillages Lithiques: Notice sur les Travaux Scientifique* 10 (Paris, 1978): 54-59.

2241 **Tomimura, Deu.** [Recent activities in Egyptology, 3: Problems on the origin of the dynastic culture in Egypt.] *Palaeologia* 6 (Osaka, 1957): 318-25. [In Japanese]

2242 **Tomkins, Henry G.** <289> Remarks on Mr. Flinders Petrie's collection of ethnographical types from the monuments of Egypt. *JRAI* 18 (1889): 206-38.

2243 **Torr, Cecil.** Sur quelques prétendue navires égyptiens. *L'Anthropologie* 9 (1898): 32-35. [See also entries 1573 and 1579.]

2244 **Toussoun, Omar.** Notes sur les déserts de l'Egypte. *BIE* 8-10 (1932): 14, 189 and 202.

2245 **Trigger, Bruce Graham.** *History and Settlement in Lower Nubia. Yale University Publications in Anthropology* 69 (New Haven, 1965).

2246 ———. New light on the history of settlement in Lower Nubia. In Robert A. Fernea (ed.), *Contemporary Egyptian Nubia.* (HRAFlex Book MR8-001, vol. 1), (New Haven, 1966): 21-58.

2247 ———. *Beyond History: The Methods of Prehistory.* New York, 1968. Transl. as *Além da Historia: os Métodos da Préhistoria.* Sao Paulo, 1973.

2248 ———. New light on the history of Lower Nubia. *Anthropologica,* n.s., 10 (1968): 81-106.

2249 ———. The personality of the Sudan. In Daniel F. McCall, Norman R. Bennett and Jeffrey Butler (eds.), *Eastern African History. Boston University Papers on African History* 3 (New York, 1969): 74-106.

2250 ———. *Nubia under the Pharaohs.* Boulder, Colorado and London, 1976.

2251 ———. Egypt and the comparative study of early civilization. In Kent R. Weeks (ed.), *Egyptology and the Social Sciences: Five Studies.* (Cairo, 1979): 23-56.

2252 ———. The Narmer Palette in cross-cultural perspective. In Manfred Görg and Edgar Pusch (eds.), *Festschrift Elmar Edel.* (Bamberg, 1979): 409-19.

2253 ———. *Gordon Childe: Revolutions in Archaeology.* New York, 1980.

2254 ———. The rise of civilization in Egypt. In J. Desmond Clark (ed.), *The Cambridge History of Africa,* 1: *From the Earliest Times to c. 500 B.C.* (Cambridge, 1981): 478-547. Repr. in Supplement entry 2514.

Tringham, Ruth. See entry 2265.

2255 **Tristram, Henry Baker.** *The Natural History of the Bible; Being a Review of the Physical Geography, Geology, and Methodology of the Holy Land; With a Description of Every Animal and Plant Mentioned in Holy Scripture.* London, 1867.

2256 **Tulli, A.** Una coorte musteriana nel P. Museo Egizio Vaticano. *Atti. d. S. Ital. p. il Progresso dell Sc., XXIV Reunione, Palermo, 12-18 Ottobre 1935-XXXI,* 5 (Rome, 1936): 20-36.

2257 ———. Un 'Manipolo di Capsiani' nel Pont. Museo Egizio Vaticano. *Atti. d. S. Ital. P. il Progresso delle Sc.* 16 (Rome, 1937): 233-48.

2258 **Tutundžić, S.P.** A potsherd of a painted vase from Maadi and D class pottery. *Bull. Faculty of Arts, Cairo Univ.* 28 (1966): 115-28.

2259 ———. [The rendering of animal skin on two white cross-lined vases with dancing scenes.] (1968): 41-46. [In Russian]

2260 ———. Ways of relations between Upper Egypt and Palestine during the late Chalcolithic period. In entry 1898, pp. 651-60.

2261 **Tylor, Edward B.** Stone age basis for oriental study. *Annual Report of the Smithsonian Institution* (1893): 701-8.

U

2262 **Ucko, Peter J.** Predynastic Cemetery N7000 at Naga-ed-Dêr. *CdE* 42 (1967): 345-53.

2263 ————. *Anthropomorphic Figurines of Predynastic Egypt and Neolithic Crete with Comparative Material from the Prehistoric Near East and Mainland Greece. Occas. Paper, RAI* 24 (London, 1968).

Reviewed: *Amer. Anthrop.* 72 (1970): 1181-82 by W.K. Simpson.
Anthropos 65 (1970): 1022-23 by Johannes Maringer.
Antiquity 44 (1970): 68-69 by C.C. Lamberg-Karlovsky.
BiOr 27 (1970): 187-88 by Ingrid Gamer-Wallert.
Bull. School of Oriental and African Studies 33 (1970): 603-4 by John Oates.
JEA 56 (1968): 198-201 by E.J. Baumgartel.
Man 4 (1969): 297-98 by Colin Renfrew.
Mitt. anth. Gesell. Wien 100 (1970): 436 by Andreas Lippert.

————. See entries 106 and 234.

2263a **Ucko, Peter J.** and **G.W. Dimbleby** (eds.). *The Domestication and Exploitation of Plants and Animals.* Chicago, 1969.

2264 **Ucko, Peter J.** and **H.W.M. Hodges.** Some predynastic Egyptian figurines: Problems of authenticity. *J. Warburg and Courtauld Insts.* 26 (1963): 205-22.

2265 **Ucko, Peter J., R. Tringham** and **G.W. Dimbleby** (eds.). *Man, Settlement and Urbanism.* London, 1972.

2266 **[Univ. College, London].** *Catalogue of Antiquities of the Earliest Dynasties, Found by Professor Flinders Petrie at Abydos, Mr. Randall-Maciver at el Amrah , (Egyptian Exploration Fund), and Mr. J. Garstang at Beit Khallaf, (Egyptian Research Account), 1901. Exhibited at University College, Gorner Street, London, W.C., July 1st to 27th, Hours 10-5.* London, 1902.

V

2267 **Valori, Berto.** Osservation soi rapporti preistorici fra l'Egitto e la Libia. *Archivo per l'Anthropologie e la Etnologie* 58 (Firenze, 1928): 291-95.

Van Bomberghen, M. See entry 1189.

2268 **Van Campo, M.** Pollen analysis in the Sahara. In entry 2388, pp. 45-64.

2269 **Van Campo, M., P Guinet** and **J. Cohen.** Fossil pollen from late Tertiary and Middle Pleistocene deposits of the Kurkur Oasis. In entry 419, pp. 515-20.

2270 **Van der Meer, P.E.** *The Ancient Chronology of Western Asia and Egypt.* Leiden, 1947.

2271 ————. At what time has the reign of Menes to be placed? *Orientalia Neerlandica* (1948): 23-49.

2272 **Vandier, Jacques.** *Le Religion Egyptienne.* (*Mana: Introduction à l'Histoire des Religions, Les Anciennes Religions Orientales,* 1). (Paris, 1944).

2273 ————. *Manuel d'Archéologie Egyptienne,* I: *Les Epoques de Formation;* 1: *La Préhistoire,* 2: *Les Trois Premières Dynasties.* 2 vols. Paris, 1952-.

Reviewed: *CdE* 57 (1954): 63-65 by P. Gilbert.
CdE 57 (1954): 65-77 by J.-Ph. Lauer.

————. See entry 678.

2274 **Van Gerven, Dennis P., David S. Carlson** and **George J. Armelagos.** Racial history and biocultural adaptation of Nubian archaeological populations. *J. African Hist.* 14 (1973): 555-64.

Van Meer, Willem. See entry 870.

Van Noten, F. See entries 1021 and 1438.

2275 **de Vasconcellos, Leite.** Présentation d'une palette égyptienne ovoide. *C.r. du Congr. Intern. d'Archéol., 2e Session, Cairo* (1909): 194-95.

2276 ————. L'Aterian en Egypte. *L'Anthropologie* 41 (1931): 433-34.

2277 **Vaufrey, R.** Les gisements paléolithiques de l'Oasis de Kharga (Egypte). *L'Anthropologie* 42 (1932): 647-84.

2278 **Vayson, André.** Faucille préhistorique de Solférino. Etude comparative: Egypte. *L'Anthropologie* 29 (1918): 407-13.

2279 ————. A propos des trièdres néolithiques et du 'Chalossien' d'Egypte. *BSPF* 29 (Paris,

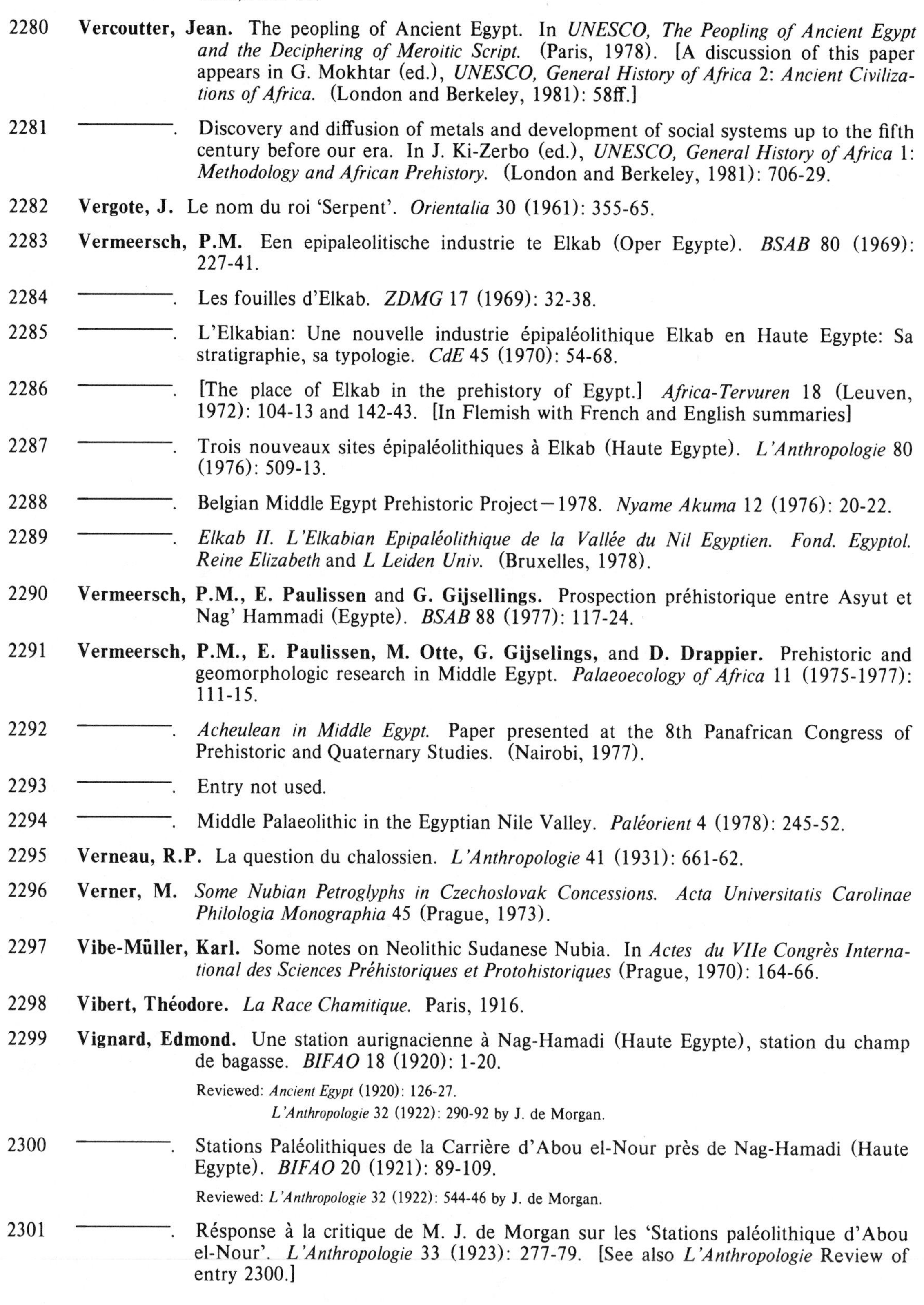

1932): 500-01.

2280 **Vercoutter, Jean.** The peopling of Ancient Egypt. In *UNESCO, The Peopling of Ancient Egypt and the Deciphering of Meroitic Script.* (Paris, 1978). [A discussion of this paper appears in G. Mokhtar (ed.), *UNESCO, General History of Africa* 2: *Ancient Civilizations of Africa.* (London and Berkeley, 1981): 58ff.]

2281 ————. Discovery and diffusion of metals and development of social systems up to the fifth century before our era. In J. Ki-Zerbo (ed.), *UNESCO, General History of Africa* 1: *Methodology and African Prehistory.* (London and Berkeley, 1981): 706-29.

2282 **Vergote, J.** Le nom du roi 'Serpent'. *Orientalia* 30 (1961): 355-65.

2283 **Vermeersch, P.M.** Een epipaleolitische industrie te Elkab (Oper Egypte). *BSAB* 80 (1969): 227-41.

2284 ————. Les fouilles d'Elkab. *ZDMG* 17 (1969): 32-38.

2285 ————. L'Elkabian: Une nouvelle industrie épipaléolithique Elkab en Haute Egypte: Sa stratigraphie, sa typologie. *CdE* 45 (1970): 54-68.

2286 ————. [The place of Elkab in the prehistory of Egypt.] *Africa-Tervuren* 18 (Leuven, 1972): 104-13 and 142-43. [In Flemish with French and English summaries]

2287 ————. Trois nouveaux sites épipaléolithiques à Elkab (Haute Egypte). *L'Anthropologie* 80 (1976): 509-13.

2288 ————. Belgian Middle Egypt Prehistoric Project—1978. *Nyame Akuma* 12 (1976): 20-22.

2289 ————. *Elkab II. L'Elkabian Epipaléolithique de la Vallée du Nil Egyptien. Fond. Egyptol. Reine Elizabeth* and *L Leiden Univ.* (Bruxelles, 1978).

2290 **Vermeersch, P.M., E. Paulissen** and **G. Gijsellings.** Prospection préhistorique entre Asyut et Nag' Hammadi (Egypte). *BSAB* 88 (1977): 117-24.

2291 **Vermeersch, P.M., E. Paulissen, M. Otte, G. Gijselings,** and **D. Drappier.** Prehistoric and geomorphologic research in Middle Egypt. *Palaeoecology of Africa* 11 (1975-1977): 111-15.

2292 ————. *Acheulean in Middle Egypt.* Paper presented at the 8th Panafrican Congress of Prehistoric and Quaternary Studies. (Nairobi, 1977).

2293 ————. Entry not used.

2294 ————. Middle Palaeolithic in the Egyptian Nile Valley. *Paléorient* 4 (1978): 245-52.

2295 **Verneau, R.P.** La question du chalossien. *L'Anthropologie* 41 (1931): 661-62.

2296 **Verner, M.** *Some Nubian Petroglyphs in Czechoslovak Concessions. Acta Universitatis Carolinae Philologia Monographia* 45 (Prague, 1973).

2297 **Vibe-Müller, Karl.** Some notes on Neolithic Sudanese Nubia. In *Actes du VIIe Congrès International des Sciences Préhistoriques et Protohistoriques* (Prague, 1970): 164-66.

2298 **Vibert, Théodore.** *La Race Chamitique.* Paris, 1916.

2299 **Vignard, Edmond.** Une station aurignacienne à Nag-Hamadi (Haute Egypte), station du champ de bagasse. *BIFAO* 18 (1920): 1-20.

Reviewed: *Ancient Egypt* (1920): 126-27.
L'Anthropologie 32 (1922): 290-92 by J. de Morgan.

2300 ————. Stations Paléolithiques de la Carrière d'Abou el-Nour près de Nag-Hamadi (Haute Egypte). *BIFAO* 20 (1921): 89-109.

Reviewed: *L'Anthropologie* 32 (1922): 544-46 by J. de Morgan.

2301 ————. Résponse à la critique de M. J. de Morgan sur les 'Stations paléolithique d'Abou el-Nour'. *L'Anthropologie* 33 (1923): 277-79. [See also *L'Anthropologie* Review of entry 2300.]

2302 ———. Une nouvelle industrie lithique, le 'Sébilien'. *BIFAO* 22 (1923): 1-76.

2303 ———. Une station aurignacienne à Nag-Hamadi (Haute Egypte). Station du champ de bagasse. *L'Anthropologie* 33 (1924): 275-77.

2304 ———. Un galet perforé de la Province de Minih. *BSPF* 24 (1927): 169.

2305 ———. Silex de Nag-Hamadi. *BSPF* 24 (1927): 236.

2306 ———. Une nouvelle industrie lithique, le Sébilien. *BSPF* 25 (1928): 200-20.
Reviewed: *L'Anthropologie* 39 (1929): 165 by M. Boule.

2307 ———. Station aurignacienne du champ de bagasse à Nag-Hamadi (Haute Egypte). *BSPF* 26 (1929): 299-306.

2308 ———. Stations paléolithiques de la carrière d'Abou el-Nour, près de Nag Hamadi (Haute Egypte). *BSPF* 27 (1930): 301-20.

2309 ———. L'Origine et le but du microburin tardenoisien. *CrASP, 54e Session, Nancy, 1931* (Paris, 1931): 330-31.

2310 ———. Deux éléments de faucilles énéolithiques de la Haute-Egypte. *BSPF* 29 (1932): 99-102.

2311 ———. L'Eau rémanente dans les silex paléolithiques d'Egypte. *BSPF* 30 (1933): 288-96.

2312 ———. Les microburins tardenoisiens du Sébilien. Fabrication, emplois, origine du microburin. *Congrès Préhistorique de France, Xe Session* (Paris, 1934): 66-106.
Reviewed: *L'Anthropologie* 45 (1935): 141-42 by R. Vaufrey.

2313 ———. Le paléolithique en Egypte. *MIFAO* 66 (1934): 165-75.

2314 ———. Le microburin est-il Sébilien? *BSPF* 32 (1935): 649-58.

2315 ———. Le Levalloisian du Gébel-Silsilé. Région de Kom-Ombo (Province d'Assouan, Haute Egypte). *BSPF* 52 (1955): 214-18.

2316 ———. Menchia, une station aurignacienne dans le nord de la plaine de Kom Ombo (Haute Egypte). *Congrès Préhistorique de France, XIVe Session, Strassbourg, 1953* (Paris, 1955): 634-53.

2317 ———. Les Stations et Industries Sébiliennes du Burg el Makkazin, Région de Kom Ombo (Haute Egypte). *BSPF* 52 (1955): 436-52.

2318 ———. Un Kjoekkenmodding sur la rive droit du Wadi-Shait dans le nord de la plaine de Kom Ombo (Haute Egypte). *BSPF* 52 (1955): 703-08.

2319 ———. Les stations de taille de la plaine nord-est de Kom Ombo (Haute Egypte). *BSPF* 53 (1956): 588-98.

2320 ———. Patine des silex d'Egypte. *BSPF* 54 (1957): 380-81.

2321 ———. Pointe de vue nouveau sur l'industrie du Champ de Bagasse de Nag Hamadi (Haute Egype). *BSPF* 54 (1957): 298-313.

2322 ———. Destruction de gisements préhistoriques en Egypte. *BSPF* 59 (1962): 190.

2323 ———. Couteau prédynastiques égyptien. *BSPF* 60 (1963): 112-13.

2324 **Vigoroux, F.** *La Bible et l'Egyptologie.* Paris, 1876.

2325 ———. *La Bible et les Découvertes Modernes en Palestine, en Egypte et en Assyria.* Paris, 1877; 2nd ed. 1878; 3rd ed. 1881-1882.

2326 **Vikientiev, Vladimir.** <293> Les monuments archaiques, 1: La tablette en ivoire de Naquada. *ASAE* 33 (1933): 208-34.

2327 ———. Etudes d'epigraphie protodynastique. *ASAE* 45 (1948): 25-33.

2328 ———. Les monuments archaiques, 3: A propos, du soi-disant nom de Ménès dans la tablette de Naqada. *ASAE* 48 (1948): 665-85. [See also entry 926.]

2329 ———. Les monuments archaiques, 4: Donation du souffle de la vie au peuple, illustrée par l'incision dans la traché-artère (trachéotamie). *BIE* 32 (1951):171-200.

2330 ———. Les monuments archaiques, 5: Donation du souffle ou ouverture des plantes. *BIE* 32 (1951): 201-28.

2331 ———. Les monuments archaiques, 6: La tablette en ivoire d'un haut fuctionnare du roi de la 1re dynastie *Weneuty-Ouénéphès*. *BIE* 36 (1955): 293-315.

2332 ———. Etudes d'épigraphie protodynastique, 1: Quelques cas où se lit *d3i* et signifie 'suc'. *ASAE* 55 (1958): 25-33.

2333 ———. Etudes d'épigraphie protodynastique, 2: Deux tablettes en ivoire (I. Dyn.) et les linteaux de Medamud (XII-XIIIe Dyn.). *ASAE* 56 (1959): 1-30.

2334 **Vincent, A.** L'Egypte primitive. *Revue des Deux Mondes* (1951): 338-45.

2335 **Virchow, Rudolf.** Vorhistorische Zeit Aegyptens. *Verh. Berlin Gesell. für Anthrop.* (1888): 344-93.

2336 ———. Anthropologie Ägyptens. *C.B. Ges. Anthrop.* 19 (1888): 105-12.

2337 ———. *Über die ethnologische Stellung der prähistorischen und protohistorischen Ägypter, nebst Bemerkungen über Entfärbung und Verfärbung der Haare.* *APAW* 1 (Berlin, 1898).

2338 **Vogel, J.C.** and **H.T. Waterbolk.** Haua Fteah series, Libya. Ed Dabba, Libya. *Radiocarbon* 5 (1963): 170-72.

2339 **Volney,** Compte de **Constantin François Chasseboeuf.** <294> *Voyage en Syrie et en Egypte, faits pendant les années 1783 à 1785.* Paris, 1787.

2340 **Vyčichl, Werner.** [This article was not seen] *AÄA* 1 (1938): 131-32 and 172-75.

2341 ———. Notes sur la préhistoire de la langue égyptienne. *Orientalia* 23 (1954): 217-22.

2342 **Waddell, L.A.** *The Makers of Civilisation in Race and History.* London, 1929.

2343 ———. *Egyptian Civilization, its Sumerian Origin and Real Chronology and Sumerian Origin of Egyptian Hieroglyphs.* London, 1930.

2344 **Wainwright, Gerald Avery.** <296> *A Report on the Antiquities of Lower Egypt.* Oxford, 1907.

2345 ———. Pre-dynastic beads in Egypt. *Man* 11 (1911): 177-78.

2346 ———. Pre-dynastic iron beads in Egypt. *BAAS, Report of the 80th Meeting, Portsmouth, 1911* (London, 1912): 515-16.

2347 ———. Pre-dynastic iron beads in Egypt. *Revue Archéol.*, 4th ser., 19 (1912): 255-59.

2348 ———. *Balabish. EEF* 37 (London, 1920).

2349 ———. The red crown in early prehistory times. *JEA* 9 (1923): 26-33.

2350 ———. Obsidian. *Ancient Egypt* (1927): 77-93.

2351 ———. The coming of iron. *Antiquity* 10 (1936): 5-24.

2352 ———. The origin of storm-gods in Egypt. *JEA* 49 (1963): 13-20.

———. See entries 1615, 1796 and 1797.

2353 **Waite, Fred.** *Egyptian Predynastic Pottery [in the Otago Museum.] Otago Museum Handbook* no. 1 (Dunedin, N.Z., 1950).

2354 **Wake, C. Staniland.** On the origin of the classificatory system of relationship used among primitive peoples. *JRAI* 8 (1879): 144-79.

2355 **Waley-el-Dine, S.** Zur Entstehung der ägyptischen Kunst. *Du* 35 (Zürich, 1975): 57-65.

Walter, Heinz. See entry 1880.

2356 **Ward, P.** and **A. Pesce.** Wadi al-Khail. Libyan Rock Art. *Arab World* n.s., 35 (London, 1972): 7-9.

2357 **Ward, William A.** Ancient sea-trade between Egypt and Syria. *Middle East Forum* 40 (Beirut, 1964): 23-28.

2358 ———. Relations between Egypt and Mesopotamia from prehistoric times to the end of the Middle Kingdom. *JESHO* 7 (1964): 1-45 and 121-135.

2359 **Warren, E.** An investigation on the variability of the human skeleton, with special reference to the Naqada race discovered by Prof. Fl. Petrie on his explorations in Egypt. *Phil.*

Trans. 189B (1898): 135-227.

Waterbolk, H.T. See entry 2338.

2360 **Webb, Wilfred Mark.** The 'New Race': A prehistoric people of Egypt. *English Illus. Mag.* 22 (1900): 135-43.

2361 **Weeks, Kent R.** Preliminary report on the first two seasons at Hierakonpolis. 2: The early dynastic palace. *JARCE* 9 (1971-1972): 29-33.

2362 **Weigall, Arthur Edward Pearse Brome.** <299> *Travels in the Upper Egyptian deserts.* Edinburgh and London, 1909; 2nd ed. 1913.

———. See entry 120.

2363 **Weill, Raymond.** <300> Hierakonpolis et les origines de l'Egypte. *Revue Archéol.,* 3rd ser., 41 (1902): 117-24.

2364 ———. Notes sur les monuments de la periode thinite. *RecTrav* 29 (1907): 26-53.

2365 ———. *Des Monuments et de l'Histoire des IIe et IIIe Dynasties Egyptiennes.* Paris, 1908.

2366 ———. Les originales de l'Egypte pharaonique, I, la IIe et la IIIe Dynasties. *Annales du Musée Guimet, (Bibliothèque d'Etude)* 25 (Paris, 1908).

2367 ———. Monuments noveaux des premières dynasties. *Sphinx* 15 (1911): 1-35.

2368 ———. Nouvelles lumières sur les nom royaux des trois premières dynasties. *CdE* 6 (1931): 290-93.

2369 ———. *Recherches sur la Ire Dynastie et les Temps Prépharaoniques.* 2 vols. *BdE* 38 (Cairo, 1961).

2370 **Weissen-Szumlanska, Marcelle.** *Origines Atlantiques des Anciens Egyptiens.* Paris, 1965.

2371 **Wendorf, Fred** (ed.). *Contributions to the Prehistory of Nubia.* Dallas, 1965.

2372 ———. Mission to Nubia. *Orbit* 6, no. 4 (1965): 18-19.

2373 ———. Late paleolithic sites in Egyptian Nubia. In entry 2375, pp. 791-953.

2374 ———. A Nubian final paleolithic graveyard near Gebel Sahaba, Sudan. In entry 2375, pp. 954-95.

2375 ———. *The Prehistory of Nubia. SMU Contrib. Anth.,* 2; *Fort Burgwin Res. Ctr. Publ.* 5. 2 vols., plus atlas. (Dallas, 1968).

Reviewed: *Antiquity* 44 (1970): 158-60 by W.Y. Adams.
AJA 73 (1969): 380-81 by Hans Goedicke.
J. Afr. Hist. 10 (1969): 487-89 by A.J. Arkell.
Man 4 (1968):142-43 by F.A. Evans.
Mitt. Anth. Gesell Wien 100 (1970): 460-61 by Andreas Lippert.

2376 ———. The Prehistory of the Nile Valley. *Science* 162 (1968): 1032-33.

2377 ———. Summary of Nubian Prehistory. In entry 2375, pp. 1040-59.

2378 ———. *New Concepts in Egyptian Prehistory. Arid Lands Symposium III.* Texas Tech. Univ. Press, 1970.

2379 ———. Dates for the Middle Stone Age of East Africa. *Science* 187 (1975): 740-42.

2380 ———. The use of ground grain during the Late Paleolithic of the Lower Nile Valley in Egypt. In J. Harlan, J.M.J. de Wet, and A.B.L. Stemmler, *Origins of African Plant Domestication.* (The Hague, 1976): 269-88.

2381 ———. Food production in the Palaeolithic? Excavations at Wadi Kubbaniya: 1981. *NARCE* 116 (1981/2): 13-21.

———. See entries 1001, 1987, and 1989.

2382 **Wendorf, Fred** and **J. Desmond Clark.** The implication of Nile prehistory for Africa and the Levant. *Current Anthropology* 12, 3 (1971): 408-411.

2383 **Wendorf, Fred, J.D. Clark,** and **S. Brandt.** *From Hunters to Farmers: Considerations of the Causes and Consequences of Food Production in Africa.* (Berkeley, in Press).

2384 **Wendorf, Fred, A.E. Close,** and **R. Schild.** *The Afian: A Study of Stylistic Variation in Nilotic Industry. SMU Papers in Anthropology.* (Dallas, 1979).

2385 **Wendorf, Fred, A.E. Close, R. Schild, R. Said, C.V. Haynes, A. Gautier,** and **N. el-Hadidi.** Late Pleistocene and recent climatic changes in the Egyptian Sahara. *Geogr. J.* 143 (1977): 211-34.

2386 **Wendorf, Fred** and **F. Hassan.** Holocene ecology and prehistory in the Egyptian Sahara. In entry 2449, pp. 407-419.

2387 **Wendorf, Fred, F. Hassan,** and **A. Hassan.** Geochronology of Terminal Pleistocene and Early Holocene industries in the Southeastern Mediterranean Basin. *Congrès Préhistorique de France, XXe Session.* (In press).

2388 **Wendorf, Fred** and **Anthony Marks** (eds.). *Problems in Prehistory: North Africa and the Levant.* Dallas, 1975.

2389 **Wendorf, Fred, G.J. Race, E.I. Fry,** and **S.B. Humphreys.** Paleopathology of ancient Nubian human bone studied by chemical and electron microscopic methods. *Journal of Human Evolution* 1 (1972): 263-279.

2390 **Wendorf, Fred** and **Rushdi Said.** Paleolithic remains in Upper Egypt. *Nature* 215 (1967): 244-47.

2391 **Wendorf, Fred, R. Said, C.C. Albritton,** and **R. Schild.** Remarks on the holocene geology and archaeology of the northern Fayum desert. *Archaeologia Polona* 12 (1972).

2392 **Wendorf, Fred, R. Said, C.C. Albritton, R. Schild,** and **M. Kobusiewicz.** A preliminary report on the Holocene geology and archaeology of the Northern Fayum Desert. In C.C. Reves (ed.), *Playa Lake Symposium,* (Texas Tech. Univ., 1972): 41-61.

2393 **Wendorf, Fred, Rushdi Said,** and **Romuald Schild.** Egyptian prehistory: some new concepts. *Science* 169 (1970): 1161-71.

2394 ————. The geology and prehistory of the Nile valley in Upper Egypt. *Archaeologia Polona* 12 (1970): 43-60.

2395 ————. Late paleolithic sites in Upper Egypt. *Archaeologia Polona* 7 (1970): 19-42.

2396 ————. Problems in dating the Late Paleolithic in Egypt. *Radiocarbon Variations and Absolute Chronology, Nobel Symposium* 12 (1970): 55-77.

2397 **Wendorf, Fred** and **Romuald Schild.** The use of ground grain during the Late Paleolithic of the Lower Nile Valley, Egypt. *IXth International Congress of Anthropological and Ethnological Sciences* (Chicago, 1973).

2398 ————. New explorations in the Egyptian Sahara. In entry 2388, p. 462.

2399 ————. The Paleolithic of the Lower Nile Valley. In entry 2388, pp. 127-70.

2400 ————. The Middle Paleolithic of Northeastern Africa: New Data and Concepts. *Union Internationale des Sciences Préhistoriques et Protohistoriques, IXe Congrès, Colloque III, Nice* (Nice, 1976).

2401 ————. (eds.), *Prehistory of the Nile Valley.* [with sections by B. Issawi.] New York, 1976.

2402 ————. Archaeology and Pleistocene stratigraphy of the northern Fayum Depression. In entry 2401, pp. 155-226.

2403 ————. The Middle Paleolithic of the Lower Nile Valley and the adjacent desert. In H. de Lumley (ed.), *Papers of the IX Congrès Internationale des Sciences Préhistoriques et Protohistoriques* (Nice, 1977).

2404 ———. Kulkuletti und Gademotta —'Platz der Teufel'. *Das Altertum* 23 (1977): 12-19.

2405 ———. *The Prehistory of Dakhla Oasis and Adjacent Desert.* Warsaw, 1977.

2406 ———. Ein jungsteinzeitlicher Siedlungsplatz am Djebel Nabta. In *Sahara: 10000 Jahre zwischen Weide und Wüste. (Handbuch zu einer Ausstellung des Rautenstrauch — Joest — Museums für Völker Kunde in Zusammenarbeit mit dem Institut für Ur- und Frügeschichte der Universität zu Köln und dem Museum Alexander Koenig, Bonn).* (Köln, 1978): 197-204.

2407 ———. *Prehistory of the Eastern Sahara.* [Studies in Archaeology.] New York and London, 1980.

2408 ———. Summaries and conclusions. In entry 2416.

2409 ———. The earliest food producers. *Archaeology* 34 (1981): 30-36.

2410 ———. *The Prehistory of an Egyptian Oasis.* Warsaw, 1981.

2411 ———. Emergence of food production in the Egyptian Sahara. In entry 2383.

2412 ———. The Middle Paleolithic of the Lower Nile Valley and the adjacent desert. In *F. Bordes Festscrift.* (In press).

2413 ———. A Preliminary report on the Aterian sites at Bir Tarfawi. *Archaeologia Polona* (In press).

2414 ———. Some implications of Late Paleolithic cereal exploitation at Wadi Kubbaniya, Egypt. *Proceedings of the International Symposium on the Origin and Early Development of Food-Producing Cultures in North-eastern Africa.* (In press).

2415 ———. *A Summary of Sudanese Prehistory.* (In press).

2416 **Wendorf, Fred, Romuald Schild** and **A.E. Close.** *Loaves and Fishes: The Prehistory of Wadi Kubbaniya.* Dallas, 1980.

2417 ———. An ancient harvest on the Nile. *Science 82* (1982): 68-73.

2418 **Wendorf, Fred, Romuald Schild** and **H. Haas.** A new radiocarbon chronology for Prehistoric sites in Nubia. *J. of Field Archaeology* 6 (1979): 219-23.

2419 **Wendorf, Fred, Romuald Schild, Nabil el-Hadidi, Angela E. Close, Michael Kobusiewicz, Hanna Wieckowska, Bahay Issawi,** and **Herbert Haas.** Use of barley in the Egyptian Late Palaeolithic. *Science* 205 (1979): 1341-47.

2420 **Wendorf, Fred, Romuald Schild, C. Vance Haynes,** and **R. Said.** Archaeological and geological investigations in the Egyptian Sahara. *NARCE* 89 (1974): 20-28.

2421 **Wendorf, Fred, Romuald Schild,** and **Rushdi Said.** Problems of dating the Late Palaeolithic in Egypt. In I. Olson (ed.), *Radiocarbon Variations and Absolute Chronology, Nobel Symposium* 12 (Stockholm, 1970): 57-79.

2422 **Wendorf, Fred, Romuald Schild, Rushdi Said, C. Vance Haynes, A. Gautier** and **H. Kobusiewicz.** The prehistory of the Egyptian Sahara. *Science* 193 (1976): 103-14.

2423 **Wendorf, Fred, Joel L. Shiner, Anthony J. Marks, Jean de Heinzelin,** and **Waldemar Chmielewski.** The combined Prehistoric Expedition: Summary of the 1963-64 field season. *Kush* 13 (1965): 28-55.

2424 **Wendt, E.** and **C.A. Reed.** Two prehistoric archaeological sites in Egyptian Nubia. *Postilla* 102 (Peabody Museum, Yale Univ., 1966): 1-46.

2425 **Wenke, Robert J.** *Patterns in Prehistory: Mankind's First Three Million Years.* Oxford, 1980.

2426 **Wenke, Robert J.** and **Mary Ellen Lane.** Fayum Expedition, 1981. *NARCE* 116 (1981/2): 22-25.

2427 **Westendorf, Wolfhart.** Paletten, Schmink-. *LdÄ* 4 (1975-): 654-56.

2428 **Wetterstrom, Wilma.** Early agriculture in Upper Egypt: A note on palaeoethnobotanical studies at predynastic sites in the Nagada area. *Assoc. Intern. pour l'Etude de l'Egyptienne Préhistorique* 1: *'L'Egypte Avant la Préhistoire.'* (1980).

Wheat, Joe Ben. See entry 1113.

2429 **Whitehead, G.D.** and **Addison.** Meroitic remains. *SNR* 9 (1926): 51-58.

Whittle, E.H. See entry 507 and Supplement entry 2515.

2430 **Widmer, Werner.** Ein Gefäss der späten Negadezeit. *MIO* 14 (1968): 365-71.

2431 **Wiedemann, Alfred.** <304> Observations on the Nagadah Period. *PSBA* 20 (1898): 107-22.

2432 ———. Die Urzeit Aegyptens und seine älteste Bevölkerung. *Die Umschau* 3 (1899): 764-67 and 785-89.

2433 ———. Zur Nagada-Periode. *OLZ* 3 (1900): 85-87.

2434 ———. Die Steinzeit Aegyptens. *Globus* 96 (Braunschweig, 1909): 298-99.

2435 ———. Das Neolitische Aegypten. *Bonner Zeitung,* (February 23, 1913).

2436 ———. *Das alte Aegypten.* Heidelberg, 1928.

Reviewed: *L'Anthropologie* 33 (1923): 237-38 by M. Boule.

2437 **Wieckowska, Hanna.** Site Dibeira 4, Site Dibeira West 6. In entry 2375, pp. 757-66.

———. See entries 570, 2041 and 2419.

2438 **Wieckowska, Hanna** and **K. Morgan Banks.** Report on site E-78-4. In entry 2416, pp. 119-50.

2439 **Wiercinski, Andrzej.** Introductory remarks concerning the anthropology of ancient Egypt. *BSGE* 31 (1958): 73-84.

2440 ———. Analiza struktury rasowej ludności Egiptu w epoce przeddynastycznej. Polska Akademia Nank Zahtad Anthropologii. *Materialy i Prace Antropologiczne* 56 (Wroctaw, 1963). [with English Summary]

Reviewed: *L'Anthropologie* 69 (1965): 202.

2441 ———. The analysis of racial structure of early dynastic populations in Egypt. *Materialy i Prace Antropologiczne* 71 (Wroclaw, 1965): 3-48.

2442 ———. The problem of anthroposcopic variations in ancient Egyptians. In entry 332, pp. 143-65.

2443 **Wijngarden, W.D. Van.** Oud-Egyptisch Steenen Vaatwerk. *Oud Heidkundige Mededeelingen nit's Rijsk Museum vax Oudheden te Leiden* (1926): 79-84.

2444 **Wild, H.** Choix d'objets pré-pharaoniques appartenant à des collections de Suisse. *BIFAO* 47 (1948): 11-58.

2445 **Wildung, Dietrich.** *Ägypten vor den Pyramiden. Münchner Ausgrabungen in Ägypten.* Mainz, 1981.

Reviewed: *JARCE* 17 (1980): 98 by Hans Goedicke.

2446 **Wilhelm II** [German Emperor]. *Vergleichende Zeittafeln der Vor- und Frühgeschichte Vorderasiens, Ägyptens und der Mittelmeerländer, unter Mitwirkung der 'Doorner Arbeitsgemerinschaft' hrsg. vom Vorsitzenden Kaiser Wilhelm II.* Leipzig, 1936.

2447 **Wilkinson,** Sir **John Gardner.** *The Egyptians in the Time of the Pharaohs, Being a Companion to the Crystal Palace, Egyptian Collection.* London, 1857.

Williams, M.A.J. See entries 8 and 1949.

2448 **Williams, M.A.J.** and **D.A. Adamson.** Late Pleistocene dessication along the White Nile. *Nature* 248 (1974): 584-86.

2449 **Williams, M.A.J.** and **H. Faure.** *The Sahara and the Nile: Quaternary Environments and Pre-*

historic Occupation in Northern Africa. Rotterdam, 1980.

2450 **Wilson,** Rev. **J.** Hypothesis of an European influence on an early Egyptian art. *BAAS, Report of the 59th Meeting, Newcastle-upon-Tyne, 1889* (London, 1890): 778-9.

2451 **Wilson, John A.** Egypt. In H.A. Frankfort, et al., *The Intellectual Adventures of Ancient Man.* Chicago, 1946.

2452 ————. Buto and Hierakonpolis in the geography of Egypt. *JNES* 14 (1955): 209-36.

2453 ————. *The Burden of Egypt.* Chicago, 1951. Published in paperback as *The Culture of Ancient Egypt.* Chicago, 1956.

2454 ————. Civilization without cities. In C. Kraeling and R. McC. Adams, *City Invincible* (Chicago, 1960).

2455 ————. *Signs and Wonders upon Pharaoh: A History of American Egyptology.* Chicago, 1964.

2456 **Winckell, A.** *Preadamites: Or, a Demonstration of the Existence of Man before Adam.* Chicago, 1880.

2457 **Winckelmann, Johann Joachim.** *Histoire de l'Art chez les Anciens.* Paris, 1802. Transl. by G. Henry Lodge as *The History of Ancient Art.* Boston, 1856.

2458 **Wingate, Orde.** In search of Zerzura. *Geogr. J.* 83 (1934): 281-308.

2459 **Winkler, Hans Alexander.** Felsbilder und Inschriften aus des Ostwüste Oberägyptens. *FuF* 12 (1936).

2460 ————. *Völker und Völkerbewegungen im vorgeschichtlichen Oberägypten im Lichte neuer Felsbilderfunde.* Stuttgart, 1937.

2461 ————. *Rock-drawings of Southern Upper Egypt.* 2 vols. *EES* (London, 1938-39). [See also entry 1676 for appendix.]

————. See entry 140.

2462 **Winlock, Herbert Eustis.** <309> The origin of the ancient Egyptian calendar. *Proc. Amer. Phil. Soc.* 83 (1940).

2463 **Wittfogel, Karl.** *Oriental Despotism: A Comparative Study of Total Power.* New Haven, 1957.

Wolf, John E. See entry 184.

2464 **Worrell, William H.** *A Study of Races in the Ancient Near East.* Cambridge, 1927.

2465 **Wortham, John David.** *The Genesis of British Egyptology.* Norman, Oaklahoma, 1971. Published in Britain as *British Egyptology, 1549-1806.* London, 1971.

2466 **Wreschner, E.** [Bone-tools from early and middle palaeolithic sites. Problems and documentation.] *Mitekufat Haeven* 2 (Jerusalem, 1973): 47-60. [In Hebrew]

2467 **Wright, Julia McNair.** *Bricks from Babel: A Brief View of the Myths, Traditions and Religious Beliefs of Races, with Concise Studies in Ethnography.* New York, 1885.

Y

2468 **Yadin, Yigael.** The earliest records of Egypt's penetration into Asia? *IEJ* 5 (1955): 1-16.

Summaries in *B. Fac. Arts,* Cairo 16 (1954): 155-16 by A. Badawy.
Wiener Völkerkundliche Mitt. 2 (1954): 220 by Erick Winter.

2469 **el-Yahky, Farid.** Remarks on the armless figurines represented on Gerzean boats. *JSSEA* 2 (1981): 77-84.

2470 **Yeiven, S.** Early contacts between Canaan and Egypt. *IEJ* 10 (1960): 193-203.

2471 ———. Further evidence for Narmer at 'Gat'. *Oriens Antiquus* 2 (1963): 205-13.

Reviewed: *Sefarad* 25 (1965): 162 by J.M. Lacave.
Z. Altestaunentliche Wiss. 76 (1964): 89 by J.A. Soggin.

2472 ———. The ceremonial slate-palette of King Narmer. In *Studies in Egyptology and Linguistics in Honor of H.J. Polotsky.* (Jerusalem, 1964): 22-53.

2473 ———. A new Chalcolithic culture at Tell 'Erany and its implications for early Egypto-Canaanite Relations. *IVth World Congr. of Jewish Studies, Papers* 1 (Jerusalem, 1967): 45-48.

2474 ———. Additional notes on the early relations between Canaan and Egypt. *JNES* 27 (1968): 37-50.

Yousri, F. See entry 1990.

Yoyotte, Jean. See entry 2007.

Z

2475 **Zaborowski-Moindron, Sigismond.** Races préhistoriques de l'ancienne Egypte. *BSAP,* 4th ser., 9 (1898): 597-616.

Reviewed: *L'Anthropologie* 10 (1899): 481-82.

2476 ————. Origines africanes de la civilisation de l'ancienne Egypte. *Revue Scient.,* 4th ser., 11 (Paris, 1899): 189-96.

2477 ————. L'Origine des anciens égyptiens. *BSAP,* 5th ser., 1 (1900): 212-21.

2478 ————. Races de la primitive Egypte, suivant MM. Flinders Petrie, J. Kollmann et Chantre. *BSAP,* 5th ser., 5 (1904): 600-610.

Zaghloul, el-Sayed Abbas. See entry 1011.

Zampini, P. See entries 583-84.

2479 **Zandee, J.** Seth als Sturmgott. *ZÄS* 90 (1963): 144-56.

2480 **Ziegert, H.** Pleistocene climatic changes and human industries in the central Sahara (Eastern Fezzan and Northern Tibesti). *Actes du Premier Colloque International d'Archéologie Africane, Fort-Lamy 11-16 Decembre 1966* (Fort-Lamy, 1969): 374-87.

2481 ————. Überblick zur jüngeren Besiedlungsgeschichte des Fezzan. *Berliner Geogr.* 8 (1969): 49-58.

2482 ————. Zur Pleistozän-gliederung in der zentralen Sahara. (Ostfezzan und Nord-Tibesti). *Actes du Congrès Intern. des Sciences Préhistoriques et Protohistoriques* 7 (1970): 252-54.

2483 ————. Human cultural development and climatic conditions in the Sahara during Pleistocene times. In T.F.J. Dessauvagie and A.J. Whiteman (eds.), *Proc. of the Conference on African Geology, Ibadan, 7-14 Dec. 1970* (Ibadan, 1972): 461-67.

2484 **Zittel, K.A. von.** Lettre sur les collections de Figari Bet à Florence. Forêt pétrifiée et silex taillés. *BIE* 3 (1874-75): 145.

2485 ————. Sur les silex taillés trouvés dans le désert Libyque. *C.r. du Congr. Anthrop.* 7e session (Stockholm, 1874): 76-79.

2486 **Zivie, Christiane M.** Memphis. *LdÄ* 3 (1975-): 24-41.

Supplement

2487 **Arcelin, A.** *La question Préhistorique.* Paris, 1873.

2488 **Bell, Barbara.** The oldest records of the Nile floods. *Geogr. J.* 136 (1970): 569-73.

2489 **Chowdhury, K.A.** and **G.M. Buth.** Cotton seeds from the Neolithic in Egyptian Nubia and the origin of Old World cotton. *Biol. J. Linn. Soc.* 3 (London, 1971): 303-12.

2490 **Clark, J. Desmond.** The Cultures of the Middle Palaeolithic/Middle Stone Age. In J. Desmond Clark (ed.), *The Cambridge History of Africa,* 1: *From the Earliest Times to c. 500 B.C.* (Cambridge, 1982): 248-341.

2491 **Davis, Whitney.** A 'late predynastic' decorated pot in the British Museum. *GM* 40 (1980): 15-20. [See also entry 2498.]

2492 **Fairservis, Walter A., Jr.** *Hierakonpolis: The Graffiti and the Origins of Egyptian Hieroglyphic Writing. The Hierakonpolis Project. Occasional Papers in Anthropology* 2 (Vassar College, Poughkeepsie, New York, 1983).

2493 **Gould, Stephen Jay.** *The Mismeasure of Man.* New York, 1980.

2494 **von Herder, Johann Gottfried.** *Reflections on the History of Mankind.* [Abridged, and with an Introduction, by Frank E. Manuel.] Chicago, 1968.

2495 **Hugot, H.J.** *L'Afrique Préhistorique.* Paris, 1970.

2496 **Isaac, Glynn Ll.** The earliest archaeological traces. In J.D. Clark (ed.), *The Cambridge History of Africa,* 1: *From the Earliest Times to c. 500 B.C.* (Cambridge, 1982): 157-247.

2497 **King, Leonard W.** *A History of Sumer and Akkad.* London, 1923.

2498 **Lacovara, Peter.** British Museum 35324, again. *GM* 59 (1982): 41-50. [See also entry 2491.]

2499 **Mellaart, James.** Egyptian and Near Eastern chronology: A dilemma? *Antiquity* 53 (1979): 6-18.

2500 **Muzzolini, A.** L'Age des peintures et gravures du Djebel Ouenat et la problème du *Bos Brachyceros* au Sahara. In *Centenaire de l'Enseignement de la Préhistoire à Toulouse, Hommage au Professeur L.R. Nouger = Travaux de l'Institut d'Art Préhistorique,* 22 (Toulouse 1980): 347-71.

2501 ———. Essai de classification des peintures bovidiennes du Tassili. *Bull. Soc. Préh. de l'Ariège.* 36 (1981): 93-113.

2502 ———. Les chars préhistoriques du Sahara: Archéologie et techniques d'attelage. In: G. Camps and M. Gast (eds.), *Actes du Colloque de Sénanque 21-22 Mars 1981* (Aix-en-Provence, Université de Provence, 1982): 45-56.

2503 ————. Les datations au 14C sur roches carbonatées en zone aride: corrections à appliquer et incertitudes. *Archaeometry* 24, 1.

2504 ————. Les peintures des 'Têtes rondes' et les peintures de l'ère 'pastorale' dans l'Acacus (Libye). Chronologie relative et chronologie absolue. *Ars Praehistorica* 1 (1982): 99-122.

2505 ————. Sur un quadrige 'Grec,' du Style Iheren-Tahilahi, au Tassili du N.-O. *Ars Praehistorica* 1 (1982): 189-97.

2506 ————. Les climats sahariens durant l'Holocène et la fin du Pléistocène. *Travaux du Laboratoire d'Anthropologie de Préhistoire et d'Ethnologie des Pays de la Méditerranée occidentale* (Aix-en-Provence, C.N.R.S.) 2 (1982): 1-38.

2507 **Renouf, Peter le Page.** A second note on the royal title [nsw-byt]. *PSBA* 14 (1892): 396-402.

2508 ————. The royal titles [nswt-bit]. *PSBA* 16 (1893): 53.

2509 **Sauter, Marc R.** *Préhistoroire de la Méditerranée: Paléolithique-Mésolithique.* Paris, 1948.

2510 **Seligman, C.G.** and **M.A. Murray.** Note upon an early Egyptian standard. *Man* 11 (1911): 165-71.

2511 **Siepel, Wilfred.** *Grab und Wohnhaus: Die Anfänge Ägyptens.* Konstanz, 1979.

2512 **Smith, P.E.L.** The Late Palaeolithic and Epi-Palaeolithic of northern Africa. In J.D.Clark (ed.), *The Cambridge History of Africa,* 1: *From the Earliest Times to c. 500 B.C.* (Cambridge, 1982): 157-247.

2513 **Smith, William Stevenson.** *A History of Egyptian Sculpture and Painting in the Old Kingdom,* Cambridge, Mass., 1946; 2nd ed. 1949.

2514 **Trigger, Bruce G., B. J. Kemp, D. O'Connor, A.B. Lloyd.** *Ancient Egypt: A Social History.* Cambridge 1983.

2515 **Whittle, E.H.** Thermoluminescent dating of Egyptian predynastic pottery from Hemamieh and Qurna-Tarif. *Archaeometry* 17 (1975): 119-22.